D0291486

# HOLINESS
# AND
# HIGH COUNTRY

# HOLINESS
# AND
# HIGH COUNTRY

by

**A. F. Harper, Ph.D., D.D.**

BEACON HILL PRESS

OF KANSAS CITY

Kansas City, Mo.

First Printing, 1964

ISBN: 978-0-8341-0232-3

Printed in the United States of America

20  19  18  17  16

## Dedication

To some who have heard me preach these truths and have found the blessing of entire sanctification,

To others who have been encouraged to press further into the life of holiness,

To all who yearn to be "perfect in Christ Jesus," I dedicate these pages.

## Acknowledgments

An author's debts for ideas are always too many to pay. I have lived and learned in the surrounding environment of a holiness church. I have heard her preachers and read after her writers. All that I have here recorded reflects the impact of this ministry upon my own mind and spirit. I acknowledge my debt to every unremembered servant of Christ whose holiness ministry of teaching, preaching, or writing has touched my life.

I wish to thank the following publishers for permission to quote from the sources listed below. These items are identified by title and by author where they appear in the book.

Abingdon Press, *The Pure in Heart*
Beacon Hill Press, numerous books and articles
Wm. B. Eerdmans, *The Spirit of Holiness*
Harper & Row, Publishers, *A Testament of Devotion*
Light and Life Press, *Holiness, the Finished Foundation*
Warner Press, *The Meaning of Sanctification,*
             *Studies in Christian Theology*

Poetry has always been an effective language of the soul. I am indebted to every glad spirit who, moved by the Holy Spirit, has penned the lines of devotion that I have used. For permission to reprint copyrighted materials thanks are due to the following publishers and persons:

Hope Publishing Co.
Hymntime Publishers
John T. Benson, Jr.
Lillenas Publishing Co.
Lillian Plankenhorn
Singspiration, Inc.
The Rodeheaver Co.

Permission has been graciously given for the use of various copyrighted versions of the Bible as follows:

*The Amplified New Testament*
    Copyright 1958 by the Lockman Foundation, La Habra, California.

*The Berkley Version in Modern English*
    Copyright 1958, 1959 by Zondervan Publishing House, Grand Rapids, Michigan.

*The Bible: A New Translation,* by James Moffatt
    Copyright 1950, 1952, 1953, 1954 by James A. R. Moffatt. Printed by Harper and Row, Publishers, Inc., New York.

*The Bible: An American Translation,* by Smith-Goodspeed
Copyright 1923, 1927, 1948 by the University of Chicago.
Printed by University of Chicago Press.

*New English Bible*
Copyright by the Delegates of the Oxford University
Press and the Syndics of the Cambridge University Press,
1961.

*The New Testament in Modern English,* by Phillips
Copyright by J. B. Phillips, 1958. Used by permission of
The Macmillan Company.

*The New Testament in the Language of the People,* by Charles
B. Williams
Copyright 1937 by Bruce Humphries, Inc. Assigned 1949
to Moody Bible Institute, Chicago.

*Old Testament and New Testament in Basic English*
Copyright 1950 by Dutton Publishers, New York.

*Revised Standard Version*
Copyright 1946 and 1952 by the Division of Christian Education of the National Council of Churches.

*Explanatory Notes upon the New Testament* by John Wesley
Copyright 1941 by The Epworth Press, London.

*The Weymouth New Testament in Modern Speech*
Copyright by Harper and Brothers, Publishers.

I express appreciation to Dr. Samuel Young, who encouraged me to put these periodical materials into book form;
to Dr. Norman Oke, who, as book editor for the Nazarene
Publishing House, gave helpful suggestions in the early stages
of the project; to Miss Margaret Cutting, who prepared copy
for the publisher; and to my wife, Laura, who waited patiently
"for the book to be finished" so that she might again have a
little time with her husband.

# Preface

I was brought up under holiness teaching. As reflected on page 128, God called me to the ministry and I accepted that call as I was seeking the blessing of entire sanctification. This ministry of the Holy Spirit has meant so much to my own life that I have sought to share its joy and wonder with others.

For a number of years my best opportunity to preach the gospel has been through writing. About one-third of this material appeared first in the *Advanced Quarterly* and *Bible School Journal* of the Church of the Nazarene. It was published in 1952 and again in a revised form in 1956 as a series of studies in Christian holiness. It was suggested to me then that the material should be published in book form for more permanent availability.

The idea of the day-by-day presentation I borrowed from Dr. E. Stanley Jones, who has organized several of his books this way. The content is planned to be a systematic presentation but divided into daily, bite-size pieces. I have observed that sometimes a sentence gives the Holy Spirit an open door to the human heart when a whole sermon has failed to budge it. I hope that this will happen often to the readers of these pages.

I have prayed again and again that this book might have an evangelistic appeal; that the nature and form of the truths here presented shall create a yearning for "all the fullness of God," and that this yearning shall bring many readers into that glad company of whom Jesus spoke: "Blessed are they which do hunger and thirst after righteousness: for they shall be filled." My second prayer is that readers who have found God in sanctifying grace shall from time to time find new understanding of this gift from God and be encouraged to press further into the high country of Christian holiness. Perhaps some who are called to teach and preach this message may find help from these pages to interpret the experience and life to those whose feet they seek to guide into the way of holiness.

The book is primarily designed to be read—and its truths to be prayed about—day by day throughout the year. But the reader may also have occasion at times to look for discussions in specific areas of the truth. The table of contents, the running heads, and the Index of Scripture References will provide help at this point. Chapters one through five deal with the doctrine of the deeper life. Chapters six, seven, and eight discuss the steps by which one may enter this experience with God. Chapters nine through thirteen attempt to point out scriptural guidance for a satisfying and effective Spirit-filled life. The last two chapters explore in some depth the holiness teaching implicit and explicit in the Bible passages selected.

I send the book on its way with a continuing prayer for its ministry. May these pages be used in some small measure to bring nearer the answer to our Lord's prayer, "Thy kingdom come. Thy will be done in earth, as it is in heaven."

A. F. HARPER

# Contents

READ: Matthew 5:1-12

*Happy are the kind-hearted, for they will have kindness shown to them! Happy are the pure in heart, for they will see God!* (Matthew 5:7-8, *The Gospels*, J. B. Phillips, 1952 edition)

## Happy New Year

Happy New Year! I will say it a score of times today. Friends will wish me the same. Will our greetings be only friendly formalities or will they be prophecies of good things to come in the months ahead? The answer depends very little on my circumstances. This year I may have a serious illness, or be forced to retire, or fail to get a promotion. These will be disappointments but they cannot thwart the intent of my friends' greetings. It can still be a happy new year.

Happiness is not something that depends significantly on where I am or what is done to me. It does not come from the outside in, but rather from the inside out. Happiness is God's good gift to those who are rightly related to Him and to the people around them. I cannot find happiness by searching for it. I cannot even pray for happiness and expect God to give it. I can, however, earnestly seek to find God's will for my life. In doing His will I may confidently expect to find life's ultimate satisfaction. I can give myself in honest effort to help another and discover happiness in helpfulness. But the happiness is always a by-product of loving God and sharing myself with my fellowman.

If I know what I am saying when I wish my friend "Happy New Year!" I am wishing that this shall be a year in which he shall walk with God and do something for folk who are near him. If I am to have the happy new year that my friends have wished for me I must open the floodgates through which happiness flows in. I must keep my spirit open to the presence of God and keep my heart open to the needs of men.

### Resolution for today

*I resolve this year to follow Jesus' formula for happiness. I shall seek to love God with all my heart, with all my mind, with all my strength; and to love my neighbor as myself.*

**January 2**

READ: Psalms 42:1-2

*They shall hunger no more, neither thirst any more;
... and God shall wipe away all tears from their eyes*
(Revelation 7:16-17).

## The Wonder of God's Presence

We saw yesterday that happiness in the new year depends on keeping our spirits wide open to God. With deep insight, St. Augustine wrote: "God has made us for himself and we are restless until we find ourselves at home in Him." Ah, what a day when we shall be "before the throne of God, and serve Him day and night in his temple"! Then shall all our restless hungers be satisfied; then shall all our thirsts be quenched. God himself shall satisfy our every longing; His presence shall wipe away all tears from our eyes. Heaven will be heaven because God is there.

But we know as we begin a new year that it is not enough to wait for heaven. We need God here and now. Always men have needed Him; and always God has found ways to make himself known to those who hunger for Him. "When the fulness of the time was come, God sent forth his Son" (Galatians 4:4). When the Son left our earth, He sent the Holy Spirit to dwell in us.

Today, God's Spirit can fill our hearts. Here and now, He can walk with us. Because of His help, hunger is easier to bear, and thirst is not impossible torture. Our crying is hushed, and our pain is eased. The most blessed hours in this life are those in which God's presence seems most fully to surround our hungering spirits. As John Wesley lay on his deathbed he cried out, "The best thing of all is that God is with us." And Wesley was right. Therefore we begin the new year with this assurance:

> *He leadeth me! Oh, blessed tho't!*
> *Oh, words with heav'nly comfort fraught!*
> *Whate'er I do, where'er I be,*
> *Still 'tis God's hand that leadeth me.*
>
> —JOSEPH H. GILMORE

14

READ: Philippians 3:12-14

*My one thought is, . . . to press on to the goal for the prize of God's high call in Christ Jesus* (Philippians 3: 13-14, Moffatt).

## God's High Call

*All that you do, do with your might;*
*Things done by halves are never done right.*

As these lines come back from childhood memories, we approve them almost instinctively. We know that Oliver Wendell Holmes was right:

*Let us do our work as well,*
*Both the unseen and the seen;*
*Make a house where gods may dwell,*
*Beautiful, entire and clean.*

Deep within the mind of every right-thinking person is the conviction that anything worth doing at all is worth doing well. If this be true of other worthy endeavors, how much more should it be true of my religion?

We who have once felt God's presence with us can never be content without Him; and we who have enjoyed something of His love know an ever-recurring hunger for more of that grace. Peter writes to his fellow Christians: "Like newly born children, thirst for the pure, spiritual milk to make you grow up to salvation. You have had a taste of the kindness of the Lord: come to him then—come to that living Stone . . . come and like living stones yourselves, be built into a spiritual house" (I Peter 2:2-5, Moffatt).

Peter mixed his metaphors but he knew the urgency of this spiritual hunger. And we know it. With Paul my own heart responds: "My one thought . . . is to press on to the goal for the prize of God's high call in Christ Jesus."

*More about Jesus would I know,*
*More of His grace to others show;*
*More of His saving fullness see,*
*More of His love who died for me.*
—E. E. HEWITT

READ: Matthew 16:24-26

*Then said Jesus unto his disciples, If any man will come after me, let him deny himself, and take up his cross, and follow me* (Matthew 16:24).

## Holy Obedience

Yesterday on a radio broadcast I heard Dale Evans testify to a moving religious experience in her adult life. As background she said: "I had, as a girl of ten, taken Christ as my Saviour; but I had never taken Him as my Lord." I am sure it is this same difference in the dimensions of the Christian life of which Thomas R. Kelly, a Quaker, testifies movingly.

"Meister Eckhart wrote: 'There are plenty to follow our Lord half-way, but not the other half. They will give up possessions, friends and honors, but it touches them too closely to disown themselves.' It is just this astonishing life which is willing to follow Him the other half, sincerely to disown itself, this life which intends *complete* obedience, without *any* reservations, that I would propose to you in all humility, in all boldness, in all seriousness. I mean this literally, utterly, completely, and I mean it for you and for me—commit your lives in unreserved obedience to Him. . . .

"When such a commitment comes in a human life, God breaks through, miracles are wrought, world-renewing divine forces are released, history changes. There is nothing more important now than to have the human race endowed with just such committed lives. . . . To this extraordinary life I call you—or He calls you through me—not as a lovely ideal, a charming pattern to aim at hopefully, but as a serious, concrete program of life, to be lived here and now, in industrial America, by you and by me.

"In some, says William James, religion exists as a dull habit, in others as an acute fever. Religion as a dull habit is not that for which Christ lived and died" (*A Testament of Devotion*).

### Question for today

*Have I taken Christ as my Saviour, but not really as my Lord? Is my Christian life the dull habit or the acute fever? Am I the kind of Christian that Christ wants me to be?*

READ: Matthew 13: 44-46

*The kingdom of heaven is like unto a merchant man, seeking goodly pearls: who, when he had found one pearl of great price, went and sold all that he had, and bought it* (Matthew 13: 45-46).

## Am I Serious About Serving God?

A stranger getting his shoes shined was curious about a church convention in town. He asked the shine boy: "Who are all these people that I see wearing badges?"

The boy replied: "Dey is some kind of 'ligious group, Boss."

"I know," the man answered, "but what kind?"

The boy's response was: "I ain't quite shuh, Mistah. But as neah as Ah can figah, dey is some kind of souped-up Christians!" It was not a bad testimony that these convention delegates had left in a shoeshine shop.

Would anyone see in my Christian life a "souped-up job"? Do my acquaintances have reason to believe that my commitment to God is something more than the ordinary stock model? More important still, Does Christ know that His will is supreme in my life? Can I honestly say that I am in earnest about serving God?

A Sunday school teacher recently said of the Christian life: "To be filled with the Holy Spirit is as good as it can get." And it is. Apart from all-out abandonment to God there is no real satisfaction in religion. But in such abandon there is joy. It is this joy that Jesus was talking about when He said: "The Kingdom of heaven is like treasure buried in the field, which a man finds, but buries again, and, in his joy about it, goes and sells all he has and buys that piece of ground" (Weymouth).

Who would not "buy" such an all-out religion? What Christian would turn away when Christ points him to the treasure that he has been seeking?

> *All for Jesus! All for Jesus!*
> *All my being's ransomed pow'rs:*
> *All my tho'ts and words and doings,*
> *All my days and all my hours.*
>
> —MARY D. JAMES

**January 6**

READ: Hebrews 6:1-3

*Therefore leaving the principles of the doctrine of Christ, let us go on unto perfection ... And this will we do, if God permit* (Hebrews 6:1, 3).

## A Higher-up Religion

Dr. Lloyd Byron tells of a lady in one of our large cities who came under conviction for heart holiness. She was clearly converted, but felt that there must be a religious experience beyond what she possessed. She sought counsel from different ones, but none could help her. One day she met a lady whom she knew to be a genuine, zealous Christian; she stopped her with this question: "Can you tell me anything about a higher-up religion?"

"Higher-up religion"—that is the hunger of the sincere Christian when he finds that his devotion and service to God are less than they ought to be. Dr. Harry E. Jessop testifies: "It was not long [after I was saved] before I began to feel that, glorious as my new experience in conversion had been, God was now holding before me something of a deeper nature than that which I had already enjoyed. While my love for Christ was such that it pained me to know that I had grieved Him, my spiritual life was far from constant, and my communion was not sustained."

Half a loaf is better than no bread. Some religion is better than none. But low-level religion is not very satisfying. The Bible does not offer a better-than-thou religion, but it does promise a better-than-yesterday experience. The Christian's aim is never to be more holy than others. But our goal is always to be more like Christ. God offers me "a higher-up religion" whenever I am discontented with the lowlands.

*More about Jesus let me learn,*
*More of His holy will discern;*
*Spirit of God, my Teacher be,*
*Showing the things of Christ to me.*

—E. E. HEWITT

READ: Romans 12:1-2

*I plead with you therefore, brethren, by the compassion of God, to present all your faculties to Him as a living and holy sacrifice acceptable to Him—a spiritual mode of worship* (Romans 12:1, Weymouth).

## Life's Divine Center

Thomas R. Kelly writes: "If the Society of Friends has anything to say, it lies in this region primarily. Life is meant to be lived from a Center, a Divine Center. Each one of us can live such a life of amazing power and peace and serenity, of integration and confidence and simplified multiplicity, on one condition—that is, *if we really want to*. . . . We have all heard this holy Whisper at times. At times we have followed the Whisper, and amazing equilibrium of life, amazing effectiveness of living set in. But too many of us have heeded the Voice only at times. Only at times have we submitted to His holy guidance. We have not counted this Holy Thing within us to be the most precious thing in the world. We have not surrendered *all else,* to attend to it alone. Let me repeat. Most of us, I fear, have not surrendered all else, in order to attend to the Holy Within.

"John Woolman did. He resolved so to order his outward affairs as to be, *at every moment,* attentive to that voice. He simplified life on the basis of its relation to the Divine Center. Nothing else really counted so much as attentiveness to that Root of all living which he found within himself. And the Quaker discovery lies in just that: the welling-up whispers of divine guidance and love and presence, more precious than heaven or earth. John Woolman . . . found that we can be heaven-led men and women, and he surrendered himself completely, unreservedly to that blessed leading, keeping warm and close to the Center" (*A Testament of Devotion*).

> *Now rest, my long divided heart;*
> *Fixed on this blissful Center, rest;*
> *Nor ever from my Lord depart,*
> *With Him of ev'ry good possessed.*
> —PHILIP DODDRIDGE

**January 8**

READ: Ezekiel 36: 25-27

*And God, which knoweth the hearts, bare them witness, giving them the Holy Ghost, . . . purifying their hearts by faith* (Acts 15: 8-9).

## A Statement of Faith

God has put into our hearts a hunger for himself. This yearning is never satisfied by a halfway religion. Real joy comes only when we make a complete surrender of ourselves to God. But the Bible teaches that we may have genuine satisfaction when we thus surrender. Earnest seekers after God testify that they have found their hearts' desire. Many Christian groups have formulated statements of this truth.

In the *Book of Discipline* of the Free Methodist church we read: "Entire sanctification is that work of the Holy Spirit, subsequent to regeneration, by which the fully consecrated believer, upon exercise of faith in the atoning blood of Christ, is cleansed in that moment from all inward sin and empowered for service. The resulting relationship is attested by the witness of the Holy Spirit and is maintained by obedience and faith. Entire sanctification enables the believer to love God with all his heart, soul, strength and mind, and his neighbor as himself, and prepares him for greater growth in grace" (Par. 33).

Holiness people everywhere gladly join with the Free Methodists in this proclamation of faith from their hymnal, *Hymns of the Living Faith:*

> *Ye who know your sins forgiven,*
> *And are happy in the Lord,*
> *Have you read the precious promise,*
> *Which is left upon record?*
> *I will sprinkle you with water,*
> *I will cleanse you from all sin,*
> *Sanctify and make you holy,*
> *I will dwell and reign within.*
>
> —WALTER H. TALCOTT

READ: Acts 15: 7-9

*And God, which knoweth the hearts, bare them witness, giving them the Holy Ghost, . . . purifying their hearts by faith* (Acts 15: 8-9).

## Holiness and Entire Sanctification

God is holy and He desires men to become like himself in this respect. Here is a doctrine of well-nigh universal acceptance. Every branch of the Christian Church would officially recognize the supreme place of holiness when we use the term in this broad and general sense. However, we also use the term to designate a specific experience in which the heart of the Christian is made holy by an act of God. This experience is more commonly known as entire sanctification.

It is at the point of our belief in sanctification as a definite work of grace, experienced in this life, that holiness people are unique in doctrine. We believe not only that God calls men to a holy life, but also that the Bible teaches well-defined spiritual crises by which men enter and move forward into such a life.

The Scriptures are clear that if men are to please God they must repent of their sins and be forgiven. When this takes place, God regenerates spiritual life within the soul. God's Word teaches us that after this there is a second crisis (hence the expression *second-blessing holiness*) in which the Christian must consecrate himself wholly to God, be filled with the Holy Spirit, and thus be entirely sanctified.

In our text, Peter testified to having received this kind of experience. He also told of others who had received the same blessing in the same way: "And God, which knoweth the hearts, bare them witness, giving them the Holy Ghost, even as he did unto us; . . . purifying their hearts by faith."

### Affirmation for today

*What God has revealed so clearly in the Bible, I gladly accept as my rule of faith and my guide for life.*

**January 10**

READ: II Peter 1:1-4

*Whereby are given unto us exceeding great and precious promises: that by these ye might be partakers of the divine nature, having escaped the corruption that is in the world through lust* (II Peter 1:4).

## Conformed to God's Nature

"Entire sanctification is that work of the Holy Spirit by which the child of God is cleansed from all inbred sin through faith in Jesus Christ. It is subsequent to regeneration, and is wrought when the believer presents himself a living sacrifice, holy and acceptable unto God, and is thus enabled through grace to love God with all the heart and to walk in His holy commandments blameless.

"Be it Resolved, That the General Conference . . . now in its twenty-first quadrennial session, do hereby declare and reaffirm our faith and adherence to those Doctrines that have been held as fundamental.

"We reaffirm our faith in the doctrine of entire sanctification, by which work of grace the heart is cleansed by the Holy Spirit from all inbred sin through faith in Jesus Christ when the believer presents himself a living sacrifice, holy and acceptable unto God, and is enabled through grace to love God with all his heart and to walk in His holy commandments blameless. By the act of cleansing it is to be interpreted and taught by the ministry and teachers that it is not a 'suppression' or a 'counteraction' of 'inbred sin' so as to 'make it inoperative'; but 'to destroy' or 'to eradicate' from the heart so that the believer not only has a right to heaven, but is so conformed to God's nature that he will enjoy God and heaven forever. These terms are what we hold that cleansing from all sin implies" (*Wesleyan Methodist Discipline*).

> *The cleansing stream I see, I see!*
> *I plunge, and O it cleanseth me;*
> *O praise the Lord, it cleanseth me,*
> *It cleanseth me, yes, cleanseth me.*
> —PHOEBE PALMER

READ: Titus 2: 11-14

*For the saving grace of God hath appeared to all men, instructing us that, having renounced ungodliness and all worldly desires, we should live soberly, and righteously, and godly in the present world* (Titus 2: 11-12, Wesley's translation).

## Holiness in This Life

There are many sincere Christians who admire the ideal of a Spirit-filled life. They believe that every Christian should aspire to it. But their faith is not strong enough to claim it as a possibility for this life. If this be our mood, let us consider the appeal of a man who left a holiness testimony in the mid-twentieth century.

"If any man question whether it is possible to attain to such a state of holiness in this world, let him remember that this is our world of probation, and that here the blood of Jesus was shed and here the Holy Spirit is poured out. Here all the conditions are possible and here all the propitiation of Christ and all the efficiency of the Holy Spirit are available.

"What merit can the future have that we do not have now? We have the blood of Jesus. What more of merit can saints in heaven have? What power to renovate spirit can they have in heaven that we do not have here? We have the Holy Spirit, the infinite refining fire, what can they have in heaven that can be more efficient?

"The world is sinful! That is true, but 'greater is he that is in you than he that is in the world.' Our own natures are depraved! True, but 'the blood of Jesus Christ his Son cleanseth us from all sin.' We are too unworthy and weak! True, but 'The grace of God that bringeth salvation hath appeared to all men, teaching us that, denying ungodliness and worldly lusts, we should live soberly, righteously, and godly, in this present world' " (J. B. CHAPMAN).

> *Saviour, to Thee my soul looks up,*
> *My present Saviour, Thou!*
> *In all the confidence of hope,*
> *I claim the blessing now.*
>
> *—Wesley's Hymns*

**January 12**

READ: John 17:15-17

*Be ye therefore perfect, even as your Father which is in heaven is perfect* (Matthew 5:48).

## Sanctification and Christian Perfection

In their confession of faith under the heading "Sanctification and Christian Perfection," Christians of the Evangelical United Brethren church affirm: "We believe sanctification is the work of God's grace through the Word and the Spirit, by which those who have been born again are cleansed from sin in their thoughts, words and acts, and are enabled to live in accordance with God's will, and to strive for holiness without which no one will see the Lord.

"Entire sanctification is a state of perfect love, righteousness and true holiness which every regenerate believer may obtain by being delivered from the power of sin, by loving God with all the heart, soul, mind and strength, and by loving one's neighbor as one's self. Through faith in Jesus Christ this gracious gift may be received in this life both gradually and instantaneously, and should be sought earnestly by every child of God.

"We believe this experience does not deliver us from infirmities, ignorance and mistakes common to man, nor from the possibilities of further sin. The Christian must continue on guard against spiritual pride and seek to gain victory over every temptation to sin. He must respond wholly to the will of God so that sin will lose its power over him; and the world, the flesh and the devil are put under his feet. Thus he rules over these enemies with watchfulness through the power of the Holy Spirit" (*Discipline*, 1963, Par. XI).

> *There is a place of quiet rest,*
> *Near to the heart of God;*
> *A place where sin cannot molest,*
> *Near to the heart of God.*
>
> —C. B. MCAFEE

24

READ: John 17:15-20

*Sanctify them through thy truth: thy word is truth* (John 17:17).

## We Believe

"We believe that entire sanctification is that act of God, subsequent to regeneration, by which believers are made free from original sin, or depravity, and brought into a state of entire devotement to God, and the holy obedience of love made perfect.

"It is wrought by the baptism with the Holy Spirit, and comprehends in one experience the cleansing of the heart from sin and the abiding indwelling presence of the Holy Spirit, empowering the believer for life and service.

"Entire sanctification is provided by the blood of Jesus, is wrought instantaneously by faith, preceded by entire consecration; and to this work and state of grace the Holy Spirit bears witness.

"This experience is also known by various terms representing its different phases, such as 'Christian Perfection,' 'Perfect Love,' 'Heart Purity,' 'The Baptism with the Holy Spirit,' 'The Fullness of the Blessing,' and 'Christian Holiness.'

.    .    .    .    .    .    .    .    .    .    .    .

"There is a marked distinction between a perfect heart and a perfect character. The former is obtained in an instant, the result of entire sanctification, but the latter is the result of growth in grace.

"Our mission to the world is not alone to spread scriptural holiness as a doctrine, but also to be 'an example of the believers, in word, in conversation, in charity, in spirit, in faith, in purity.' Our people should give careful heed to the development of holiness in the fear of the Lord, to the promotion of the growth of Christian graces in the heart, and to their manifestation in the daily life" (*Manual*, Church of the Nazarene).

### Affirmation for today

*I believe it is God's will to cleanse my heart from sin, to fill me with His Holy Spirit, thus giving me power for Christian life and service.*

**January 14**

READ: Philippians 3: 12-15

*Reaching forth unto those things which are before, I press toward the mark . . . Let us therefore, as many as be perfect, be thus minded* (Philippians 3:13-15).

## Purity and Maturity

We saw yesterday that God plans to make us like himself by filling us with the Holy Spirit now. This experience comes as a result of God's offer and in response to our faith for it. When the Holy Spirit thus comes, He cleanses us from inherited sin and purifies our hearts. It is to such purified Christians that Paul appeals, "Let us therefore, as many as be perfect, be thus minded." But we know that this purity is only the beginning of the sanctified life. Purity of heart is *not* maturity in Christian life and conduct.

After entire sanctification, the healthy, sanctified Christian has many experiences through which his conduct becomes more perfectly harmonized with the will of God. A fuller knowledge of God's will comes as we read the Bible; and we must move up to keep pace with this new light. An unexpected trial comes, and we must turn quickly to God for courage and strength to come through the new battle with victory. All such experiences are steps in the process of spiritual growth by which a man becomes more like the holy God in whose image he was created.

But while all of these are steps in the process, the crisis experience of entire sanctification is so fundamental that all of the others are vitally dependent upon it. When we have been sanctified wholly, Christian growth is normal as we press on toward the "measure of the stature of the fulness of Christ." But until we have been sanctified wholly Christian life at best is anemic; all too often it weakens and dies.

> *Forgive, and make my nature whole;*
> *My inbred malady remove;*
> *To perfect holiness and love.*
> *To perfect holiness and love.*
>
> —*Wesley's Hymns*

God's Call

READ: I Thessalonians 5: 21-24

*And the very God of peace sanctify you wholly. . . .
Faithful is he that calleth you, who also will do it
(I Thessalonians 5: 23-24).*

## Sanctification Is for All Believers

Within the family of holiness churches there are several
that identify their faith in their name. Among these is the
Pilgrim Holiness church. Their affirmation of faith in Christian holiness is composed basically of brief statements sup-
ported by scripture references. Here are some representative
passages.

"*Entire sanctification is subsequent to regeneration,* 'I
pray for them: I pray not for the world, but for them which
thou hast given me. . . . Sanctify them through thy truth'
(John 17: 9-17) *and is effected by the baptism of the Holy
Spirit,* 'One mightier than I cometh . . . he shall baptize you
with the Holy Ghost and with fire' (Luke 3: 16-17; also I Peter
1: 2; Romans 15: 16).

"*It is for all believers,* 'Sanctify them through thy truth.
. . . Neither pray I for these alone, but for them also which
shall believe on me through their word' (John 17: 17, 20;
also I Thessalonians 4: 3, 7; 5: 23-24), *and is an instantaneous
experience, received by faith,* 'And when the day of Pentecost
was fully come, they were all with one accord in one place.
And suddenly . . . they were all filled with the Holy Ghost'
(Acts 2: 1-4; also 15: 8-9).

"*It cleanses the heart of the recipient from all sin,* 'If we
walk in the light, as he is in the light, we have fellowship one
with another, and the blood of Jesus Christ his Son cleanseth
us from all sin (I John 1: 7, 9; also Acts 15: 8-9), *sets him apart,
and endows him with power for the accomplishment of all to
which he is called.* 'But ye shall receive power, after that the
Holy Ghost is come upon you: and ye shall be witnesses unto
me' (Acts 1: 8, also Luke 24: 49)" (*Manual,* Pilgrim Holiness
church).

*We praise Thee for the radiance
That from the hallowed page,
A lantern to our footsteps,
Shines on from age to age.*
WILLIAM WALSHAM HOW

**January 16**

READ: Acts 15: 8-9

*But as he which hath called you is holy, so be ye holy
in all manner of conversation; because it is written,
Be ye holy; for I am holy* (I Peter 1: 15-16).

## The Holy Spirit and Holiness

Dr. Albert F. Gray of the Church of God (Anderson,
Indiana) has written as follows in a series of doctrinal studies
for their people:

"As heaven is a holy place, sin cannot enter there. Only
the pure in heart have promise of seeing God. It is therefore
necessary that men become holy here and now, for without
holiness no man shall see the Lord. . . . We think of holiness
as freedom from sinful actions. . . . Holiness also applies to
the state of one's heart. . . . A holy or sanctified heart is pure,
having been cleansed through the blood of Christ.

"A life of holiness must have a beginning. Initial holiness
is the result of the new birth. In this experience one receives
a new life, which gives him power over sin and enables him
to live holily every day. . . . All conscious, willful sinning
ceases when one becomes a child of God.

"However the new convert is not slow to discover that
there are defects in his disposition and habits that need further
correction. There are tendencies to evil, against which he
must struggle and to which he does not give the consent of his
will. . . . Such defects are seen in the lives of the Apostles
before Pentecost and are found commonly in the lives of all
who have not received the baptism of the Spirit.

"There are two ways in which these defects are overcome:
by the very definite experience of the infilling of the Spirit,
and by growth in grace. The one is instantaneous, the other
·gradual. . . . The cleansing accompanying the baptism is
usually called sanctification, though this is a limited use of
the term. After the heart has been purified from ·all sin and
the nature has been cleansed in sanctification, there is room
for development and improvement of one's attitudes and conduct. This is growth in grace" (*Studies in Christian Theology,*
Warner Press).

READ: Psalms 99: 2, 5, 9

*O Lord my God, mine Holy One . . . Thou art of purer eyes than to behold evil, and canst not look on iniquity* (Habakkuk 1: 12-13).

## God Is Holy

Why does the supreme importance of holiness impress itself upon those who study the Bible, and the work of God in the human spirit? The answer is to be found in the very nature of God himself.

God is holy. Holiness is an intrinsic part of His being. We sometimes speak of God's holiness as His wholeness or completeness; there is nothing desirable that is missing from the character of God. But in His relationship to us we usually use the word to describe God's moral goodness. He never desires wrong and never does wrong. The Bible assures us, "God cannot be tempted with evil" (James 1: 13); He is holy. God never wishes to be dishonest and never acts dishonestly; He is holy. We always see our clearest picture of God when we are looking at the character of Christ. Of Him it is written, "Thou hast loved righteousness, and hated iniquity; therefore God, even thy God, hath anointed thee with the oil of gladness above thy fellows" (Hebrews 1: 9).

God desires only the best for every man and woman. He loves us sincerely because He is holy. Because sin blights and will eventually destroy all who remain sinners, God is utterly opposed to sin; He is holy. God is perfect righteousness and perfect love; that is what we mean by His holiness. As we meditate upon the kind of God whom we serve we sing with the Psalmist, "Oh how great is thy goodness, which thou hast laid up for them that fear thee!" (Psalms 31: 19).

> *Holy, Holy, Holy! Tho' the darkness hide Thee,*
> *Tho' the eye of sinful man Thy glory may not see,*
> *Only Thou art holy; there is none beside Thee*
> *Perfect in pow'r, in love, in purity.*
> —REGINALD HEBER

READ: Exodus 19:3-6

*I am the Lord your God: ye shall therefore sanctify yourselves, and ye shall be holy; for I am holy* (Leviticus 11:44).

## Ye Shall Be Holy

Have you ever found an unexpected treasure or a bit of beauty in some hidden spot? Here in our text are both. Lifting its face to the sun above the unattractive surface scum of an out-of-the-way pond, blooms a lily of purest white. Here in the middle of a maze of ceremonial law God has given us the central purpose for His people, "Ye shall be holy."

He is the God of all the earth but in a special sense He becomes the Father of those who obey His voice and keep His covenant. His chosen people in Old Testament times were to sanctify themselves—to set their lives apart for true worship. They were to be a unique people because they were to seek to be like a holy God.

That is what holiness means. Insofar as a man can resemble God, we are to be like Him in our attitudes toward right and wrong. We are to resemble Him in His love for persons. We were created in order that we might be "partakers of the divine nature."

God created us to be like himself in holiness—not equal to God, but similar to Him—a little lower only than the angels in heaven. God is unalterably committed to righteousness and His nature is perfect love. When He created us, He planned that we should be persons like himself in our complete devotion to righteousness.

**Prayer for today**

*O God, Thou hast made me to be like thyself. Thy will for me shall be my will. Help me to set my life apart, to devote it fully to Thee. Because I seek to be wholly Thine, make me holy as Thou art holy. In Jesus' name I pray. Amen.*

READ: I Thessalonians 5:15-26

*Abstain from all appearance of evil. And the very God of peace sanctify you wholly* (I Thessalonians 5:22-23).

## Entire Sanctification

The Salvation Army has formulated its faith in an experience of holiness as follows: "The Bible, as well as the experience of Christians generally, shows that regeneration, although a very great change, is not the complete purifying of man's nature. Thus Paul writes to some of his converts: 'And I, brethren, could not speak unto you as unto spiritual, but as unto carnal, even as unto babes in Christ' (I Corinthians 3:1).

"When a man is regenerated, he receives from the Holy Spirit *power* to conquer outward sin, yet sinful feelings and desires may still be present. The *love* of God is shed abroad in his heart, and he enjoys the presence and help of *the Holy Spirit,* but that love and the Holy Spirit have not always full control, and consequently cannot *fill* the soul. The man becomes in some measure a *partaker of God's nature,* but ungodlike inclinations and tendencies may still remain.

"We believe that it is the privilege of all believers to be 'wholly sanctified' and that their 'whole spirit and soul and body' may 'be preserved blameless unto the coming of our Lord Jesus Christ' (I Thessalonians 5:23).

"That is to say, We believe that after conversion there remain in the heart of the believer inclinations to evil, or roots of bitterness, which, unless overpowered by divine grace, produce actual sin; but that these evil tendencies can be entirely taken away by the Spirit of God, and the whole heart, thus cleansed from everything contrary to the will of God, or entirely sanctified, will then produce the fruit of the Spirit only. And we believe that persons thus entirely sanctified may, by the power of God, be kept unblamable and unreprovable before Him" (*Handbook of Doctrine*).

> *Deepen in me Thy work of grace,*
> *Teach me to do Thy will;*
> *Help me to live a spotless life,*
> *Thy holy laws fulfil.*
> —*The Salvation Army Tune Book*

**January 20**

READ: Leviticus 20: 7-8

*Let your heart therefore be perfect with the Lord our God, to walk in his statutes* (I Kings 8: 61).

## The Old Testament Call

Is God's call to live a holy life something new and strange? No. The call may be new to me and holiness may seem strange to men without spiritual life. But to the people of God the call is not new.

Abraham heard God's call to leave a heathen people and a heathen country. After he had served the Lord for some years, God spoke to him again saying, "I am the Almighty God; walk before me, and be thou perfect" (Genesis 17:1).

Israel had experienced God's deliverance from Egyptian bondage. God had led them across the Red Sea and through the wilderness. Now they were about to enter the promised land. At this point God said to them "Sanctify yourselves therefore, and be ye holy: for I am the Lord your God. And ye shall keep my statutes, and do them: I am the Lord which sanctify you" (Leviticus 20: 7-8).

To a later generation another of God's servants brought the divine call. "That all the people of the earth may know that the Lord is God, and that there is none else. Let your heart therefore be perfect with the Lord our God, to walk in his statutes, and to keep his commandments" (I Kings 8: 60-61).

To His people of every age God promises, "I will take away the stony heart out of your flesh, and I will give you an heart of flesh. And I will put my spirit within you, and cause you to walk in my statutes, and ye shall keep my judgments, and do them" (Ezekiel 36: 26-27).

**Prayer for today**

*O God, my Father, my spirit longs to be like Thee. With the saints of all the ages I pray, Make me holy as Thou dost desire me to be.*

READ: Luke 24: 45-49
*For this is the will of God, even your sanctification*
(I Thessalonians 4: 3).

## The New Testament Call

God calls His people to high-level living and names it sanctification. To Israel, He said, "Sanctify yourselves therefore, and be ye holy" (Leviticus 20: 7-8). In calling for clean living by New Testament church members, God declares through His apostle, "For this is the will of God, even your sanctification" (I Thessalonians 4: 3).

The Bible uses striking language to describe this high-level spiritual experience. To Abraham, God said, "Walk before me, and be thou perfect." When Jesus gave us the Sermon on the Mount, He summarized these applications of a perfect love in the call to holiness: "Be ye therefore perfect, even as your Father which is in heaven is perfect" (Matthew 5: 48).

Whatever else the call to Christian perfection may mean, it is the call for our lives to be well pleasing to God. Solomon exhorted his people, "Let your heart therefore be perfect with the Lord our God." Paul challenges us, "Be ye transformed by the renewing of your mind, that ye may prove what is that good, and acceptable, and perfect, will of God" (Romans 12: 2).

God calls us to be pure in heart, but not through our own efforts. He asks us to allow Him to work a miracle of love in our spirits. Hear His promise: "A new heart also will I give you, and a new spirit will I put within you." Hear also a New Testament testimony: "And God, which knoweth the hearts, bare them witness, giving them the Holy Ghost, even as he did unto us; and put no difference between us and them, purifying their hearts by faith" (Acts 15: 8-9).

*I hear Thy welcome voice,*
*That calls me, Lord, to Thee,*
*For cleansing in Thy precious blood*
*That flowed on Calvary.*

—L. HARTSOUGH

**January 22**

READ: Luke 1: 67-75

*Blessed be the Lord God . . . for he hath visited and redeemed his people . . . that we . . . might serve him . . . in holiness and righteousness . . . all the days of our life* (Luke 1: 68-75).

## Holiness Is Central

The doctrine of holiness has been called "the central idea of Christianity," "the supreme message of the church," "the keystone in the arch of God," and "the holy of holies of the Christian church." Why do men who study the Bible and God's work in the human heart thus magnify the supreme importance of this experience and life? It is because holiness is the central truth in our Christian faith.

A great saint and a careful theologian testified that he was converted one day and went on into the experience of Christian holiness the next. He often said that he got converted so that he could get sanctified. In this attitude he was entirely scriptural. We are saved in order that we may be sanctified wholly, just as we are sanctified in order to live a life of holiness.

There are other great and vital truths in God's plan for our salvation: Christ atoned for our sins; He died for our redemption; through His sacrifice we may be justified by faith. These are important; but standing alone they are incomplete. They are important in the same sense that every mile of a journey is important. But without the doctrine of holiness they are as a man who travels far toward home, only to end his journey one mile short of his hearthstone. Holiness is as that last mile; it is not the entire journey, but it is an advanced stage of our salvation for which all of the earlier steps have been taken.

> *He who has pardoned surely will cleanse thee,*
> *All of the dross of thy nature refine.*
> *Cleansed from all sin, His power will enter,*
> *Fill you and thrill you with power divine.*
> —MRS. C. H. MORRIS

READ: II Corinthians 6:16—7:1

*Since we have these promises, beloved, let us cleanse ourselves from every defilement of body and spirit, and make holiness perfect in the fear of God* (II Corinthians 7:1, R.S.V.).

## Scriptural Holiness

Because the experience of being filled with the Holy Spirit is so directly related to holy living, we often speak of entire sanctification as though it were equivalent to a holy life. Technically this is not true. But there is an important sense in which such an identification is correct. The Bible teaches that there is only one way a man can fully meet God's requirements of holiness in his inner life and conduct. He must be filled with the Holy Spirit.

Not every verse in the Bible which speaks of holiness is a direct proof text for the doctrine of entire sanctification. But because the experience of Christian holiness is so directly related to holy living, every reference to the holy life is relevant to the experience of holiness. And every scriptural reference to holiness in man is either direct or indirect evidence for the crisis experience.

It is this central place of entire sanctification in God's basic purpose for men which leads Dr. H. E. Jessop to say: "There is no passage of scripture, viewed in relation to its historic background, examined in the light of its widest context, and read and interpreted in accord with the general teaching of the writer, which does not teach either the need, possibility or possession of the experience for which the Wesleyan doctrine so uncompromisingly stands."

Since this second blessing is the indispensable prerequisite to God's requirements, every scriptural exhortation to holy living—when read or heard by the unsanctified—becomes an exhortation to the second blessing. And the sincere Christian heart responds:

> *Bid my inbred sin depart,*
> *And I Thy utmost word shall prove,*
> *Upright both in life and heart,*
> *And perfected in love.*
>
> *—Wesley's Hymns*

READ: Luke 1: 67-75

*God . . . hath visited and redeemed his people . . . that we being delivered out of the hand of our enemies might serve him without fear, in holiness and righteousness before him, all the days of our life* (Luke 1: 68-75).

## Redemption and Sanctification

We believe that entire sanctification is provided in the atonement of Christ. The Bible teaches that conversion and entire sanctification are both parts of God's plan of redemption for us. In our scripture reading Zacharias saw in prophetic vision that the birth of Jesus was to be a visitation from God for the redemption of His people. This redemption was to come through Christ and was to be the fulfillment of God's promise to Abraham.

Paul recognized that the promise was even more ancient than Abraham, and declared: "He hath chosen us in him before the foundation of the world" (Ephesians 1: 4). That choice and the promise of a Saviour involved not only forgiveness for sins, but it included our sanctification also. God's Word states clearly, "Wherefore Jesus also, that he might sanctify the people with his own blood, suffered without the gate" (Hebrews 13: 12). And again, God sent His Son into the world in order that we "might serve him without fear, in holiness and righteousness before him, all the days of our life." Christ died to save us; Christ died to sanctify us also. He saves us in order that we may be sanctified wholly; He sanctifies us so that we may "be holy and without blame before him in love."

The truth of divine revelation is clear, "For God hath not called us unto uncleanness, but unto holiness. He therefore that despiseth, despiseth not man, but God, who hath also given unto us his holy Spirit" (I Thessalonians 4: 7-8).

*Be it according to Thy word,*
*Redeem me from all sin;*
*My heart would now receive Thee, Lord!*
*Come in, my Lord, come in!*

—*The Salvation Army Tune Book*

READ: Genesis 17:1-8
*I am the Almighty God; walk before me, and be thou perfect* (Genesis 17:1).

## Be Thou Perfect

Here is high country! It is a breath-taking command, but it is God's command. What does it mean when God asks a man to be perfect? The Hebrew word is *tamin*. It is translated "perfect," "upright," or "sincere." The word is used elsewhere of God's character as well as for man, suggesting the possibility of a man resembling his God.

God does not here or elsewhere in the Bible ask absolute perfection of any man—not under any circumstances, or in any state of grace. Only God is beyond error. What was asked of Abraham and what God requires of us is that we shall walk before Him and live the kind of life that He has planned for men. *The Berkeley Version* translates it, "live in my presence and be upright"; the Revised Standard Version, "walk before me, and be blameless." A perfect life in God's sight is a life conformed wholly to His will and made possible by His presence. Can any man quarrel with that?

Adam Clarke comments: "Be just such as the *holy* God would have thee to be, as the *almighty* God can make thee, and live as the *all-sufficient* God shall support thee; for He alone who makes the soul holy can preserve it in holiness. . . . And who can doubt the possibility of its attainment, who believes in the omnipotent love of God, the infinite merit of the blood of atonement, and the all-pervading and all-purifying energy of the Holy Ghost?"

**Truth for today**

*In only three things is the child of God expected to be perfect: obedience, faith, and love.*—E. S. DUN-HAM.

READ: John 16: 12-14

*When he, the Spirit of truth, is come, he will guide*
*you into all truth* (John 16: 13).

## Will You Follow the Guide?

An earnest Christian bowed at a public altar seeking God's
perfect will for his life. In the intensity of his hunger he
cried out, "O Lord, sweep into my soul full force!" Is not
this the appropriate prayer for every sincere follower of
Christ? Entire sanctification follows when we let God have
complete control of our lives.

This is the way to Christian holiness, as holiness people
understand it. This we believe to be God's will for us—the
sanctification of our lives. We believe the Bible testifies that
full fellowship with God can be found in this fashion.

Holiness people have no monopoly on hunger for the
deeper spiritual life. God is the great Magnet who draws on
toward complete union with himself every man who responds
to His seeking love. We have no corner on the divine blessings, but we bear glad witness to the satisfaction that we
have found.

We believe that the Bible teaches the doctrine of Christian holiness. We find in the Scripture guidance that seems
clear to us as to how in this life we may come into such a
deeper fellowship with God. We have sought the leadership of the Holy Spirit to direct us in this search. We have
tried to give ourselves to God in such full obedience that
He could thereafter have the real controls of our lives. We
have believed that God cleanses and fills every life insofar
as that life is open to Him. We testify that God has answered
our prayer.

*When God is mine, and I am His,*
*Of paradise possessed,*
*I taste unutterable bliss,*
*And everlasting rest.*

—CHARLES WESLEY

READ: Psalms 27: 7-9
*When thou saidst, Seek ye my face; my heart said
unto thee, Thy face, Lord, will I seek* (Psalms 27: 8).

## Thy Face, Lord, Will I Seek

We saw yesterday that many Christian people bear glad
testimony to God's work of sanctifying power in their lives.
This is not something which they have achieved; it is the gift
of God. We believe, however, that men do not find God by
drifting, but rather by searching. While God is ever seeking
to find us, we are found of Him when we turn to Him and
when we seek for Him. We find forgiveness and recon-
ciliation when we ask for them. We find cleansing and sanctification when we come to God for these gifts of His grace.

Having found this kind of help from God, we invite you
to try it for yourself. As you meditate on these truths and
pray about the meaning of these passages from the Bible, do
they become God's word to you? If so, will you follow the
impulse of your spirit and take a further step toward God?

Perhaps your experience may parallel what happened in
the life of another. Bud Robinson testified that the first time
he heard the message of Christian holiness he declared that
no one could get it and keep it. The second time he heard
the truth he said: "Maybe some folk could have this experience, but it is not for me." With the third message his
faith began to take hold. Said he: "I believe it is for me.
I'll have it or die." He died to himself and received the
blessing.

> *He wills that I should holy be;*
> *That holiness I long to feel—*
> *That full divine conformity*
> *To all my Saviour's righteous will.*
> —CHARLES WESLEY

READ: I Corinthians 13:4-7

*O worship the Lord in the beauty of holiness—And let the beauty of the Lord our God be upon us* (Psalms 96:9; 90:17).

## The Beauty of Holiness

In the introduction to his book, *The Pure in Heart*, W. E. Sangster has said the best way for a man to study holiness is to look long at those who are holy and then to consult his own heart and mind on the reactions which he feels. That is because holiness is inherently attractive.

Can you now recall the man or woman whom you think of as the best Christian you have ever known? Perhaps a pastor or some little-known layman who walked with God. Are you thinking now of such a person? If you have that person in mind, will you answer this question: How often as you have thought of his life have you said, I wish I could be like that? To see the beauty of holiness makes the heart hungry for it.

If that beauty in a friend attracts us, how much more are our hearts stirred as we look steadily at the life of our Lord? On the mount of transfiguration Peter saw that beauty and wanted to capture it permanently. "Master, it is good for us to be here . . . let us make three tabernacles" (Mark 9:5). Thomas was discouraged, ready to surrender his faith. But a moment in the presence of the Master rekindled his magnificent obsession. He wanted more and not less as he gave the glad cry, "My Lord and my God" (John 20:28).

To see the beauty of holiness makes the heart hungry for it, and that hunger becomes a prayer:

> *Oh, to be like Thee! Oh, to be like Thee,*
> *Blessed Redeemer, pure as Thou art!*
> *Come in Thy sweetness, come in Thy fullness;*
> *Stamp Thine own image deep on my heart.*
> —T. O. CHISHOLM

Sin in the Soul

January 29 *2*

READ: Isaiah 6:1-7

*Mine eyes have seen the King, the Lord of hosts* (Isaiah 6:5).

## Holy, Holy, Holy

"God inflames the soul with a burning craving for absolute purity. One burns for complete innocency and holiness of personal life. No man can look on God and live, live in his own faults, live in the shadow of the least self-deceit. . . . The blinding purity of God in Christ, how captivating, how alluring, how compelling it is! The pure in heart shall see God? More, they who see God shall cry out to become pure in heart, even as He is pure, with all the energy of their souls.

"This has been an astonishing and unexpected element for me. . . . No average goodness will do, no measuring of our lives by our fellows, but only a relentless, inexorable divine standard. No relatives suffice; only absolutes satisfy the soul committed to holy obedience. Absolute honesty, absolute gentleness, absolute self-control, unwearied patience and thoughtfulness in the midst of the raveling friction of home and office and school and shop.

"Boldly must we risk the dangers which lie along the margins of excess, if we would live the life of the second half. For the life of obedience is a holy life, a separated life, a renounced life, cut off from worldly compromises, distinct, heaven-directed in the midst of men.

"He who walks in obedience, following God the second half, living the life of inner prayer of submission and exultation, on him God's holiness takes hold as a mastering passion of life. Yet ever he cries out in abysmal sincerity, 'I am the blackest of all the sinners of earth. I am a man of unclean lips, for mine eyes have seen the King, Jehovah of Hosts.' For humility and holiness are twins in the astonishing birth of obedience in the heart of men. So God draws unworthy us, in loving tenderness up into fellowship with His glorious self" (Thomas R. Kelly, *A Testament of Devotion*).

**January 30**

READ: Isaiah 6:1-7

*Woe is me! . . . I am a man of unclean lips, and I dwell in the midst of a people of unclean lips* (Isaiah 6:5).

## I See Sin in My Soul

It is said that the grandson of Ernest Renan, who was also a skeptic, knocked one day at the door of a rectory. When the priest answered the door, the young man said, "Come out; I want to talk to you about a problem." But the priest replied, "No, you come in; I want to talk to you about your sins." Men do not seek a remedy until they are aware of an illness.

Man needs to be sanctified wholly because he has a sinful nature. God is a holy God. His purpose is that we shall be holy people. But because of sin in our souls we are, apart from the power of His Holy Spirit, utterly incapable of living holy lives. Our fallen human nature is deeply dyed in sin, polluted, and loathsome. To be free from the carnal nature we must first recognize it. But how?

I become most aware of the "sin that dwelleth in me" when I see the holiness of God most clearly. It was when Isaiah realized, "Holy, holy, holy, is the Lord of hosts," that he cried out, "I am a man of unclean lips." To see the power of God is always to see our own human weakness. To see the goodness of God is to awaken in us the sharp pain of our human uncleanness, pollution, and profanity.

Let him who has never felt this need go on until the light of God someday breaks in upon his soul. But let him who has felt the exceeding sinfulness of his own nature join in the prayer:

> *Oh, make me clean! Oh, make me clean!*
> *Mine eyes Thy holiness have seen.*
> *Oh, send the burning, cleansing flame,*
> *And make me clean in Jesus' name!**

—GEORGE BENNARD

*© 1940 Renewal, The Rodeheaver Co. Used by permission.

READ: Genesis 1:27; 2:16-17; 3:6

*So God created man in his own image, in the image of God created he him* (Genesis 1:27).

## The Origin of Inherited Sin

As our first parents came from the hand of the Creator they were like God in their attitudes toward right and wrong. God endowed them with a quality of spirit which inclined them to goodness. This ready and glad conformity to the divine will is clearly reflected in Eve's spontaneous reaction to Satan's suggestion that God was stingy and unfair.

Moffatt translates Satan's approach in Genesis 3:1 thus: "And so God has said that you are not to eat from any tree in the park?" At once the woman's natural impulse for truth and her inherent loyalty to God showed themselves in her reply. "We may eat of the fruit of the trees of the garden [God has given us plenty]. But of the fruit of the tree which is in the midst of the garden [just that one tree], God hath said, Ye shall not eat of it."

In spite of man's original inclination to righteousness, God had planned that holy living must be the result of man's own free choice. Satan came to our first parents with a subtle temptation and they chose evil. They weighed the known will of their Creator against the suggestion of Satan and turned away from God. The seed of human sin was sown with that choice; we are still reaping the tragic harvest.

What was true in the Garden of Eden is equally true today. No state of grace puts us in a place where our choices become unreal. In the experience of entire sanctification God graciously restores this blessing of an inward inclination to holy living. But not even for righteousness will God debase our essential human dignity by canceling our power of choice.

**Thought for today**

*Our choices are the hinges upon which the doors of destiny swing.*

READ: Genesis 3: 6-13

*I heard thy voice in the garden, and I was afraid* (Genesis 3:10).

## Evidences of Carnality

Sin always raises barriers between our souls and God. In the place of joyous fellowship in the presence of God, our first parents were now afraid of the Creator's voice. They sought to hide from Him. The carnal mind, which is the enemy of God, always makes us afraid of Him. We are afraid of God because we know that inside of us there is a spirit of opposition to Him.

Instead of accepting personal responsibility for their wrong choices, an evil disposition in our first parents sought to place the blame on others. Adam blamed Eve; "The woman whom thou gavest to be with me, she gave me of the tree, and I did eat." When God turned to Eve and asked, "What is this that thou hast done?" she too passed the blame along: "The serpent beguiled me, and I did eat."

The first man and woman had once been happily obedient, accepting God's suggestion as the rule of life. They now had an evil spirit of resistance and had to be driven by force to obey. Formerly a mere knowledge of God's will had been enough for obedience. Now only the threat of a flaming sword was sufficient to prevent forthright rebellion.

The inward disposition of man had changed. Sin, entering through the door of choice, deranged the whole of man's nature. His original holiness was lost. Some quality of spirit that attracted him to God had died. The image of God in which we were created was broken and our moral likeness to the Creator was marred. Man had fallen.

### Questions for today

*Am I afraid of God? Am I unwilling to accept responsibility for my conduct? Do I have a spirit of rebellion against God's will? Are these attitudes fruits of the Holy Spirit or of a carnal spirit?*

READ: Romans 5:12, 19

*By one man sin entered into the world, and death by sin; and so death passed upon all men* (Romans 5:12).

## Death Passed upon All

Whenever man sees clearly the alternative between right and wrong and deliberately chooses wrong, something dies in his soul. And the more clearly the issue is seen, the more fatal is the choice of the wrong. Because the wrong choice of our first parents was made in spite of maximum opportunity to do God's will, there was maximum tragedy in the soul.

This sin not only affected our first parents, but the evil consequences of this wrong choice have entered tragically into the lives of all men. God chose to bind our world together with interacting bonds of mutual influence. "None of us liveth to himself, and no man dieth to himself" (Romans 14:7). We lift others when we rise, and we drag our friends down when we fall. In a world of mutual influence we could not have one without the other.

Our first parents sinned and fell from their high level of holiness. The serious nature of that Fall is shown by the language with which the Bible describes it. The Fall brought death to man—both physical death and also that deeper tragedy of separation from God which the Scriptures call spiritual death.

The effects of that most serious of all wrong choices was most widespread in its influence for ill. The Word of God makes clear the tragic extent of that tragic choice. By one man sin entered the world, and death by sin; and so death passed upon all men."

### Thought for today

*Sinning, even in its most private forms, is like putting poison into a city's water supply. Sooner or later everyone is worse for the pollution.*

**February 3**

READ: Psalms 51: 5-10

*Create in me a clean heart, O God; and renew a right spirit within me* (Psalms 51:10).

## I Was Born in Sin

The Scriptures clearly teach that there is in the nature of fallen man a universal tendency to evil. "And God saw that the wickedness of man was great . . . and that every imagination of the thoughts of his heart was only evil continually" (Genesis 6:5). Because carnality is the common lot of all men, I know that I too was born with this evil in my soul.

Since my sins have been forgiven, have I asked God to give me a clean heart? Can I testify now that, by faith, "the blood of Jesus Christ his Son cleanseth . . . from all sin" (I John 1:7)? If not, carnality is still present. I am not guilty by reason of my evil nature, because I was born with it. But I am responsible for remaining carnal when I am aware of this sinful nature and know that God has made provision to cleanse it.

As David reflected upon his outbroken sin, his mind turned to this inner spirit of evil which lay behind the act. In his hour of moral introspection he cried out, "Behold, I was shapen in iniquity; and in sin did my mother conceive me." The Psalmist was not trying to shrug off responsibility for his own sin by passing the blame to his parents. His mood was one of utter sincerity and confession. He saw clearly his whole sin problem. He knew that he could not save himself from the penalty of the sins he had committed nor could he be certain that he would not commit those sins again.

David recognized what we too must acknowledge. From the beginning of his life he had had an unclean heart and a wrong spirit. He needed that heart cleansed and that spirit made right.

READ: Psalms 51: 5-10

*Behold, I was shapen in iniquity; and in sin did my mother conceive me* (Psalms 51: 5).

## Selfishness Shows Early

Let him who questions the truth of universal inherited sin in the soul consider the selfish behavior of even young children. A child's natural philosophy of life seems to be, What's mine is my own, and what's yours is mine too if I can get my hands on it!

At six years of age our little girl was in vacation Bible school. To help the children develop habits of unselfishness the teachers taught them this song:

*If I had a scooter new,*
*I would sometimes share with you.*
*If I had an apple bright,*
*I would let you have a bite.*

Gail sang the song happily around home—it seemed to me she sang it fifty times a day! She had no scooter to test her willingness to share; and extra apples could be had for the asking, so they posed no problem. But Gail had a bicycle that she loved dearly and she had a hard time being willing to let her friends take rides on it.

One day I thought I would help the Bible school teachers with their project in Christian education. I said, "Gail, let's sing the song this way: 'If I had a *bike* so new, I would sometimes share with you." What was a child's response? Her face clouded, her lips trembled, and tears welled up in her eyes as she sobbed, "No, Daddy. I don't want to sing the song that way!"

What brought that resistance? It was the sinful spirit of selfishness reflecting itself in even a young child.

**Affirmation for today**

*I recognize that all men are born in sin. I do now accept God's provision to create in me a clean heart.*

**February 5**

READ: Mark 7: 21-23

*For from within, out of the heart of men, proceed evil thoughts . . . covetousness, wickedness, deceit* (Mark 7: 21-22).

## Evil Acts Come from Within

Jesus often turned the thoughts of His listeners to the fact that carnality is the source of sin—that evil acts are caused by an evil condition in man's spirit. Of this inventory of the carnal heart, Paul Rees has said, "It reads like a sewer inspector's write up."

"For from within, out of the heart of men, proceed evil thoughts, adulteries, fornications, murders, thefts, covetousness, wickedness, deceit, lasciviousness, an evil eye, blasphemy, pride, foolishness: all these evil things come from within, and defile the man."

Elsewhere our Lord asked, "How can ye, being evil, speak good things? for out of the abundance of the heart the mouth speaketh. A good man out of the good treasure of the heart bringeth forth good things: and an evil man out of the evil treasure bringeth forth evil things" (Matthew 12:34-35). "Thou blind Pharisee, cleanse first that which is within . . . that the outside . . . may be clean also" (Matthew 23:26).

Dr. B. F. Neely says carnality is that which "rises up and tries to open the door every time the devil knocks from without." We can have clean lives only when we get at the troublemaker and through divine grace get rid of the traitorous doorkeeper.

When we sense how prone we are even *at our best* to fall short of holy living, should it not make us hunger for *all the resources* that God can give us?

**Prayer for today**

*Create in me a clean heart, O God; and renew a right spirit within me* (Psalms 51: 10).

READ: Romans 7:18-25

*Now if I do that I would not, it is no more I that do it, but sin that dwelleth in me* (Romans 7:20).

## Carnality Is My Enemy

The Bible explains to us how man fell. Jesus makes it clear that this fallen, sinful nature is a deep-seated source of sins in our lives. In our scripture lesson Paul testifies that this carnal nature in the soul is a foreign element by which man is enslaved. It works in opposition to our best interests and our highest desires.

"I often find that I have the will to do good, but not the power. That is, I don't accomplish the good I set out to do, and the evil I don't really want to do I find I am always doing. Yet if I do the things that I don't really want to do then it is not, I repeat, 'I' who do them, but the sin which has made its home within me" (Phillips).

This description of the work of the carnal mind certainly refers to Paul's experience before he was converted. There is power in regeneration to save a man from continuous sinning. But the passage does depict clearly the essentially evil and alien nature of sin in the soul. Paul's sensitive spirit recognized this antagonism to God and goodness before he met Christ. The presence and power of this sinful nature, even after one has been saved, is the widespread testimony of born-again Christians.

Paul was certain that this evil inclination was a foreign intrusion and no essential part of himself; its effects came from a force beyond his control. In his helplessness he implored, "O wretched man that I am! who shall deliver me from the body of this death?"

Does my own spirit echo Paul's cry? If so, I may also find Paul's answer, "I thank God [it is] through Jesus Christ our Lord."

**February 7**

READ: Romans 7: 14-15

*I delight in the law of God after the inward man: but I see another law in my members, warring against the law of my mind* (Romans 7: 22-23).

## Do I Have Evidences of Carnality?

The Bible clearly teaches the doctrine of the fall of man and the universality of the carnal mind. The great need of every unsanctified Christian is that he shall recognize the presence and nature of inherited sin in himself and find deliverance from it. But how does one become aware of indwelling sin?

The specific ways in which carnality manifests itself may vary from one person to another, but always it shows up in an attitude that is un-Christlike. In one it is anger and in another pride. Sometimes carnality is revealed in a dwarfed Christian life in which one has failed to grow in grace. Some have been convicted by their lack of Christian concern and others by frequent defeats under temptation. Often the telltale evidence is jealousy, doubt, or unyielded ambition.

The carnal mind is Satan's open door to the unsanctified soul, and Satan is shrewd enough to attack us at our weakest point.

The need is there, and if we keep our hearts open God will reveal it to us. In a little booklet *Instructions to Christian Converts,* Dr. Dougan Clark writes, "Every sincere Christian must have this need and, if you do not draw back from it, the Holy Spirit will lead you and guide you into the grace of sanctification as a second definite work."

**Prayer for today**

*Search me, O God, and know my heart: try me, and know my thoughts: and see if there be any wicked way in me, and lead in the way everlasting* (Psalms 139: 23-24).

READ: Romans 8:5-7

*The carnal mind is enmity against God: for it is not subject to the law of God, neither indeed can be* (Romans 8:7).

## Resistance to Light on Holiness

In his book, *Perfect Love*, J. A. Wood writes "Being so often convicted of my need of perfect love, and failing to obtain it, I, after a while, like many others, became somewhat skeptical in regard to the Wesleyan doctrine of entire sanctification, as a *distinct* work, subsequent to regeneration . . . I became somewhat prejudiced against the Bible terms *sanctification, holiness* and *perfection* . . . If a pious brother exhorted the preachers to seek sanctification . . . I was distressed in spirit, and disposed to find fault."

Here is an indication of carnality. Antagonism and resistance to the truth of heart holiness is one of the sure evidences that we need the second blessing. God's Word declares, "The carnal attitude is inevitably opposed to the purpose of God, and neither can nor will follow His laws for living" (Romans 8:7, Phillips).

When God begins to reveal the light of Bible holiness to the unsanctified Christian, the carnal spirit begins to argue, to resist, to reject. If God has begun to talk to us about our need and we find in our hearts such a negative attitude, we must earnestly seek God's help to destroy that spirit. We must ask Him to take from our hearts all antagonism to His full will for our lives.

*My stubborn will at last hath yielded;*
*I would be Thine, and Thine alone;*
*And this the prayer my lips are bringing,*
*"Lord, let in me Thy will be done."*
—MRS. C. H. MORRIS

**February 9**

READ: Romans 7: 22-24

*Let all bitterness, and wrath, and anger . . . be put
away from you* (Ephesians 4: 31).

## Carnal Anger

Often carnality reveals itself in spiritual failure that
brings a deep sense of need to the struggling Christian. Dr.
D. I. Vanderpool relates his own experience as follows:
"Having a quick temper and a feeling that I was quite
important, I kept in trouble most of the time. My life of sin
was brought to an end when I was converted at the age of
seventeen. . . . I was supremely happy in my new-found joy.

"I had been converted only a few days when a fellow
with whom I had had trouble insulted me. My first impulse
was to fight, but something reminded me that I was now a
Christian and must not fight. For a full minute the war was
on in my heart. I shall never forget the warring in my
members; but I took the insult, said nothing, and went on
my way. I was filled with fear when I considered how near
I came to doing something which I would always have regretted.

"Knowing that I had that vicious something still in my
heart alarmed me and put me on my guard. Two or three
times within ten days I had upsets because of my quick temper, but after prayer and repentance I found forgiveness and
the joy bells would ring again in my heart. I loathed the thing
within my heart that constantly strove to upset me" (*Flames
of Living Fire*, Beacon Hill Press).

> *Have you ever felt the power of the Pentecostal fire,*
> *Burning up all carnal nature, cleansing out all base*
> *desire,*
> *Going thro' and thro' your spirit, cleansing all its*
> *stain away?*
> *Oh, I'm glad, so glad to tell you it is for us all today.*
> —L. L. PICKETT

READ: Revelation 3: 13-16, 19-20

*Ye . . . are . . . such as have need of milk, and not of strong meat* (Hebrews 5: 12).

## The Sin of Stagnation

In the advancement of God's work, the weakness of the Christian is often a greater problem than the wickedness of the world. The Bible declares, "Although you ought to be teachers of others because you have been Christians so long, you actually need someone to teach you over and over again the very elements of the truths that God has given us, and you have gotten into such a state that you are in constant need of milk instead of solid food" (Hebrews 5: 12, Williams).

It was a realization of this condition that showed to Hannah Whitall Smith her need of holiness. She describes her experience thus:

"I was converted in my twenty-sixth year . . . But my heart was ill at ease . . . I did not grow in grace; and at the end of eight years of my Christian life, I was forced to make the sorrowful admission that I had not even as much power over sin as when I was first converted. In the presence of temptation, I found myself weakness itself.

"It was not my outward walk that caused me sorrow, though I can see now that was far from what it ought to have been; but it was the sins of my heart that troubled me—coldness, deadness, want of Christian love . . . roots of bitterness, want of a meek and quiet spirit . . . Sin still had more or less dominion over me, and I did not come up to the Bible standard."

### Prayer for an anemic Christian

*For this cause I bow my knees unto the Father of our Lord Jesus Christ, . . . that he would grant you, according to the riches of his glory, to be strengthened with might by his Spirit in the inner man; . . . that ye might be filled with all the fulness of God* (Ephesians 3: 14, 16, 19).

**February 11**

READ: Matthew 19: 16-22

*Who then is willing to consecrate his service this day
unto the Lord?* (I Chronicles 29: 5)

## Unyielded Ambitions

Dr. J. A. Huffman testifies: "From the time of my boy-hood conversion, I had lived a good, conscientious Christian life, by God's help. . . . But early in my Christian experience I sensed the need of a consecration which I did not possess. . . . I willed to do God's will; but, contradictory as it may seem, I was unwilling to let Him have His way in all the details of my life. I had ambitions, choices, and plans . . . which I dared not commit to Him, lest they should fail of His approval. This brought unhappiness.

"It was at a campmeeting where holiness was being preached and testified to that I became convinced that the . . . thing for me to do . . . was to consecrate myself entirely to God, thus abandoning myself fully to Him, to be His and His alone. . . . This might mean the foreign mission field. It might spoil all my cherished plans; but at that altar, that day, the consecration was made.

"It is a great joy to testify that God's plans and purposes for my life, as they have been revealed gradually, have proved to be infinitely bigger, better and richer than the plans which I had made for myself. It is my belief that God has a far richer plan for every life which will be yielded to Him than the individual could possibly plan for himself" (*Flames of Living Fire*, Beacon Hill Press).

*The closer I walk the sweeter He seems.*
*Much fairer is He than all of my dreams.*
*His love lights my way when pathways are dim,*
*The closer I walk to Him .\**

—HALDOR LILLENAS

*© 1931 and 1958 by Lillenas Publishing Co.

READ: Luke 15: 25-32

*Jealousy is cruel as the grave. Its flashes are flashes of fire, a most vehement flame* (Song of Solomon 8: 6, R.S.V.).

## Jealousy

The essence of carnality is selfishness—a self-centered spirit that will not yield to God's will, nor give fair consideration to other persons. It is a basic deficiency in Christlike kindliness. It is a lack of the kind of love that wishes the best for a fellow human being. Because this love is lacking, the spirit grows jealous and cannot be happy in the success or happiness of others. Jealousy has been called "the meanest feeling." The Bible describes this carnal attitude, "cruel as the grave: the coals thereof are coals of fire, which hath a most vehement flame" (Song of Solomon 8: 6).

A friend testifies that during his college days he became aware of the carnal mind because of a spirit of jealousy. He was studying for the ministry and working hard to excel as a preacher of the gospel. When given an opportunity to preach, he did his best and had good success. But he could not bring himself to be glad when a fellow student was successful in the pulpit.

He could always find flaws in the ministry of others. It was a painful revelation when he faced up to the fact that he secretly rejoiced in the discovery of these shortcomings in his friends. Through the soul-searching ministry of the Holy Spirit he saw that the underlying cause was carnality. He deplored this wrong spirit that he found. He sought for deliverance and God gave it. That deliverance is available to all who are grieved by inward sin.

*I hate the sin which grieves Thy loving heart;*
*Speak, precious Lord, and bid it all depart.*
*Thy temple cleanse and make my heart Thy home;*
*Come, King of Kings, and reign thyself alone.**
—GEORGE BENNARD

*© 1940 Renewal, The Rodeheaver Co. Used by permission.

**February 13**

READ: James 1: 5-8

*A double-minded man is unstable in all his ways* (James 1: 8).

## Instability

Instability is one of the common failures of the Christian life, and carnality is the cause of much of it. A subtle love for the things of the world robs the spirit of its loyalty to Christ. Commissioner Brengle of the Salvation Army testified, "After I was converted to God I did not want any evil thing, but there was something in me that did." The recognition of this double mindedness has awakened many a new Christian to the existence of carnality and has started him on his search for heart holiness.

Dr. Harry E. Jessop recalls: "From the first moment of the realization of saving grace, I wanted all that God could give me, and soon found myself yearning for a deeper life in Him. It was not long before I began to feel that, glorious as my new experience of conversion had been, God was now holding before me something of a deeper nature than that which I already enjoyed.

"While my love for Christ was such that it pained me to know that I had grieved Him, my spiritual life was far from constant, and my communion was not sustained. Frequently the conflicts into which I came did not end in such a manner as to bring glory to the Lord. I was conscious of a lack of power in service, and of a strange inward conflict which did not seem consistent with New Testament standards" (*Flames of Living Fire,* Beacon Hill Press).

God has for us something better than halfway religion. When we give ourselves wholly to Him, He gives himself fully to us.

> *All to Jesus I surrender.*
> *Make me, Saviour, wholly Thine;*
> *Let me feel the Holy Spirit,*
> *Truly know that Thou art mine.*
> —J. W. VAN DEVENTER

READ: Luke 22: 55-62

*Peter said unto him, Though I should die with thee, yet will I not deny thee* (Matthew 26: 35).

## Moral Defeat

In *The Caine Mutiny,* Willie Keith said to May Wynn, "I'm a sort of pale Christian." The description fits Peter when we remember his behavior that night in the courtyard of the high priest. The words of our text were brave words, and Peter meant them when he said them. But Peter did not know his own weakness, nor the treachery of an unsanctified heart. It was perhaps midnight when he made this earnest declaration of loyalty. Before the sun was up he had broken his promise, and failed his Lord. Where there had once been a fire of devotion, a saddened Peter now had only "the white cold ashes of moral defeat." He went out and wept bitterly.

How many a man has found in this story the true mirror of his own spiritual failure? William McDonald, holiness pioneer and author of *Scriptural Way of Holiness,* testifies for many another: "I had been struggling to be holy from the night I was converted to God, and had been preserved from any willful departure from God. . . . But I had tried a hundred times to be holy and failed every time." In his prayer he cried out: "I am very sorry, but oh, God, I have no confidence in the flesh or any of my efforts! I have tried and tried until my heart is sick. I know I will never be any better, nor do any better unless my heart is made better."

It is well to weep over our failure. It is better when God reveals to us the cause. It is a rapturous joy when through the power of His Holy Spirit God enables us to live a life of victory.

> *With aching heart and spirit sore distressed,*
> *I came to Thee and Thou didst give me rest.*
> *Now, Lord, I pray and long with deep desire*
> *To be made clean by Thy refining fire.* *
> —GEORGE BENNARD

*© 1940, renewal, The Rodeheaver Co. Used by permission.

**February 15**

READ: John 20: 24-28

*Take heed, brethren, lest there be in any of you an evil heart of unbelief* (Hebrews 3:12).

## Doubt and Unbelief

Dr. P. F. Bresee had been in the ministry for a number of years when he fought the great battle of his life with carnality. God had blessed his ministry with many souls, but he came to realize that he did not have sufficient grace to handle inbred sin. He says:

"I had a big load of carnality on hand always. It had taken the form of pride, anger and worldly ambitions. At last, however, it took the form of doubt. It seemed as though I doubted everything. . . . I had come to the point where I seemingly could not go on. My religion did not meet my needs. It seemed as though I could not continue to preach with this awful question of doubt on me, and I prayed and cried to the Lord.

"I was ignorant of my own condition. I did not understand in reference to carnality. . . . But in my ignorance the Lord helped me, drew me and impelled me, and, as I cried to Him that night, He seemed to open heaven on me, and gave me, as I believe, the baptism with the Holy Ghost.

"It not only took away my tendencies to worldliness, anger and pride, but it also removed my doubt. For the first time, I apprehended that the conditions of doubt were moral instead of intellectual, and that doubt was a part of carnality that could only be removed as the other works of the flesh are removed."

**Prayer for today**

*O Thou Spirit of truth, cleanse my heart of uncertainty and unbelief. Make thyself real to me. Then shall I serve Thee gladly all the days of my life. In Jesus' name. Amen.*

READ: John 8:34

*O wretched man that I am! who shall deliver me from the body of this death? I thank God [it is] through Jesus Christ our Lord* (Romans 7:24-25).

## "Who Shall Deliver Me?"

Men and women of every age have been confronted by the tragic fact of carnality in the soul. Some in early Christian life and some after years of struggle have cried out with Paul, "Wretched man that I am! Who can save me from this deadly lower nature?" Then with Paul they have shouted, "Thank God! it has been done through Jesus Christ our Lord!" (Romans 7:24-25, Williams)

There *is* deliverance. God allows the sin of our souls to harass and embarrass us only in order that we shall cry out for release. He hurts us only in order that He may help us through the pain that He causes. The Bible assures us, "Whom the Lord loveth he chasteneth, and scourgeth every son whom he receiveth. If ye endure chastening, God dealeth with you as with sons." And this chastening is given us for the precise purpose "that we might be partakers of his holiness" (Hebrews 12:6-7, 10).

The discovery of unyielded ambitions, inner conflicts, carnal anger, or any other un-Christlike attitude is the occasion which God uses to reveal to us our spiritual need. No matter how the revelation may come, it is to be looked upon as a convicting ministry of the Holy Spirit to lead us into the experience of entire sanctification.

Let us then in this hour of unpleasant revelation yield ourselves to God's diagnosis and prescription. He is the faithful Physician of the soul.

*Search me, O God, and know my heart today;*
*Try me, O Saviour, and know my thoughts, I pray.*
*See if there be some wicked way in me;*
*Cleanse me from ev'ry sin, and set me free.*
—EDWIN ORR

**February 17**

READ: I Corinthians 3: 1-3

*For whereas there is among you envying, and strife, and divisions, are ye not carnal, and walk as men?* (I Corinthians 3: 3)

## What's in a Name?

What do we learn about the nature of inherited sin from a study of the names by which it is known?

Our English words *carnal* and *carnality* come from the Latin *carnis*, which means "flesh." Paul also calls this evil disposition *the lust of the flesh* (Galatians 5:16). These Biblical uses of the words do not indicate physical flesh. The Bible nowhere teaches that the human body is sinful. The carnal mind is, rather, the mind of the natural man, contrasted with the mind of a man who has been filled with the Spirit of God.

The Bible also speaks of the carnal nature as *sin*. We must be careful to distinguish this *sin* from the plural term *sins*. Sins are our own willful transgressions of God's law for which we are responsible and therefore guilty. Sin, on the other hand, is the natural tendency in us to oppose God, a tendency with which we were born. Since we did not personally choose it, we bear no guilt because of it. When the term sin is used this way in the Greek, the definite article *the* often appears with it. In the sixth chapter of Romans the expression *the sin* occurs fourteen times and is the key to the Apostle's argument. The term sin is used to describe carnality because (1) the carnal nature came from an act of sin and (2) carnality is by nature an active tendency to commit sins.

Because we are born with this tendency, theology has called it *inherited sin* and *inbred sin*. Because the tendency originated in our first parents, it is called *original sin* or the *Adamic nature*. Because it is a perversion of human nature as God first created us, we call it *depravity* and *inherited depravity*.

**Thought for today**

*Call it what you will—carnality, sin, inherited depravity, or just a bad attitude—if you have it, you ought to get rid of it.*

READ: Hebrews 12:14-17

*Looking diligently lest any man fail of the grace of God; lest any root of bitterness springing up trouble you, and thereby many be defiled* (Hebrews 12:15).

## What's in a Name? (continued)

The term *sin* by which we designate carnality is called *race sin* because it occurs in all persons of the human race. It is called *inherent sin* because it comes with and inheres in our fallen human nature. We call it *sin in believers* because carnality is not removed when our sins are forgiven; unsanctified believers still have in them this sinful tendency.

The writer of Hebrews speaks of carnality as a "root of bitterness." It is a figure of speech that has been the basis for much holiness preaching—and with good reason. Carnality is like a root because: (1) It is sometimes not apparent and hence we may deceive ourselves that it is not there. (2) It has a life principle in it that puts forth shoots of its own kind. (3) If one would effectively get rid of the bitter shoots that spring up, he must do more than chop them off when they appear; he must get rid of the root cause—pull it up, destroy it, eradicate it.

But we must never allow our figures of speech to lead us into thinking of carnality as a physical thing. It is not like a cancer on the hand that can be cut off or a decayed tooth that can be pulled out. Such physical figures are only crutches for the imagination. Carnality is a quality of the spirit, a disposition of mind, an attitude, an inclination.

This spirit nature of carnality is clear from the evils our scripture suggests. Carnality causes trouble in the spirit of a man. Always this defilement reflects itself in wrong attitudes toward God and His people. The illustration of Esau describes a man who was conscious of making a wrong choice, and later regretting it. When we look for our clearest understanding of the sin principle and its cure, we must keep in the realm of conscious experience—or close to it.

**February 19**

READ: Ephesians 4: 22-24

*Put off your old nature which belongs to your former manner of life* (Ephesians 4: 22, R.S.V.).

## Put Off the Old Man

One of Paul's figures of speech as translated in the Authorized Version has caused some merriment and a little ludicrous misunderstanding. The first and clearest statement is in Romans 6: 6: "Our old man is crucified with him, that the body of sin might be destroyed, that henceforth we should not serve sin." The same figure is used in Ephesians 4: 22 and Colossians 3: 9. The misunderstanding is due to our American slang in which a father is sometimes discourteously referred to as "the old man."

Almost all the new versions show us the true nature of the "old man" of sin. Paul is talking about the old nature which went along with, and was a cause of the old sinful lives of these people—their lives before they became Christians. God's Word exhorts Christians to "put off your old nature" (R.S.V.), "that old human nature" (*New English Bible*), "your old self" (Williams), "the old nature" (Berkeley and (Moffatt), "your former nature" and "your old unrenewed self" (*Amplified New Testament*), "your original evil nature" (Weymouth).

It is clear that in the experience of entire sanctification some change is to be made inside of us. We are to have new natures which are as well adapted to the new life as the old sinful nature was adapted to sinful conduct.

How are desires for evil to be rooted out of my conscious experience? How can I be changed so that I want the things that God wants? How are good inclinations born? How do temptations to sin wither and die before they become so much a part of me that they are really my sincere desires? These are the real questions involved when we speak of carnality being destroyed. It is a big assignment—but we have a big God!

READ: Psalms 42:1-2

*Blessed are they which do hunger and thirst after righteousness: for they shall be filled* (Matthew 5:6).

## Where There Is Need, There Is Satisfaction

"Set over against the holy demand of the holy God is the inescapable fact that the regenerate man is not holy. The regenerate life he has received is holy, but an unholy element remains in him. This is admitted in the Articles of Religion of the Church of England and other Episcopal bodies, with those of the Methodist tradition. The Book of Common Prayer says of original or birth-sin, 'this infection of nature doth remain, yea in them that are regenerated.' These words describe as clearly as did Wesley the condition of the unsanctified heart.

"The need of heart purity has been sensed to the point of agony by thousands of devout Christians who never heard the doctrine of full salvation proclaimed. The diaries and journals of many betray their dissatisfaction of soul and their desire for deliverance. Sighs for heaven bulk large in their confessions, for there they hope to be free from sin.

"Is there nothing this side of heaven to match the need and meet the desire of believers who are keenly conscious of inbred sin? Is there no provision that reaches to the height of God's demand and to the depth of man's hunger? If not, we are of all men most miserable. If there is, we can say to God as did Augustine, 'Grant what thou commandest, and then command what thou wilt.'

"God is faithful who has promised, and the promise stimulates the desire for the fullness of love. He will not mock the hunger He has aroused. He says, 'Blessed are they which do hunger and thirst after righteousness: for they shall be filled'" (*Holiness the Finished Foundation*, J. PAUL TAYLOR).

> *Breathe on me, Breath of God,*
> *Till I am wholly thine,*
> *Until this earthly part of me*
> *Glows with thy fire divine.*
> —*Hymns of the Living Faith*

**February 21**

## My Testimony

### By E. Stanley Jones

"I came to Christ bankrupt. My capacity to blunder drove me to his feet, and to my astonishment he took me, forgave me, and sent my happy soul singing its way down the years. By grace was I saved, through faith, and that not of myself—it was the gift of God.

"I walked in the joy of that for months and then the clouds began to gather. There was something within me not redeemed, something else down in the cellar that seemed to be sullenly at war with this new life. I was at war with myself.

"I think I can see what happened. We live in two minds —the conscious and the subconscious. The subconscious is the residing place of the driving instincts: self, sex, and the herd. These instincts have come down through a long racial history and they have bents toward evil.

"Into the conscious mind there is introduced at conversion a new life, a new loyalty, a new love. But the subconscious mind does not obey this new life. Its driving instincts drive for fulfillment apart from any morality built up in the conscious mind. There ensues a clash between the new life in the conscious mind and the instincts of the subconscious. The house of man-soul becomes a house divided against itself.

"I wondered if this was the best Christianity could do— to leave one in this divided condition? I found to my glad surprise the teaching concerning the Holy Spirit, and I found that the area of the work of the Holy Spirit is largely, if not entirely, in the subconscious. I found that if I would surrender to the Holy Spirit this conscious mind—all I knew and all I did not know—He would cleanse at these depths I could not control. I surrendered and accepted the gift by faith. He did cleanse as a refining fire. In that cleansing there was a unifying. Conscious and subconscious minds were brought under a single control and redemption. That control was the Holy Spirit. I was no longer at war with myself. Life was on a permanently higher level. It was no longer up and down. The soul had caught its stride. I went on my way singing a new song. That song has continued. It is fresher today than then." (From *The Meaning of Sanctification*, Charles Ewing Brown).

READ: Romans 6:1-2

*Shall we continue in sin, that grace may abound?*
*God forbid. How shall we, that are dead to sin, live*
*any longer therein?*  (Romans 6:1-2)

## We Need to Be Freed from Sin

For the past several weeks we have seen that, due to the Fall, there is within the soul of man a deep-seated tendency to sin. The Scriptures clearly teach it. Paul writes, "The carnal mind is enmity against God" (Romans 8:7). What the Bible teaches, our own human experience confirms. We have seen it at work in ourselves and in others.

This inner spirit of evil seeks to destroy our concern for righteousness. Even when desires for goodness arise, carnality saps the moral energy of the soul. We find in ourselves a kind of spiritual paralysis so that we cannot do the good things that we desire. Paul describes it thus: "For to will is present with me; but how to perform that which is good I find not. For the good that I would I do not: but the evil which I would not, that I do" (Romans 7:18-19).

How is God ever to gather a people who are like Him in moral character—righteous and loving—when man has within him such a spirit of antagonism to goodness? How can a man ever serve God when he has such an inability to follow the ideals which his mind says are right?

Until such deep-seated inability is removed we have no sound hope for God's will to be done in us. If our first parents failed to live holy lives even with God's moral image intact, how shall we succeed, deprived of His likeness and depraved as a consequence?

If we are to live above sin, we need to have the carnal spirit destroyed. We need to have it replaced with something akin to an instinct for goodness as an integral part of the soul. Such a moral and spiritual transformation is our only hope for securing that quality of spirit of which Jesus spoke when He said, "Blessed are the pure in heart: for they shall see God" (Matthew 5:8).

**February 23**

READ: Psalms 24: 3-5

*Blessed are they which do hunger and thirst after righteousness: for they shall be filled* (Matthew 5: 6).

## Can We Be Free from Sin?

We saw yesterday our deep need to be freed from sin. But how can it be? Is it possible to be pure in heart? Can the human spirit be cleansed of carnality? Can a man inclined to evil be changed so that he desires only the good? Can our inborn antagonism to God be exchanged for an enduring devotion to Him? Is such spiritual transformation of the soul possible? Is it scriptural?

Our knowledge of God tells us that it must be possible. We need it desperately and the very urgency of our need argues that it must be so. God has never disappointed any of man's deep hungers. For our thirst He has given water; for the eyes He has provided beauty; for hunger He has given food; for hearing He has filled the world with music. Shall He who provides so bountifully for the needs of the body and mind make no provision for the deepest need of the soul?

Can hearts once filled with evil be cleansed and filled with the Spirit of God? Jesus assures us that it is so—all that is required of us is that we must earnestly desire it. "Blessed are they which do hunger and thirst after righteousness: for they shall be filled."

The Bible teaches that it is our privilege to be free from sin. We have made that faith a part of our church doctrine. "We believe that entire sanctification is that act of God, subsequent to regeneration, by which believers are made free from original sin, or depravity, and brought into a state of entire devotement to God, and the holy obedience of love made perfect" (*Manual, Church of the Nazarene*).

READ: John 17: 13-17

*Blessed are the pure in heart: for they shall see God* (Matthew 5: 8).

## Jesus Taught Freedom from Sin

When I accept Christ as Lord of my life, I am through with the sin business. Paul asks, "How shall we, that are dead to sin, live any longer therein?" (Romans 6: 2) And Paul learned his theology from Jesus.

Our Lord expected persons who had found God to quit sinning. To the man whom He healed at the Pool of Bethesda, Jesus said, "Behold, thou art made whole: sin no more, lest a worse thing come unto thee" (John 5: 14). To the woman taken in adultery He said, "Neither do I condemn thee: go, and sin no more" (John 8: 11). The clear implication is, if you are through with sinning, you are forgiven. Does it not follow just as clearly that, if you are forgiven, you should be through with sinning?

Forgiveness for the past should keep us from sin in the future. But evil is strong and men are frail. Our Lord knew that only the power of God in a sanctified soul can keep a man from sin in this life. His prayer for His disciples was, "I pray not that thou shouldest take them out of the world, but that thou shouldest keep them from the evil. . . . Sanctify them through thy truth: thy word is truth."

Jesus taught us, "Blessed are the pure in heart: for they shall see God" (Matthew 5: 8). Origen commented on this passage: "A defiled heart cannot see God . . . he must be pure who wishes to enjoy a proper view of a pure Being." Freedom from sin in this life is the proper preparation for heaven.

### Affirmation for today

*I want for my life what Christ wants for me. I trust the power of the Holy Spirit to keep me from sin.*

**February 25**

READ: Romans 6: 6-8

*Now if we be dead with Christ, we believe that we shall also live with him* (Romans 6: 8).

## Christians No Longer Live in Sin

In the fifth chapter of Romans, Paul emphasizes that our salvation is by faith; that despite the worst sins we have committed, we may have "peace with God through our Lord Jesus Christ." But Paul was afraid that some readers would make this doctrine of salvation by faith the excuse for a "sinning religion." In the sixth chapter he therefore said a dozen times that followers of Christ are to be *dead to sin.*

What does the Bible mean by such expressions? What does it mean to be dead to sin? This much is clear, dead men are no longer troubled by the problems of the living. No stronger term of separation can be used. The Apostle asks, "How shall we that are dead to sin, live any longer therein?" (Romans 6:2) The question carries its own obvious answer. He that is dead to sin no longer lives in sin.

Can we read the sixth chapter of Romans thoughtfully and conclude that sinning is consistent with a profession of Christian faith? Surely God means to say to us that salvation through Christ somehow takes a man out of the sin business. God's full work of grace in our lives is designed to do away with sin—all sin in the soul. This is the clear truth that God's Word teaches. But we can be truly dead to sin only when the inner source of sin has been removed, when the old carnal self is dead indeed. Therefore the soul of man cries out:

> O God, my heart doth long for Thee,
>  Let me die, let me die;
> Now set my soul at liberty,
>  Let me die, let me die.
>
> —JEANETTE PALMITER

READ: Romans 6: 3-6

*He that is dead is freed from sin* (Romans 6: 7).

## Dead to Sin

Sinfulness and Christlikeness are mutually exclusive alternatives. God's plan of salvation is to free us from sin and to make us Christlike. The destruction of the carnal mind is a decisive step in that process. Paul asks, "How shall we, that are dead to sin [*the sin,* carnality], live any longer therein?"

The surprise in the Apostle's question is because he knew the thorough way that God proposes to deal with carnality. The treatment is as radical as death itself and that is why God's Word uses the figure. Matthew Henry comments, "Death makes a mighty change; such a change doth sanctification make in the soul, it cuts off all correspondence with sin."

Dr. A. M. Hills adds: "Can such . . . a dying mean anything less than that . . . depravity can be so destroyed by sanctifying grace, that the Christian can become as dead to any internal impulse to sin as a corpse is dead to the attractions of the world that once charmed him?

"A man that is dead is uninfluenced and unaffected by the affairs of this life. He is insensible to sounds and tastes and pleasures. . . . The voices of condemnation or praise do not reach him.

"And a Christian can be so delivered from the propensity to be charmed by the world that he is as one dead. The thing that once stirred within him at the approach of temptation has been 'crucified' and 'destroyed,' and he is dead to all but holiness and usefulness and God."

This is what it means to die out to self, to die out to the world, to be dead to sin. Does it seem like an impossible goal? It is high country but not too high for a man who walks with God. The Bible presents it as the true Christian ideal within reach of every child of God.

**February 27**

READ: Romans 6: 11-13

*Reckon ye also yourselves to be dead indeed unto sin* (Romans 6: 11).

## Reckon Yourselves to Be Dead

The Bible tells us that we can be dead to sin. But this is not the only truth of Christian holiness which God's Word presents. In the same breath that Paul declares Christians to be dead to sin, he urges those same Christians, "Likewise *reckon ye* also yourselves to be dead indeed unto sin."

Why do dead Christians need to reckon themselves to be dead? The answer is, Because they are still living persons and still subject to temptation. Paul knew and we know that there is no state of grace in which genuine effort is not required to live the Christian life. The eradication of carnality does not remove all struggle from the Christian's fight against sin, but entire sanctification does radically change the odds in that fight. How is the change to be known?

Carnality is a power that makes itself known in our conscious experience. When it is destroyed we should be aware of some change in our inner consciousness. And there is such a change. Paul tells us how to live so that we may be always conscious of this new sanctifying power. When temptation comes, the Apostle says, reckon that you are dead to sin, remember that you belong to Christ. This kind of reckoning gives a consciousness of inner spiritual power. It is the kind of power N. B. Herrell had experienced when he wrote:

> Take the world with all its pleasures;
> Take them, take them great and small.
> Give me Christ, my precious Saviour.
> He is sweeter than them all.

Is this not effective deadness? Can there be any better deadness to sin than this—to so love Christ that we want nothing contrary to His will?

70

READ: Romans 6:11-13

*Likewise reckon ye also yourselves to be . . . alive unto God through Jesus Christ our Lord* (Romans 6:11).

## Alive unto God

In the same verse that Paul exhorts Christians to reckon themselves dead to sin, he urges, "Reckon ye also yourselves to be . . . *alive unto God.*" The only way a man can become dead to sin is to become alive to God.

It is the power of God that destroys carnality. It is being alive to God that makes us dead to sin. This is true in the moment that we are sanctified wholly. When God's Holy Spirit fills our lives there is no way for us to feel any spirit or attitude contrary to His Spirit. And this has been the glad testimony of many a seeker after holiness.

What is true at the altar is true throughout the sanctified life. The only way a sanctified Christian remains dead to sin is as he strives to become increasingly alive to God. And this takes some reckoning!

What does it mean to be alive to God? Simply this, that I continue responsive to every intimation of His will for me. To do God's will is not always easy even for a sanctified Christian. But when His will is known I do it even when it seems hard. I do it because I remember that this is what being a sanctified Christian means.

Death to sin and to sinning is simply the negative side to life in the Spirit—and life is living, continuous, ongoing activity, changing every day, every hour, every moment. Is sanctifying grace adequate for that? *Yes!*

> *Moment by moment I'm kept in His love;*
> *Moment by moment I've life from above.*
> *Looking to Jesus till glory doth shine,*
> *Moment by moment, O Lord, I am Thine.*
> —D. W. WHITTLE

**March 1**

READ: Romans 6:14-15

*Sin shall not have dominion over you: for ye are not under the law, but under grace* (Romans 6:14).

## Shall We Sin?

We have been made free from the guilt of past sins by divine forgiveness. We are to be made free from the pollution of sin by the crucifixion of the carnal nature. Now may we reasonably expect to remain free from further specific sins? Will this new life of God in the soul be powerful enough to banish sin in every particular case? This is Paul's question in our scripture study for today. After the sin principle has been destroyed, should we expect to commit individual acts of sin? Paul vehemently shouts, "God forbid."

In entire sanctification God's Holy Spirit has been given to us and carnality has been destroyed. This work of grace is provided in order to save us from our former weakness of soul that let us so easily fall into sin. The law demanded obedience but it offered no power to help us avoid sin. Under the plan of grace we are still required to conform to the will of God, but it is a workable conformity, and God supplies the necessary power.

By the sanctifying grace of God we need not "sin daily in thought, word, and deed." Our Lord prayed for His followers to be kept from evil *while they were in the world* here and now. To this end He prayed that they might be sanctified. If the Bible teaches anything, it teaches that sin is not a necessity in the life of the Christian.

**Prayer for today**

*My foes are ever near me,*
*Around me and within;*
*But Jesus, draw Thou nearer,*
*And shield my soul from sin.*
—JOHN E. BODE

READ: Romans 6: 16-18

*Thanks be to God, that you who were once slaves of sin have become obedient from the heart* (Romans 6:17, R.S.V.).

## The Power of a Right Desire

We saw yesterday that a Christian may have the power to be kept free from sinning. What is the nature of that power?

The New Testament assures us that our relationship to God is fundamentally an attitude of the heart. Sincerity is the human measure of gospel perfection. Our love for God and our wholehearted desire to do His will meets the New Testament standard of righteousness. Paul exclaims, "Thanks be to God, that you . . . have become obedient *from the heart.*"

The miracle of sanctifying grace is that God can change a man's desires. By God's grace we can want to do His will more than we want anything else in life. When God's Holy Spirit takes possession of our lives, our desires become like His desires. If we want to avoid sin more than we want anything else, we can avoid sin. This transformation of the heart's desire is the power of the Holy Spirit that keeps us from sinning.

We can never gain such power by sheer effort, but it is a gift which we may have for the asking. Do I want to love God with all my heart? Do I want to be like Him? Do I want to be filled with His Holy Spirit? If this is my sincere desire, God will grant it.

To be completely given over to God is the way to be free from sin. This is the way to get sanctified and this is the way to keep sanctified wholly. The Bible declares, "Now that you have been set free from sin and have become slaves of God, the return you get is sanctification and its end, eternal life" (Romans 6:22, R.S.V.).

### Affirmation for today

*I desire the will of God more than any other thing. I shall live today in the light of that desire.*

**March 3**

READ: Psalms 51:1-2

*Blessed are the pure in heart: for they shall see God* (Matthew 5:8).

## Freedom from Sin—Now

We may be free from carnality whenever we sincerely desire it because sanctification is a gift from God and comes by faith in Him. This was the truth discovered by an earnest seeker. He testified: "I sincerely thought this blessing came as a result of growth into it. But I came here to this altar and in two minutes of prayer and faith I have made more progress than in the past forty years of growth."

God proposes to free us from the sinful nature now in order that He may the better save us from lives of sinning. We dare not postpone this work of grace lest we jeopardize our souls. If we are in a state of conflict—the struggle between the carnal spirit and the Holy Spirit—we must resolve that struggle as soon as possible. We must either go forward and be filled with the Holy Spirit or we shall drift back and find our lives dominated by the carnal spirit.

Some have taught that young Christians ought to wait until they have experienced enough of inbred sin to make them thoroughly sick of it. But such counsel is foolish and dangerous. To assume that we should harbor the sin of carnality in order that we may fully experience and abhor it is on the same level with the faulty logic which says we should commit great, outbroken sins in order that our pardon may be the sweeter. To harbor sin in order to enjoy freedom from it is to act like the moron who beat himself on the head with a stick because it felt so good when he quit.

*You may now receive the Spirit*
*As a sanctifying flame*
*If with all your heart you seek Him,*
*Having faith in Jesus' name.*
—L. L. PICKETT

READ: I John 1: 7-9

*If we walk in the light, as he is in the light, we have fellowship one with another, and the blood of Jesus Christ his Son cleanseth us from all sin* (I John 1: 7).

## I Have Found

Frank Dodge, Sr., is now a farmer near Fallon, Nevada. He had been a Christian only a short time when he gave this testimony:

"I was in the bar and restaurant business, including gambling, for fifteen years.

"I had accumulated possessions of the world that money could buy. But this began not to be enough. I became mean and overbearing. I could not sleep. I would take the car and go for a drive, trying to find peace. I was dissatisfied with my life; but when my wife asked me to attend church with her, I would just laugh.

"I finally became ill and was in a coma for several hours. Rev. G. Wilson came to my home when I rallied some, and asked me if I would like for her to pray for me. That prayer was all I could remember for a long time. Friends came to visit me and I couldn't remember them, but the prayer was always in my mind.

"On Easter Sunday, in 1960, I attended the Church of the Nazarene with my family. The following Sunday I attended church again and knelt at the altar to ask God for His help. He not only saved me, but He has cleansed my heart from all sin and unrighteousness and has given me a glorious freedom I had not known could be possible.

"I am now a farmer-rancher. I find my attitude toward my work has changed. I can pray and know that God will direct me through the difficult problems that arise. Before I would 'fly off the handle,' only to make bigger problems with more misery.

"I have found the peace in my heart I had been searching for. Truly, 'If we confess our sins, he is faithful and just to forgive us our sins, and to cleanse us from all unrighteousness' (I John 1: 9)."

**March 5**

READ: I John 1: 5-9

*If we walk in the light, as he is in the light, . . . the blood of Jesus Christ his Son cleanseth us from all sin* (I John 1: 7).

## Let This Be Our Prayer

If we believe the clear teaching of God's Word concerning scriptural freedom from sin and if we desire the whole will of God for our lives, we may be delivered from carnality without personally experiencing all of its evil power. We can be freed from the carnal nature early in the Christian life. In our search for entire sanctification it makes little difference whether we are driven from behind to escape moral defeat or drawn on from before to achieve spiritual victory. We need not delay. We may have freedom from sin now.

If we are converted but have never experienced scriptural freedom from sin, let us make the prayer of Isaiah Reid our own:

"O Lord, . . . especially at this time do I, Thy regenerate child, put my case into Thy hands for the cleansing of my nature from indwelling sin. I seek the sanctification of my soul. . . . Now, as I have given myself away, I will, from this time forth, regard myself as Thine. I believe the altar sanctifieth the gift. I believe the blood is applied now, as I comply with the terms of Thy salvation. I believe that Thou *dost now cleanse me from all my sin.*"

**Praise for today**

> *I rise to walk in heav'n's own light*
> *Above the world and sin,*
> *With heart made pure, and garments white,*
> *And Christ enthroned within.*
> — PHOEBE PALMER

READ: Hebrews 6:1-3

*Therefore leaving the principles of the doctrine of Christ, let us go on unto perfection* (Hebrews 6:1).

## Let Us Go On unto Perfection

God's Word exhorts us never to rest until we are mature Christians. Such a Christian life starts when we are saved from sin. We move toward its full realization to the extent that we are filled with the Holy Spirit.

It is the nature of spiritual life to create a desire for an ever deeper acquaintance with God. After we have come to know Him in forgiveness there arises a desire for yet more. God has given us this desire to lead us on into entire sanctification and to an ever-deepening life of God in the soul.

Most of the chief branches of the Christian Church believe in sanctification for God's people, but some reject the teaching of a crisis experience. For them sanctification is simply a process of growing in grace. There are others who believe that we cannot be sanctified until death. Holiness people believe that the Bible teaches an experience of entire sanctification which we may receive here and now as a second definite work of God's grace.

This experience of entire sanctification is one stage in the process of the Christian life. It is an advanced stage in relation to conversion, but a preliminary preparation in relation to later Christian life and growth. We are here concerned with the advance stage in relation to conversion. In the language of John Wesley, the experience of entire sanctification is a "second blessing properly so called."

Our text exhorts, "Let us go on unto perfection," and the writer affirms, "This we will do, if God permits." He has no doubt as to God's willingness but he knows that every spiritual advance depends on divine help.

### Affirmation for today

*God being my Helper, I shall today move forward toward His whole will for me.*

**March 7**

READ: Luke 10:17-20

*Behold, I send the promise of my Father upon you: but tarry ye in the city of Jerusalem, until ye be endued with power from on high* (Luke 24:49).

## A Blessing for Christians

When the seventy early Christians returned from their preaching mission, our Lord recognized that they were saved men. He said to them, "Rejoice because your names are written in heaven." They were already converted men, but a little later Jesus instructed them to tarry until they were endued with the power of the Holy Spirit. Many, if not all, of the seventy were present on the Day of Pentecost. They "were all with one accord in one place. And suddenly there came a sound from heaven as of a rushing mighty wind, and it filled all the house where they were sitting. . . . and they were all filled with the Holy Ghost" (Acts 2:1-4). They received the gift of the Holy Spirit after they were converted, as Jesus taught that they should.

God's revealed Word is the sure foundation upon which all Christian teaching must be based. We believe in entire sanctification as a second definite work of grace for Christian people because that is the way the Bible teaches it. John the Baptist announced, "I indeed baptize you with water unto repentance: but he that cometh after me is mightier than I, whose shoes I am not worthy to bear: he shall baptize you with the Holy Ghost, and with fire" (Matthew 3:11). Here we see clearly that the baptism with the Holy Spirit is a divine work of grace, that it is something more than repentance, and that it comes after the baptism unto repentance.

*Lord, as of old at Pentecost*
*Thou didst Thy power display,*
*With cleansing, purifying flame*
*Descend on us today.**

—CHARLOTTE G. HOMER

*© 1940, renewal, The Rodeheaver Co. Used by permission.

READ: John 17: 6, 9, 15-17

*Sanctify them through thy truth: thy word is truth*
(John 17: 17).

## Jesus' Prayer for His Followers

On the eve of His crucifixion, in the upper room, after the Last Supper, Jesus earnestly prayed for the sanctification of the eleven faithful apostles. The prayer language with which our Lord referred to these intimate companions compels us to believe that they were already God's accepted children. "Thou gavest them me; and they have kept thy word. . . . I have given unto them the words which thou gavest me; and they have received them . . . I pray not for the world, but for them which thou hast given me; for they are thine. . . . I am glorified in them. . . . none of them is lost . . . the world hath hated them, because they are not of the world."

Who can question that these men were redeemed followers of Christ? But they needed to receive the Holy Spirit in His fullness. On this same occasion Jesus prayed, "While I was with them in the world, I kept them in thy name . . . And now come I to thee . . . that they might have my joy fulfilled in themselves. I pray . . . that thou shouldest keep them from the evil. . . . Sanctify them through thy truth: thy word is truth. . . . Neither pray I for these alone, but for them also which shall believe on me through their word."

A few weeks later Jesus instructed these same men to tarry and pray until the Holy Ghost should come upon them. Ten days yet later, after they obeyed the Master's word, the Holy Ghost came to these earnest disciples and they were sanctified wholly.

**Prayer for today**

*O Jesus, may Thy prayer for my sanctification be answered this day. Pour out Thy Spirit upon me.*

**March 9**

READ: Acts 8: 5, 12, 14-17

*Then laid they their hands on them, and they received the Holy Ghost* (Acts 8:17).

## Samaritan Converts Needed to Be Sanctified

The disciples who had been sanctified on the Day of Pentecost were already followers of Christ. The baptism with the Holy Spirit came to them after their conversion. This was the order also in the Early Church following Pentecost. In verse 12 of our scripture we read, "But when they believed Philip preaching the things concerning the kingdom of God, and the name of Jesus Christ, they were baptized."

Then as now, water baptism was recognized as the acknowledgment of conversion. But before the visit of Peter and John these new Christians had experienced only the first work of grace. *The New English Bible* translates verse 16 forcefully: "Until then the Spirit had not come upon any of them. They had been baptized in the name of the Lord Jesus, that and nothing more." After these Samaritans were converted, they needed to be baptized with the Holy Ghost.

No language can tell the story as well as Luke's own inspired words. "Now when the apostles which were at Jerusalem heard that Samaria had received the word of God, they sent unto them Peter and John: who, when they were come down, prayed for them, that they might receive the Holy Ghost . . . Then laid they their hands on them, and they received the Holy Ghost."

If we believe that entire sanctification and the baptism with the Holy Ghost are fundamentally the same experience of grace, could scriptural teaching be clearer that sanctification is a crisis experience which comes after we have been converted?

> *He who has pardoned surely will cleanse thee,*
> *All of the dross of thy nature refine.*
> *Cleansed from all sin, His power will enter,*
> *Fill you and thrill you with power divine.*
> —MRS. C. H. MORRIS

READ: Acts 19:1-7

*Have ye received the Holy Ghost since ye believed?*
(Acts 19:2)

## Have You Received the Holy Spirit?

Yesterday we saw the concern of Peter and John for the sanctification of believers. Paul was also concerned that followers of Christ should receive the Holy Spirit.

Finding a little group of about a dozen believers in the city of Ephesus, he inquired concerning their spiritual life, "Have ye received the Holy Ghost since ye believed?" This verse has been a favorite text for second-blessing sermons and its phrasing is exactly true to the time sequence of Christian experience. However, the Revised Version renders Paul's question, "Did ye receive the Holy Spirit when ye believed?" Some critics of second-blessing truth assume that this more accurate translation nullifies the passage as evidence for the doctrine.

Even in this form, the passage is the clearest kind of evidence for a crisis experience of holiness. These new Christians were baptized with the Holy Spirit in a moment of time. Moreover, when the entire incident is considered, there is still conclusive evidence for entire sanctification as a second blessing, following the experience of conversion. Whatever John's baptism had done for these men, it had not given them the Holy Ghost. Even when they learned more about Christ, walked in the light, and were baptized as Christians, they were not yet sanctified. It was only *after* this experience that Paul "laid his hands upon them, and the Holy Ghost came on them."

It is a searching scriptural question with which God confronts me:

> *Have ye received, since ye believed,*
> *The blessed Holy Ghost?*
> *He who was promised, Gift of the Father—*
> *Have ye received the Holy Ghost?*
> —Mrs. C. H. Morris

**March 11**

READ: Acts 10: 1-6, 33-35, 44-47

*The Jewish believers . . . were absolutely amazed that the gift of the Holy Spirit was being poured out on Gentiles also* (Acts 10: 44, Phillips).

## Pentecost for the Gentiles

We must be careful that we do not confine the work of the Holy Spirit to our own preconceived processes and places. As faithful, thoughtful Christians we must do our best to understand how God works, and under what conditions. But God is always greater than our understanding of Him.

Was the gift of the Holy Spirit a second work of grace for Cornelius? We should not be dogmatic where there is room for disagreement. But let us look at these facts. Cornelius was a devout man and he showed a Christian attitude in his consideration for the needy. He was faithful in prayer and he fasted as he prayed (v. 30). His spiritual life was pleasing to God and he willingly walked in all the light that came to him.

But was he a Christian? He had not been baptized, and Peter's sermon to him (vv. 34-43) dealt with the basic gospel message of salvation through Christ. These facts would lead us to believe that Cornelius and his household were simply unusual gentiles who had given up idolatry, but who had not yet heard of Jesus, the Saviour. However, consider verse 35. Did not the Apostle recognize that a man who had as much light as Cornelius had, and who knew God as well as Cornelius did, could be considered a true child of God? And consider verses 36-37; "The word which God sent . . . preaching peace by Jesus Christ . . . *that word, I say, ye know.*" Had not Cornelius previously heard some gospel message?

In any case these devout persons were ready for God's Gift. The Holy Spirit was given to them just as He had been given to the believers on the Day of Pentecost.

### Affirmation for today

*I shall rejoice in the work of the Holy Spirit wherever He is given to men.*

READ: Acts 2: 14-16, 37-39

*Repent, and be baptized every one of you in the name
of Jesus Christ for the remission of sins, and ye shall
receive the gift of the Holy Ghost* (Acts 2: 38).

## Repentance Precedes Pentecost

Dr. J. B. Chapman used to say that he got saved so that
he could get sanctified wholly. His testimony was somewhat
as follows. "As a young man I listened to holiness preaching.
It sounded so good to me that I wanted to live that kind of
life. I understood that I needed to be converted before I
could become a candidate for sanctification. I therefore went
to the altar to be saved, so that I could become a seeker for
holiness."

Are not this preparation and this sequence the clear
teaching of our scripture for today? Peter had just come from
the Upper Room, where he with others had been filled with
the Holy Spirit. At the close of his first sermon following
this experience Peter's convicted listeners cried, "Men and
brethren, what shall we do?"

Peter knew the answer to that question. He knew that
these men needed to find what he had found. He had followed Jesus for three years, but even these years of disciple-
ship had not solved his own spiritual problems. However,
he had obeyed Jesus' command to tarry until the Holy Spirit
came. Now things were different!

How could his hearers find this radiant relationship with
God? Peter could only point them to the route that he had
taken. "You must repent—and, as an expression of it, let
every one of you be baptized in the name of Jesus Christ—
that you may have your sins forgiven; *and then* [italics mine]
you will receive the gift of the Holy Spirit" (Acts 2: 38, Williams).

### Promise for today

*Ye shall receive the gift of the Holy Ghost. For
the promise is unto you, and to your children, and to
all that are afar off, even as many as the Lord our
God shall call* (Acts 2: 38-39).

**March 13**

READ: John 9: 24-25

*One thing I know, that, whereas I was blind, now I
see* (John 9: 25).

## Testimony of a Scholar

Dr. Daniel Steele was one of the most scholarly pro-
ponents of Bible holiness in modern times. Preaching before
Boston University School of Theology while a member of
the faculty there, he gave his personal testimony.

"Brethren, on the subject of the fulness of the Holy Spirit
as a possible and sudden attainment in modern times, I am
not here to theorize, to philosophize, to dogmatize, but to
testify. . . .

"Six months ago I made the discovery that I was living
in the pre-pentecostal state of religious experience, admiring
Christ's character, and in a degree loving His person, but
without the conscious blessing of the Comforter. I settled
the question of privilege by a study of St. John's Gospel and
St. Paul's Epistles, and earnestly sought for the Comforter. I
prayed, consecrated, confessed my state, and believed Christ's
word. Very suddenly, after about three weeks' diligent search,
the Comforter came with power and great joy to my heart.
He took my feet out of the realm of doubt and weakness, and
planted them forever on the Rock of assurance and strength.

"My joy is a river of limpid waters, brimming and daily
overflowing the banks, unspeakable and full of glory. . . . I
am a freed man. Christ is my emancipator, bringing me into
the glorious liberty of the children of God. . . . My efficiency
in Christ's service is greatly multiplied. . . . 'Oh, that I had
known this twenty years ago!' But I thank God that after a
struggle of more than a score of years

*"I have entered the valley of blessing so sweet,*
   *And Jesus abides with me there;*
*And His Spirit and blood make my cleansing complete,*
   *And His perfect love casteth out fear."*

READ: Hebrews 6:1-3

*Therefore leaving the principles of the doctrine of Christ, let us go on unto perfection* (Hebrews 6:1).

## A Further Work of Grace

Entire sanctification is a second work of grace because it is a *further* work of grace. In our text for today God's Word admonishes us, "Therefore leaving the principles of the doctrine of Christ, let us *go on* unto perfection." We are not to remain content with the elementary attainments of the Christian life such as repentance, faith for salvation, and baptism. We are to move beyond these.

But a man cannot go on until he has previously gone somewhere. The sinner is like the southern boy who was asked by his hostess if he would like some molasses. He replied, "How kin I have mo' 'lasses when I ain't had no 'lasses yet?"

Having experienced the beginning stage of repentance and saving faith, and having witnessed to our faith in baptism, we are then to go on. The writer gives sound Christian counsel when he urges, "Let us go on and get past the elementary stage in the teachings and doctrine of Christ the Messiah, advancing steadily toward the completeness and perfection that belongs to spiritual maturity" (*The Amplified New Testament*).

Some one hundred and fifty years ago Adam Clarke succinctly asked: "What then is this complete sanctification? . . . It is the washing of the soul of a true believer from the *remains* of sin; it is the making one who is already a child of God *more holy*, that he may be *more* happy, *more* useful in the world, and bring *more* glory to his Heavenly Father."

*Lord, lift me up and let me stand,*
*By faith, on heaven's table land,*
*A higher plane than I have found.*
*Lord, plant my feet on higher ground.*
—JOHNSON OATMAN, JR.

**March 15**

READ: Acts 2:1-4

*Suddenly there came a sound from heaven . . . And they were all filled with the Holy Ghost* (Acts 2:2-4).

## God Comes in a Crisis Experience

Not only is entire sanctification received after we are converted, but the Holy Spirit comes to us in a moment of time. This was the way it happened on the Day of Pentecost. No language could be clearer than our text: "Suddenly there came a sound from heaven . . . And they were all filled with the Holy Ghost."

A crisis is a decisive moment, a turning point. Certainly this is accurate language to describe the baptism with the Holy Spirit. God requires us to make preparation, but this is to get us ready for the moment of experience. Jesus directed the disciples to make their preparation: "Tarry ye in the city of Jerusalem, until ye be endued with power from on high" (Luke 24:49). He also promised them a decisive moment of realization: "Ye shall be baptized with the Holy Ghost not many days hence" (Acts 1:5).

This pattern also prevailed later in the New Testament Church. In the house of Cornelius there was sincere preparation. A man had fasted and prayed; he had received instructions from God; he had done what God told him to do. He gathered his household and said to Peter, "Now therefore are we all here present before God, to hear all things that are commanded thee of God."

Certainly these preparations pointed to a decisive moment —and that moment arrived. The Holy Spirit came suddenly to these sincere seekers even before the altar call was made! "While Peter yet spake these words, the Holy Ghost fell on all them which heard the word" (Acts 10:44).

*The blessing by faith I receive from above.*
*Oh, glory! My soul is made perfect in love;*
*My prayer has prevailed; and this moment I know*
*The Blood is applied, I am whiter than snow.*
—JOHN NICHOLSON

## The Bible Teaches a Second Work of Grace

A seeker ready to be convinced by the authority of the Bible wrote to the *Herald of Holiness*: "Would you please either publish or send me some scripture references which verify our belief in the baptism with the Holy Spirit and sanctification as a second definite work of grace?"

Dr. W. T. Purkiser replied as follows: "This is a large order, but here are a few:

"Matthew 3:11-12—The baptism with the Spirit *follows* water baptism.

"Matthew 5:48—These words are addressed to those who are *Christians* (God is their Heavenly Father).

"Luke 11:13—The Holy Spirit is given to those who come to God *as their Heavenly Father.*

"John 14:15-18—The world cannot receive the Holy Spirit. The *disciples* can and shall.

"John 17:17—Christ prays for His *disciples* to be sanctified (see verses 3-16).

"Acts 2:1-4—All so filled with the Spirit were *disciples* of the Lord.

"Acts 8:5-17—The Samaritans were *baptized believers* before they were filled with the Spirit.

"Acts 19:5-6—The disciples at Ephesus were baptized with water by Paul, and *after that* were filled with the Spirit.

"Romans 6:6, 11, 22; 8:2-4, 6-9—Freedom from inner sin is promised to *Christians.*

"Romans 12:1-2—Consecration is a *Christian* obligation.

"II Corinthians 7:1—*Christians* are to be cleansed to perfect holiness.

"Ephesians 4:20-24—*Christians* are to put off the 'old man.'

"Ephesians 5:18—The command to be filled with the Spirit is given to believers.

"Ephesians 5:25-27—Christ gave himself to sanctify and cleanse *the Church.*"

*(More tomorrow)*

**March 17**

## The Bible Teaches a Second Work of Grace (continued)

Yesterday we reviewed some of the scriptural evidence for entire sanctification as a second work of grace. We traced the doctrine from Matthew through Paul's Ephesian letter. Today we follow the evidence still further.

"I Thessalonians 4:3, 7-8; 5:23-24—*Christians* are called to holiness, to be sanctified wholly.

"Titus 2:11-14—The grace of God provides not only *redemption* but *purity*.

"Hebrews 6:1-3—*Believers* must go on unto perfection.

"Hebrews 12:14-16—Holiness is essential to 'see the Lord,' and *to prevent backsliding*.

"Hebrews 13:12—Christ suffered to sanctify *His people* with His own blood.

"James 4:8—Sinners are to cleanse their hands; the *double-minded*, to *purify* their hearts.

"I Peter 1:14-16—God calls His *obedient children* to holiness in all manner of living.

"I John 1:7—Only *Christians* walk in the light, and as they do they are cleansed from all sin.

"I John 3:2-3—Those *with hope of seeing Christ* purify themselves, even as He is pure.

"The point of most of these references, as you see, is that they relate to those who are already converted. That what is to be done for them is a 'definite work of grace' is seen in the use of such terms as 'baptize,' 'make perfect,' 'receive' the Holy Spirit, 'fill,' 'cleanse,' 'put off,' 'put on,' etc. None of these terms suggests a gradual process which goes on through all of life and is never finished until the hour of death. They rather speak of what has a definite beginning in the experience of the believer, although its effects continue through all of life."

—W. T. Purkiser

READ: Acts 2: 38-39

*The promise is unto you, and to your children, and to all that are afar off, even as many as the Lord our God shall call* (Acts 2: 39).

## The Witness of Christians Today

We base our belief in entire sanctification as a second work of grace firmly upon the Word of God. But we rejoice to find that belief confirmed by the testimony of devout souls across the years. Some time after 1725, in answer to the question, "Does the Lord ever entirely sanctify the soul at justification?" John Wesley wrote: *"But we do not know a single instance,* in any place, of a person's receiving in one and the same moment remission of sins, the abiding witness of the Spirit, and a new and a clean heart."

Has God changed His timing in the twentieth century? Dr. S. S. White, former editor of the *Herald of Holiness,* writes: "There are hundreds whom I have heard testify that they received this blessing after they were converted. . . . Over against this great number I have only one to present who openly and aboveboard testified to the fact that he was sanctified at the same time that he was saved . . . this one man . . . was thought by some not to be too careful in his living. Even his friends were not inclined to think of him as manifesting a high state of grace."

Those who enjoy this blessing testify that they came into the experience after they were converted. In response to their faith, God gave them this added grace. Can I today testify to the sanctifying presence of the Holy Spirit in my life? If not, have I tried the way of those radiant Christians who have sought and received this gift from God?

> *On the cross He bought this blessing;*
> *He will never say us nay.*
> *He is waiting now to give it.*
> *Why not claim it, friend, today?*
> —L. L. PICKETT

**March 19**

READ: John 14:15-17

*The world cannot receive, [the Holy Spirit] because it seeth him not, neither knoweth him* (John 14:17).

## The World Cannot Receive Him

The baptism with the Holy Spirit is a second work of grace. The Bible makes this clear and our knowledge of human nature persuades us that it must be so. Why is it reasonable to believe that entire sanctification would be received as a second blessing?

The very nature of our human experience argues in favor of this doctrinal position. One must first be converted in order to experience personally the need for entire sanctification. We do not crave a satisfying meal of some new food until we have first tasted that food. We are normally not eager to become perfected musicians until we have first had some piano lessons. How can a man desire to love God with *all* his heart, soul, mind, and strength until he has experienced something of the love of God arising out of the forgiveness of his sins? Is this not what Jesus meant when He said of the Holy Spirit, "The world cannot receive [Him], because it seeth him not, neither knoweth him"?

But to His disciples Jesus declared, "Ye know him; for he dwelleth with you, and shall be in you." Only the converted man has the intimate knowledge of the richness which God's Spirit adds to life to make him desire the fullness of the Spirit. But the man who has tasted the grace of God has this knowledge and he yearns for more of God.

> *More about Jesus would I know,*
> *More of His grace to others show;*
> *More of His saving fullness see,*
> *More of His love who died for me.*
> —E. E. HEWITT

READ: Acts 8:14-17

*Now when the apostles which were at Jerusalem heard that Samaria had received the word of God, they sent unto them Peter and John: who, when they were come down, prayed for them, that they might receive the Holy Ghost* (Acts 8:14-15).

## Are Two Works of Grace Unreasonable?

The teaching of entire sanctification as a second work of grace has caused some to hesitate, and others to reject the truth. But why should we stumble over God's method of giving himself to us? In *Holiness, the Finished Foundation*, Bishop J. Paul Taylor writes: "If two or more successive stages of treatment are required to secure physical health, the patient, even though impatient with the process, will submit to the superior knowledge of his physician concerning his condition and needs. If a foreigner desires to be a full-fledged citizen, he will meet all the demands connected with filing his first and second papers. Preachers have not spent time objecting to two ordinations to qualify for all the privileges of the ordained minister, but rather have spent their time qualifying. In our space age no one has ridiculed scientists for constructing space rockets with two sections to propel astronauts into orbit around the earth.

"The trouble is not primarily an intellectual problem in arithmetic. It is not the addition of a second work of grace that troubles men, but the subtraction of the unholy element in the heart that involves the crucifixion of sinful self. The man who is determined to meet the divine requirements would submit to any number of crisis experiences that he might 'stand perfect and complete in all the will of God.' His heart and mind do not stagger at the word 'second,' but are gripped by the phrase 'work of grace.'" With **Charles Wesley** he prays:

*Finish then Thy new creation;*
*Pure and spotless let us be.*
*Let us see Thy great salvation,*
*Perfectly restored in Thee.*
—CHARLES WESLEY

**March 21**

READ: James 4: 8-10

*Cleanse your hands, ye sinners; and purify your hearts, ye double-minded* (James 4:8).

## Dual Sin Requires a Double Cure

God has always planned well for the needs of His children. He has given beauty for the eyes, music for the ears, and love for the lonely. Should we not expect Him to provide equally well for the deep needs of our spirits?

Because sin is of two kinds, God has provided two works of grace. A man who has committed sins is guilty and stands condemned. He needs to have his sins forgiven in order to become a child of God. When a man repents, and thus voluntarily turns away from his sins, God stands ready with the grace of forgiveness. He grants full pardon for all guilt and complete release from the penalty of sins committed. A man who is a sinner must have his hands thus cleansed from wicked works.

But our text says more because a man needs more. Sins are acts which are contrary to the known will of God. The Bible teaches that sin is also a disposition in the heart of man which is opposed to God's will. Even after a man's sins have been forgiven, this sinful nature remains until the heart is cleansed by the baptism with the Holy Spirit. This is the second work of grace that God has provided to deal with man's sin. Because a man is a sinner, he must have his hands cleansed; because he is double-minded, he must have his heart purified.

Seeing the clear light of these truths, I today join in the prayer:

> *Let the water and the blood,*
> *From Thy wounded side which flowed,*
> *Be of sin the double cure,*
> *Save from wrath and make me pure.*
> —AUGUSTUS M. TOPLADY

READ: Acts 11:15-18

*God gave them the like gift as he did unto us, who believed on the Lord Jesus Christ* (Acts 11:17).

## Through Decision and Faith

Dr. A. M. Hills tells of an old lady eighty years of age who testified: "I was converted when I was ten years old. I tried to grow into sanctification for sixty-nine years, and utterly failed. Then I got tired of trying to get it by growth, and last year I went to that altar and received it by faith in half an hour, and I have the blessing yet!"

This instantaneous entering into a new relationship with God is the testimony of those who have found the experience of heart holiness. And is it not what we should expect, being the kind of persons we are? Most of life's great experiences climax in some decisive moment of time. Human life begins at the moment of conception. Birth has its gradual preparation but the event itself takes place in a decisive moment. Courtship is a growing experience but it leads to the sacred moment when two persons say, "I will." The process of wearing out goes on in the human body from the time we are born, but there comes a crisis point when the body dies.

We should expect this great spiritual experience of entire sanctification to reach a critical instant because it depends upon choice and faith. Weighing alternatives is a gradual process, but a choice is made in a moment. Feeling our need and seeking to understand the truth may be a short or a long process, but there comes a point where we say, *I believe God's promise.* It is this moment of decision and faith that precipitates the crisis and brings the blessing of entire sanctification.

### Affirmation for today

*What I give, Christ takes; what He takes, He cleanses; what He cleanses, He fills. I have given myself; He has all of me; I believe God's promise; I am cleansed; He now fills me with His Holy Spirit: "Thanks be unto God for his unspeakable gift"* (II Corinthians 9:15).

**March 23**

READ: Acts 8:14-17

*Then laid they their hands on them, and they received the Holy Ghost* (Acts 8:17).

## Our Need Is Now

In New Testament times Christians who were prepared in heart received the Holy Spirit in a moment of time. It happens that way today.

We need not go far in examining the spiritual life to be fully convinced of the utter fitness of God's provision for our entire sanctification in a moment of time. Our need is now. The experience of heart holiness is preeminently the enabling grace by which we are to live the Christian life. This experience enables us to love God with all the heart because it eradicates from the soul that carnal spirit, which is not subject to the law of God. Sanctification enables us to love our neighbors because it is the perfection of love within us. The baptism with the Holy Spirit fits us for effective witnessing to the unsaved and thus prepares us to be of greatest service in God's kingdom.

All of these consequences are needed in our lives now— the sooner, the better. If they could come only gradually or not until the close of life, they would be of little help to us in building Christian character and in advancing Christ's kingdom.

God's plan is to sanctify wholly every one of His children who sincerely yearns for this blessing—to sanctify us at the earliest possible moment, so that full fellowship and service may continue for maximum years. Provision has therefore been made for this blessing to be given in a moment. God's desire is that our sanctification shall be now.

> *Thou canst fill me, gracious Spirit,*
> *Tho' I cannot tell Thee how.*
> *But I need Thee, greatly need Thee;*
> *Come, oh, come and fill me now.*
> —E. H. STOKES

READ: Luke 11:9-13

*Blessed are they which do hunger and thirst after righteousness: for they shall be filled* (Matthew 5:6).

## Make Haste, Man, Make Haste!

At Wesley's Conference in 1759 the question was asked, "Is this death to sin and renewal in love gradual or instantaneous?" The illustrative answer was, "A man may be dying for some time, yet he does not, properly speaking, die, until the instant the soul is separated from the body; and in that instant he lives the life of eternity."

The next question was, "How are we to wait for this change?" Here is the answer that Wesley gave: "Not in careless indifference, or indolent activity; but in vigorous, universal obedience, in a zealous keeping of all the commandments, in watchfulness and [painstaking], in denying ourselves and taking up our cross daily; as well as in earnest prayer and fasting, and a close attendance on all the ordinances of God. . . . It is true we receive it by simple faith; but God does not, will not, give that faith unless we seek it with all diligence in the way which he hath ordained.

"This consideration may satisfy those who inquire why so few have received the blessing. Inquire how many are seeking it in this way, and you have a sufficient answer. Prayer especially is wanting. Who continues instant therein? Who wrestles with God for this very thing? So 'ye have not, because ye ask not; or because ye ask amiss,' namely that you may be renewed before you die. *Before you die!* Will that content you? Nay, but ask that it may be done now, today, while it is called today. Do not call this 'setting God a time.' Certainly today is His time as well as tomorrow. Make haste, man, make haste! Let

> "*Thy soul break out in strong desire,*
> *Thy perfect bliss to prove;*
> *Thy longing heart be all on fire*
> *To be dissolved in love!*"
>
> —*Christian Perfection*

**March 25**

READ: Acts 1: 4-8

*Ye shall be baptized with the Holy Ghost not many days hence* (Acts 1: 5).

## We May Have Him Now

Dr. E. Stanley Jones writes of his own experience as follows: "I found a little book in a Sunday school library called *The Christian's Secret of a Happy Life* . . . I began to read it, and it set my heart on fire to get the type of life shown in its pages. When I got to the forty-second page, the inner Voice whispered, 'Now is the time to get it.' But I pleaded that I didn't know what I wanted, that this book was showing me, that as soon as I had finished reading, I would seek and then I could intelligently seek.

"But the Voice was imperious, 'Now is the time to seek.' Apparently God was willing to take me on my half-knowledge if I would give Him my whole heart." After some time spent in consecration and prayer Dr. Jones's testimony continues: "Suddenly I was filled. Wave after wave of refining fire swept through my being, even to my finger tips. It touched the whole being, physical, mental, and spiritual. I could only pace the floor with tears of quiet joy streaming down my cheeks. The Holy Spirit had invaded me and had taken complete possession. He was cleansing and uniting at depths I couldn't control" (*Flames of Living Fire*, Beacon Hill Press).

Every child of God who is unsanctified may have this experience. We need not wait to read further. Our need is now. God's provision is now. We may have Him now if with all the heart we seek Him.

> *Hover o'er me, Holy Spirit;*
> *Bathe my trembling heart and brow;*
> *Fill me with Thy hallowed presence.*
> *Come, oh, come and fill me now.*
> —E. H. STOKES

READ: Acts 1:12-14; 2:1-4

*These all continued in one accord in prayer and supplication* (Acts 1:14).

## Am I Ready to Seek Him Now?

In his testimony of yesterday Dr. E. Stanley Jones told how the Holy Spirit convicted him of the need to seek for the baptism of the Holy Spirit *now*. For several weeks we have been exploring this element of decisive action and crisis experience in God's dealings with the soul. Has it been only an exercise in correct theology or has the Holy Spirit used the truth to probe my own spirit about my own need for action *now*?

We have seen how clearly the Bible shows us that entire sanctification is God's plan for every follower of Christ. We have seen that this further experience of grace comes to us as a gift of God rather than any achievement of our own. Since God gives it freely and promises the blessing to all who love Him, we may have it *when* we ask for it. Since I am a child of God, since this is God's will for me and God's gift to me, should it not be a matter of immediate concern to me?

Our scripture for yesterday told of Jesus' promise of the Holy Spirit and of His instructions to the disciples for receiving this gift from God. Today our Bible reading recounts the obedience of those disciples and of the blessing that God poured out upon them. Jesus asked them to tarry. Our scripture records, "They went up into an upper room . . . These all continued with one accord in prayer and supplication, . . . and they were all filled with the Holy Ghost."

Here were obedience to Christ's command, united prayer for the gift of the Holy Spirit, faith that if they prayed He would come to them—and then the answer to their prayers! These disciples set out to settle this business with God as Jesus had asked them to do. Will the same action by me bring the same results for me? The answer is *Yes*.

**Affirmation for today**

*I resolve to begin seeking the baptism with the Holy Spirit* NOW.

**March 27**

READ: I Thessalonians 4: 7-8

*For God hath not called us unto uncleanness, but unto holiness* (I Thessalonians 4: 7).

## Holiness Is Not Optional

Did I make the affirmation of yesterday my own, or did I merely read the words and put off the decision? How long have I known the truth of heart holiness? How many times have I felt the urge of the Holy Spirit to seek for this blessing? Am I less concerned about the matter now than I was at some time in the past? If so, I am in the beginning of a spiritual tragedy.

One of life's most sobering facts is that we can become so accustomed to tragedy as to be unmoved by it. We can live on the threshold of spiritual opportunity and yet miss it entirely. There is grave danger that we who sit under holiness preaching shall be content to approve the theory in our minds while rejecting the fact in our lives.

God's children may enjoy wide differences in nonessentials and still be faithful Christians. But Christian holiness is not a nonessential. Entire sanctification is not an optional blessing after a Christian has heard and acknowledged the truth of the doctrine.

Christians who have no clear light on heart purity may by prayer and faith maintain a justified experience for years without going on to entire sanctification. God has a way of making holy all who sincerely walk in the light they receive. Such Christians may die and make it safely to heaven without ever having clear light on holiness. But this cannot be true of those whom God's Spirit has convicted of their need for the second work of grace. We cannot fight holiness without opposing God; we cannot consciously ignore or evade entire sanctification without drawing away from the will of God. When the truth of holiness is clearly seen, we either go forward with God or we begin to backslide from God.

**Affirmation for today**

*I will, today, walk in the light that God gives to me.*

READ: Ecclesiastes 5: 4-5

*I will pay my vows unto the Lord now in the presence of all his people* (Psalms 116:14).

## What Do I Owe My Church?

Am I a member of a holiness church? If so I have a moral obligation to maintain the blessing of heart holiness. To do less than this is to accept spiritual blessings without doing my part to maintain them. We who have shared in the message of full salvation cannot glorify God by living on a lower level. We cannot honestly discharge our moral responsibility to Christ and to a sinful world if forgiveness is all of God's grace to which we can bear witness.

As we joined the church, we listened to a godly pastor deliver this charge: "Dearly Beloved: The privileges and blessings which we have in association together in the Church of Jesus Christ are very sacred and precious. There is in it such hallowed fellowship as cannot otherwise be known." As we presented ourselves to share in that fellowship, the pastor continued: "It is necessary that we be of one mind and heart . . . We believe . . . that after the work of regeneration, there is the further work of heart cleansing, or entire sanctification, which is effected by the Holy Ghost . . . Do you heartily believe these truths? Desiring to unite with the Church . . . do you covenant to . . . seek earnestly to perfect holiness of heart and life in the fear of the Lord?" We answered, "I do."

If we are not now enjoying the blessing of heart holiness or if we are not earnestly seeking for it, we need to ask ourselves in all seriousness, What have I done with the vows that I made before God and my friends of the church?

### Prayer for today

*O God, I do remember my vow to Thee and to my church. I do now join in the sincere prayer of another child of God, "I will pay my vows unto the Lord now in the presence of all his people"* (Psalms 116:14).

**March 29**

READ: I Peter 1:13-16

*Be ye holy; for I am holy* (I Peter 1:16).

## I Must Obey God

The obligations which grow out of church membership, and my responsibilities to fellow Christians, are very real and important. But they cannot compare with the responsibility that I owe to God, who says to me, "Be ye holy; for I am holy." We are obliged to be sanctified wholly because it is God's requirement for entrance into His presence. We are exhorted to "follow peace with all men, and holiness, without which no man shall see the Lord" (Hebrews 12:14).

I do not like the expression "holiness or hell." Holiness is too glorious a reality, and hell too terrible a fact, to be glibly rolled off the tongue in a neat phrase. I do not like the expression, but I must use it because it describes a stark reality of the spiritual life.

With whom is it second-blessing holiness or hell? And why does God confront a man with this kind of alternatives? The Psalmist asks, "Who shall ascend into the hill of the Lord? or who shall stand in his holy place?" The inspired answer comes back: "He that hath clean hands, and a pure heart" (Psalms 24:3-4). Jesus said, "Blessed are the pure in heart: for they shall see God" (Matthew 5:8). If it is only the pure in heart who shall see God, then men must find heart purity or forfeit God. To be shut out of God's presence is to be eternally lost. It *is* holiness or hell.

"For if we persist in sin after receiving the knowledge of the truth, no sacrifice for sins remains: only a terrifying expectation of judgement and a fierce fire which will consume God's enemies" (Hebrews 10:26-27, N.E.B.).

READ: I Thessalonians 4:7-8

*Therefore to him that knoweth to do good, and doeth it not, to him it is sin* (James 4:17).

## To Him That Knoweth

The objection is often raised that God would not damn a saved man who, having had no light on holiness, had never been sanctified; therefore we cannot assert that it is second-blessing holiness or hell. Many able answers have been proposed to clear up this issue. But for all practical evangelical purposes it is not our question to answer. God alone can deal righteously with the consequences of ignorance among men.

Our responsibility is for the consequence of knowledge. The issue for us is not, What will God do with those who do not know? The issue is, What is God's judgment upon those who neglect or who refuse to walk in the light?

When God reveals truth to the mind, He requires us to do something about it; and the more important the truth, the greater the urgency for action. In every decision between right and wrong, between good and better, *now is the time to act.* The responsibility of God's child is to seek the truth and to obey that truth as soon as it is known.

There is no evading the fact which the Bible puts so clearly: "God hath . . . called us . . . unto holiness. He therefore that rejects [marginal reading] rejects not man, but God, who hath also given unto us his holy Spirit." We cannot turn away from the light of holiness without disobeying God. We cannot continue to disobey—even though conscience has grown numb and no longer prods us—without backsliding. If I have had clear light on entire sanctification I must walk in the light and obey. Or I shall disobey and walk into darkness. The consequences of my decision are second-blessing holiness or hell.

### Affirmation for today

*I shall this day do what I know God wants me to do.*

March 31

READ: Luke 11: 9-13

*If ye then, being evil, know how to give good gifts unto your children: how much more shall your heavenly Father give the Holy Spirit to them that ask him?* (Luke 11: 13)

## Sanctification Is a Privilege

Entire sanctification is fundamentally a privilege that God offers to us rather than a requirement exacted. This glorious grace is better than the good gifts that we plan for our children on their birthdays or at Christmas. It is true that God requires holiness of us, but it is doubtful if one can ever secure the blessing when seeking from a sheer sense of unwilling duty.

The duty of holiness must be stressed in order to arouse us if we are careless or indifferent—to show us that our hearts are already dangerously cold. But before we receive the baptism with the Holy Spirit we must sincerely desire heart purity because it is supremely desirable. Our Lord reminds us, "Blessed are they which do hunger and thirst after righteousness: for they shall be filled" (Matthew 5: 6). In answer to the question, "In what manner should we preach sanctification?" Wesley replied, "Scarce at all to those who are not pressing forward. . . . To those who are [pressing forward in the Christian life] always [present sanctification] by way of promise; always drawing, rather than driving."

It is better for a husband and wife to remain together from a sense of duty than to separate and break up a home. But all truly happy marriages are built upon the mutual desire of one to be with the other. So it is with the Holy Spirit. He comes only when He is desired, when He is wanted, when He is sought. He comes to us only when we sincerely seek Him because we want Him more than we want anything else in the world.

### Prayer for today

*As the hart panteth after the water brooks, so panteth my soul after thee, O God. My soul thirsteth for God, the living God* (Psalms 42: 1-2).

READ: I Thessalonians 5: 23-24

*And the very God of peace sanctify you wholly; and
I pray God your whole spirit and soul and body be
preserved blameless unto the coming of our Lord
Jesus Christ* (I Thessalonians 5: 23).

## I Pray God

Who were these people of Thessalonica for whom Paul
interceded? And why did the Apostle pray this special prayer
for them? They were not sinners; rather they were church
members—and in many ways they were faithful Christians.
Paul speaks of their work of faith, labor of love, patience,
hope in our Lord Jesus Christ, election of God, and following
the Lord (1: 3-6). Despite these Christian virtues, the Thessalonians needed the sanctifying grace of God, and Paul
earnestly urged this blessing upon them.

The Apostle had suffered too much for these converts
in the church to belabor them unnecessarily. He used urgent
language, just as a surgeon must use a sharp scalpel, but he
used that language only that those who read his words might
be healed.

Often Paul's Epistles turned into prayers. So it is in this
passage: "And the very God of peace sanctify you wholly;
and I pray God your whole spirit and soul and body be preserved blameless unto the coming of our Lord Jesus Christ."

Paul knew that entire sanctification was a loving gift
from the God of peace. This healer of souls also knew that
the gracious gift meant life for the spirit, health for the soul,
and blessing for the body. His heart's desire and prayer to
God for these converts whom he had won to Christ and
whom he loved as his own life was that they might know
the fullness of the blessing.

> *God of all-sufficient grace,*
> *My God in Christ Thou art;*
> *Bid me walk before Thy face,*
> *Till I am pure in heart.*
> *—Wesley's Hymns*

**April 2**

READ: Hebrews 10: 35-39

*If any man draw back, my soul shall have no pleasure in him. But we are not of them who draw back unto perdition* (Hebrews 12: 38-39).

## If Any Man Draw Back

Has the Holy Spirit convicted me of my need for entire sanctification? Have I somewhere in a holiness meeting acknowledged that need to myself and promised God that I would go home and pray it through? Was I successful in keeping that promise or am I still not sanctified? Has the devil defeated me by filling my mind with other things until the sense of urgency that I felt in the service is now gone?

We may turn away from the evangelist without spiritual loss. We may disagree with the pastor without danger to the soul. But we cannot ignore the clear truth of God's Word without drawing back. We cannot turn down or pass by the conviction of the Holy Spirit without disobeying God. To disobey the clear call to holiness even once is to begin to backslide.

When we have thus heard God's call to holiness and have failed to walk in the light, what must we do to avoid being among those "who draw back unto perdition"? The Bible is clear in its answer. "Cast not away therefore your confidence." Let us hold on to every bit of grace that God has given us. But let us also begin at once to walk in every bit of the light that God has shown us. Let us ask God now to forgive us for drawing back. Let us begin now to seek for entire sanctification. Let us continue to seek privately and publicly until we receive the baptism with the Holy Spirit.

> *I will mind God, no matter what others do;*
> *I will mind God and do as He bids me to.*
> *Whether the way be rough or steep*
> *I will mind God, I will mind God!**

—WARREN ROGERS

*© 1947, Warren Rogers. Used by permission.

READ: Luke 1: 67-75

*Blessed be the Lord God of Israel; for he hath visited and redeemed his people, . . . that we . . . might serve him without fear, in holiness and righteousness before him, all the days of our life* (Luke 1: 68, 74-75).

## Now or Later?

What kind of life does God want me to live? How can I most effectively achieve that kind of living? These are the key questions in the average Christian's theology. And much of the debate is removed even from technical theology when the issues are put this way.

Our text indicates God's will for us. He has planned for us to be a redeemed people. He has redeemed us so that we might serve Him in holiness and righteousness. The answer to the second question is clearly implied when we remember that we are to live holy and righteous *all the days of our life.*

How can any man live a holy and righteous life all of his days unless he starts now? The weakness of theories that postpone sanctification until death is that they do not make it possible for a man to serve God in holiness all the days of his life. The weakness of the theory of gradual sanctification is that it seldom challenges a man sharply enough to get him started with the life of holiness now.

If I believe in the theory of gradual sanctification, am I expecting to drift into a life of holiness? Have I ever consciously committed myself to God to accomplish that work in me as soon as possible? Have I ever asked Him to do for me as much as He could do *now* in order that I might serve Him in holiness and righteousness all the days of my life? Wesley asked the question, and in God's Word he found the answer.

> *But is it possible that I*
> *Should live and sin no more?*
> *Lord, if on Thee I dare rely,*
> *The faith shall bring the power.*
> —*Wesley's Hymns*

**April 4**

READ: Luke 11: 9-13

*I say unto you, . . . seek, and ye shall find; knock, and it shall be opened unto you* (Luke 11:9).

## The Grammar of Sanctifying Faith

In *Holiness the Finished Foundation,* Bishop J. Paul Taylor writes: "It is exceedingly important for the seeker for full salvation to master the grammar of sanctifying faith. The grammar of faith must be in the first person, singular number, present tense, indicative mood.

"When men talk in the second or third person about heart holiness, it has not come home to them personally. When they talk in the plural number, it is so general that it has no individual focus. When they talk in the future tense, it is a postponed, tentative thing. When they talk in the subjunctive, or even the imperative mood, they are only reaching for the blessing that is still out of reach. When they talk in the indicative mood, they have 'drawn near with a true heart in full assurance of faith,' and have seized the blessing.

"It is most interesting in this connection that the Wesleys twice made changes in the last line of a verse in one of their hymns. The verse originally read:

> *Quicken'd by Thy imparted flame,*
> *Saved, when possest of Thee, I am;*
> *My life, my only heaven, Thou art,*
> *When shall I feel Thee in my heart?*

In the next two editions the question was turned into the cry, 'O might I feel Thee in my heart.' In the following editions the question and the cry were superseded by the exclamation, 'And, lo! I feel Thee in my heart!' If these revisions do not represent the 'pilgrim's progress' of these founders of Methodism, they do represent the steps by which the hungry believer arrives at possession and satisfaction."

READ: Luke 11: 9-13

*If you then, imperfect as you are, know how to give your children gifts that are good for them, how much more will your Father who is in heaven give the Holy Spirit to those who ask Him!* (Luke 11:13, Weymouth)

## Take Him Now

The really worthwhile changes in the human spirit come to us as a result both of *decision* and of gradual growth. Saintly character is not achieved by a decision alone. But no saintly character is ever achieved without the decision to give myself wholly to God. A doctrine of sanctification which omits either the decision or the process is untrue to the facts of human experience.

The Wesleyan position stresses growth in grace. But it also emphasizes the importance of the personal decision as the key to the experience of entire sanctification. If a man wants to be holy he can tell God about that desire. We believe that God does not disappoint any desire to be like himself. He fills the hungry heart with His Holy Spirit, by faith, in a moment of time.

What will God do for us in that moment? Call it cleansing, call it eradication, call it enduement. Call it what you will—but try it! God will do for us all that we need to have done. He may do more than our timid theology has thought possible. He may do less than a mistaken, unscriptural dream has led us to expect. But our Lord has promised to give us the Holy Spirit.

When He has come He will guide us into all the further truth that we need. He may show us how He can do for us day at a time what He did not plan to do in a moment of time. Perhaps looking back we shall discover that He did more for us than we had dared to hope.

**Praise for today**

*Now unto him that is able to do exceedingly abundantly above all that we ask or think, according to the power that worketh in us, unto him be glory in the church by Christ Jesus throughout all ages, world without end. Amen* (Ephesians 3:20-21).

**April 6**

READ: James 1: 2-8

*Purify your hearts, ye double minded* (James 4: 8).

## The Disappointed Christian

Do you know of any disappointed Christians? Would you classify yourself in this group? If so, let God talk directly to you about your Christian experience, about your disappointment, about the only way out of it.

In our scripture, James informs us that this man is a Christian—one of his brethren. But there is something about his religious experience that is not at all commendable: he is a double-minded man. On this same theme the Apostle Paul writes of the carnal mind and the spiritual mind. There is always a conflict between these two, the one warring against the other until we have a Christian of divided loyalties, divided vision, divided affections; a double-minded man who is unstable, unsteady in all his ways.

This makes him a disappointed Christian. With his faith too weak to meet the emergencies, too wavering to depend on, how could it be otherwise? If you have similar experiences, you know just how grievous such disappointment can be.

In our text God's Word gives direction for disappointed Christians: 'Purify your hearts, ye double minded." Elsewhere Paul prays: "Let us cleanse ourselves from all fithiness of the flesh and spirit, perfecting holiness in the fear of God" (II Corinthians 7:1). We may not like the words the Bible uses, but our task is clear: we are to purify ourselves by confession, by consecration, by separation, by faith. God's work is to cleanse, to fill, to indwell, to unify, to possess.

### Prayer for today

*Lord, I have been a disappointed Christian. I long to find the way out. From the depths of my spiritual need, from the desperation of my disappointment I come for help. I open my heart to You in earnest prayer. This moment, by faith I accept the adequacy of Your infilling Holy Spirit.*

READ: Psalms 42:1-2

*Blessed are they which do hunger and thirst after righteousness: for they shall be filled* (Matthew 5:6).

## A Deepening Spiritual Hunger

Yesterday we thought about the disappointed Christian. Today we enjoy the testimony of a man who found his way out of this disappointment. Dr. W. L. Surbrook testifies: "On Sunday night, March 17, 1912 . . . about nine-twenty . . . God for Christ's sake pardoned all my sins. At a flash I was born again and at once became a new creature in Christ Jesus.

"With a background of teaching that the Holy Spirit was merely a divine emanation or influence from the Father and Son, light on His gracious work of cleansing dawned upon me slowly . . . As I walked with Him the best I knew how, He gradually deepened the hunger of my soul. To lead me into entire sanctification, He did not bless me more, but rather 'unblessed' me or in a measure withheld the blessing, and to that very degree the hunger deepened. Gradually my soul was filled with an insatiable thirst. With the ebb and flow of His blessings, the thirst deepened and the hunger increased.

"In response to this hungering and thirsting I was again found at the altar; this time I was not seeking pardon, but purity. My soul was not in the dark, and neither was there any condemnation upon it. I knew I was saved and walking in all the light while fellowshiping Him and His people, and yet I knew I needed something more. There was no guilt upon my soul, or stain upon my record, but there was inbred sin within my life that needed to be eradicated.

"It is very doubtful if I sought at that altar over twenty minutes until every condition was met; and, as faith took hold, the sweet, cleansing Holy Spirit purified my heart. As the quiet, assuring evidence came, a sweet restfulness came over my soul, and at once I knew He had sanctified me" (*Flames of Living Fire*, Beacon Hill Press of Kansas City).

**April 8**

READ: I John 1: 7-9

*If we walk in the light, as he is in the light, . . . the blood of Jesus Christ his Son cleanseth us from all sin* (I John 1: 7).

## The Prerequisites of Holiness

In our quest for holiness we have seen that God wants us to have this blessing now. What preparation must we make to receive the gift of the Holy Spirit?

Dr. J. B. Chapman has written: "The promise of cleansing is conditioned upon walking in the light. 'If we walk in the light, as he is in the light, . . . the blood of Jesus Christ his Son cleanseth us from all sin.' This walking in the light means simply obeying God to the full measure of our knowledge of His will. It implies willing and glad obedience.

"So we may summarize the prerequisites of holiness as (1) a clean, definite condition of regeneration, and (2) a heart that is willing to go all the way with God in all His revealed will. And when these two are considered together they become so closely united as to be almost one. It is essential to a clear state of justification to be ready and obedient. Reluctance and hesitation bring defeat and darkness.

"How is it with you today? Is your witness of sonship and acceptance with God bright and clear? Are you ready and willing to obey God in any and all things in which His will may be made known to you? Can you, as the poet would say, read your title clear to a mansion in the skies? If all this is descriptive of your state and relation, then you should have no hindrance in coming to God with prayer and faith to be 'made every whit whole.' There is a fullness in God's grace and mercy for you as a child of God. Do not be content without it. Claim your heritage. Lay hold upon the promise. Pray with the poet:

> *"Refining Fire, go through my heart,*
> *Illuminate my soul;*
> *Scatter Thy life through every part,*
> *And sanctify the whole."*

**110**

READ: Ephesians 5: 25-27

*Wherefore Jesus also, that he might sanctify the people with his own blood, suffered without the gate* (Hebrews 13: 12).

## Christ Died to Make Me Holy

At this Easter season we recall with deep feeling that Christ died to save us from our sins. This is the clear teaching of the Bible and the faith of the Christian Church. He died to save sinners from punishment for their sins. Did He die also to preserve His people from continued sinning? We believe that He did. We believe that forgiveness for past sins and provision to keep His followers from future sin are both provided in Christ's atonement.

Is it not reasonable to believe that when God went to such lengths to forgive the past He would provide the best possible insurance against further sinning? Is not such provision the clear meaning of the scriptures that follow?

"Christ also loved the church, and gave himself for it; that he might sanctify and cleanse it . . . that it should be holy and without blemish" (Ephesians 5: 25-27).

"And for this reason Jesus also, in order, by His own blood, to set the people free from sin, suffered outside the gate" (Hebrews 13: 12, Weymouth).

"And every man that hath this hope in him purifieth himself, even as he is pure. He that committeth sin is of the devil; for the devil sinneth from the beginning. For this purpose the Son of God was manifested, that he might destroy the works of the devil" (I John 3: 3, 8).

Christ died to save me from my sins. Did He not also die to purify and cleanse my sinful nature? The sanctified spirit shouts a glad *yes*.

*The cleansing stream, I see, I see!*
*I plunge and, oh, it cleanseth me!*
*Oh! praise the Lord, it cleanseth me!*
*It cleanseth me, yes, cleanseth me!*
—PHOEBE PALMER

**April 10**

READ: John 17: 9, 15-17

*Sanctify them through thy truth: thy word is truth*
(John 17:17).

## I Pray for Them

On the eve of the Crucifixion, as Jesus entered into His sufferings, the deepest desire of the Saviour was for the sanctification of His disciples.

In those last precious hours in the upper room before Gethsemane, He talked to them of many things: of humility, of the betrayer, of His going away, of their fruit bearing, and of the opposition to be faced. But throughout that hallowed evening our Saviour kept returning to one topic again and again. "And I will pray the Father, and he shall give you another Comforter, that he may abide with you for ever" (John 14:16). "But the Comforter, which is the Holy Ghost, whom the Father will send in my name, he shall teach you all things" (14:26). "If I go not away, the Comforter will not come unto you" (16:7).

Late in the evening the conversation was finished. There were no more words of instruction to be given. Our Lord ceased talking to men about God and began to talk to God about men.

Under the shadows of Gethsemane and of Calvary, in the hushed stillness of the night, the Saviour poured out His heart's desire to the Father. "I pray not that thou shouldest take them out of the world, but that thou shouldest keep them from the evil. They are not of the world, even as I am not of the world. Sanctify them through thy truth: thy word is truth." My heart responds to the intercession of my dying Saviour:

> *Answer that gracious end in me*
> *For which Thy precious life was given;*
> *Redeem from all iniquity;*
> *Restore, and make me meet for heaven!*
> —*Wesley's Hymns*

READ: John 17:9, 15-21

*Neither pray for these alone, but for them also which shall believe on me through their word* (John 17:20).

## Neither Pray I for These Alone

In our meditation of yesterday we saw the infinite heart of the Saviour in an agony of desire for eleven awed disciples who drew close to Him that night. He wanted them to remain in the world but to be kept from its evil. He prayed that the joy of His own fellowship with the Father might be theirs. He yearned for them to be really united with God by being filled with the Holy Spirit.

In Gethsemane, Jesus suffered as He bore the sins of the whole world. And there too He agonized over the spiritual weakness of His sleeping disciples. His concern was that they might be empowered by the gift of the Holy Spirit.

But His concern was not for them only. It was also for me. "Neither pray I for these alone, but for them also which shall believe on me through their word." In that sacred hour the Son of God prayed for me that I might be sanctified; He prayed, and He prays still, for all who need this blessing. Can we carelessly pass by the deepest concern of Him who died to save us from sin?

We who have had our sins forgiven need this blessing. We who love God must press on until our love is made perfect. Every man and woman who has turned his face toward God is called to tarry until the very image of the holy Creator is renewed in him. We who have come to Christ at Calvary must continue with Him to Pentecost.

### Prayer for today

*O my Saviour, I desire Thy full will for my life more than anything else in this world. May Thy prayer for Thy disciples be answered in me. Amen.*

**April 12**

READ: Matthew 26: 36-39

*O my Father, if it be possible, let this cup pass from me: nevertheless not as I will, but as thou wilt* (Matthew 26: 39).

## "If" or "Nevertheless"?

Gethsemane and Calvary remind us of our motives for holy living. Facing death on a cross, our Lord showed us the nature of real consecration: "O my Father, if it be possible, let this cup pass from me: nevertheless not as I will, but as thou wilt."

Absalom, the son of David, was exiled from home for three years. Homesick and ambitious for political power, he vowed a vow saying, "If the Lord shall bring me again indeed to Jerusalem, then I will serve the Lord" (II Samuel 15:8). Absalom was not the first nor the last to preface his loyalty to God with an *if*. This is conditioned loyalty. *If* the Lord blesses me, I will serve Him. *If* things go well, I will be a Christian. But conditioned loyalty is no loyalty, and conditioned consecration is not consecration.

True loyalty is seen in our Lord's utter commitment to God's will. It is seen in the action of three devoted young men who, when facing the issue of life or death, declared: "If it be so, our God whom we serve is able to deliver us from the burning fiery furnace, and he will deliver us out of thine hand, O king. *But if not*, be it known unto thee, O king, that we will not serve thy gods, nor worship the golden image which thou hast set up" (Daniel 3: 17-18).

Is my loyalty to God prefaced by the *if* of Absalom or by the *but if not* of three courageous young men? In my Gethsemanes can I follow my Lord and say, "Nevertheless not as I will, but as thou wilt"?

### Affirmation for today

*I have pledged my loyalty to God. By His grace no* IF's *shall be allowed to destroy that loyalty. By His grace I say,* NEVERTHELESS—*today, tomorrow, to the end.*

READ: John 14:25-27; 16:7

*Behold, I send the promise of my Father upon you: but tarry ye in the city of Jerusalem, until ye be endued with power from on high* (Luke 24:49).

## I Send the Promise

God has provided the blessing of entire sanctification to meet our deep human need. It was on the eve of the Crucifixion that the Holy Spirit was promised. The disciples were lonely, frightened men. They thought they were about to lose their Lord and that nothing could make up to them for that loss. It was in answer to such a pressing need that Jesus made the promise, "Let not your heart be troubled, neither let it be afraid. . . . It is expedient for you that I go away: for if I go not away, the Comforter will not come unto you; but if I depart, I will send him unto you."

It was in the last hours before Jesus was separated from the disciples on the mount of ascension that He instructed them what to do in order to have this blessing. "Tarry ye," was not a command to unwilling followers; it was a welcome word of instruction to eager Christian disciples. So it should be today.

Though we have known Christ and walked with Him, is there at this holy season of the year still a deep sense of spiritual need? Does God seem far away and unavailable? Do we yearn for a greater realization of His presence? It was to meet this need that the Holy Spirit was promised. May God's gracious provision fall like manna for the need of our hungering souls.

> *Oh, that I now the rest might know,*
> *Believe and enter in!*
> *Now, Saviour, now the power bestow,*
> *And let me cease from sin.*
> *—Wesley's Hymns*

## April 14

*6*

READ: Hebrews 6:1-3

*Therefore leaving the principles of the doctrine of Christ, let us go on unto perfection* (Hebrews 6:1).

## This Will We Do

How far have we come in our exploration of the high country of holiness? What has God shown us in the Scriptures about the place that holy living has in His grand design for our lives?

We have seen (1) that holy character was God's purpose in creating us; (2) that man lost something essential in the Fall and is now born with a spirit of antagonism to God; but (3) God has provided a way for man to be freed from such indwelling sin; (4) that the method is through a second, instantaneous work of grace; and (5) that this work of grace is God's will for all who are His redeemed children.

We come now to ask the question, How shall we enter in? As the Holy Spirit leads us into the experience, what steps must we take and by what signs shall we know that we are making progress toward our goal of heart holiness?

This is the real purpose of all our preceding study of the truth. Our better understanding of divine things is not an end in itself. We study in order to show ourselves approved unto God. The words themselves are only road signs on the highway of eternal life. We seek to understand the truth of holiness more clearly in order that we may enter in more quickly, or that we may aid others to do so. How can we be sanctified wholly? How can we guide our Christian friends to this high country? We start by wanting it. We are already moving in the right direction when we sincerely pray:

> *Purify our faith like gold;*
> *All the dross of sin remove;*
> *Melt our spirits down, and mould*
> *Into thy perfect love.*
>
> —*Wesley's Hymns*

READ: Psalms 42:1-2

*Blessed are they which do hunger and thirst after righteousness: for they shall be filled* (Matthew 5:6).

## I Must Have the Fullness of God

If in our souls we find a deep hunger for holiness—if our hearts cry, "Lord Jesus, I long to be perfectly whole," we are already on the road to the deeper life of God in the soul. But that desire must be deep and moving—true hungering and thirsting after righteousness. Only those who seek with all the heart find the fullness of God.

This must be so because entire consecration involves life-changing commitments. Into our consecration we must put everything that is nearest and everyone who is dearest to us. If we are to belong wholly to God, He must always have first place in our lives. He does not always take from us the things that we consecrate to Him; He does not always sever the ties of friendship that we place in His hands. He does not always take or sever but He always asks, "May I, if I see it is best?" And before we are sanctified wholly we must honestly and without mental reservation answer *yes*.

This is why our desire must be deep and moving. This is why we must want the Holy Spirit more than anything else in life. If our desire is faint, we are likely to come up against some obstacle and cannot go further. But if our soul hunger is deep and strong, it carries us past the hindrance.

I would this day make the prayer of Charles Wesley the prayer of my own heart:

> *Stretch my faith's capacity*
> *Wider, and yet wider still;*
> *Then with all that is in Thee*
> *My soul forever fill!*

> —*Wesley's Hymns*

**April 16**

READ: Matthew 19:16-22

*If thou will be perfect, go and sell that thou hast . . .
and come and follow me* (Matthew 19:21).

## If Thou Wilt Be Perfect

This rich young ruler who came to Jesus wanted true
spiritual life. He was already doing all that he knew to please
God: he kept the commandments and thus did not commit
acts of sin; he had faith enough in Jesus to come to Him for
some deeper experience with God. Our Lord did not question the young man's testimony but pointed out to him God's
plan for full sovereignty of the soul. "If thou will be perfect,
go and sell that thou hast . . . and come and follow me."

Jesus had previously asked Peter and John to give up
their fishing boats; He now asked this young man to give up
his farms. Peter could testify for the disciples, "We have left
all, and have followed thee" (Mark 10:28). The Master was
thus getting these disciples ready for Pentecost and He offered
the same opportunity to the rich young ruler. Had this young
man accepted the conditions, there could have been 121 filled
with the Holy Spirit in the Upper Room.

But when the young man heard the conditions "he went
away sorrowful." He was interested but he was not willing
to sell all. He wanted the prize but was unwilling to pay the
price. His desire for God was not deep enough to carry him
past hindering circumstances. He was not ready to make God's
will his own will.

The blessing comes when we go one step further than
the rich young ruler went. The blessing comes when we
surrender all in order to follow Christ.

> *My life, my love, I give to Thee,*
> *Thou Lamb of God, who died for me;*
> *Oh, may I ever faithful be,*
> *My Saviour and my God!*
>
> —R. E. HUDSON

**April 17**

READ: Deuteronomy 8: 11-14, 17-18

*Thou shalt remember the Lord thy God: for it is he that giveth thee power to get wealth* (Deuteronomy 8: 18).

## What Can I Give to God?

As a child of God, my Heavenly Father asks me to consecrate my all to Him. But how can I give anything to God? He gives me the power to earn my daily bread. God gave me the breath that I breathe; He gave me the mind that I use. My friends are gifts from God. My family is mine only by His grace. God gave His Son to save my soul. My spirit that yearns for Him was His gift to me. The very desire to give myself to Him came from Him. "Every good gift and every perfect gift is from above, and cometh down from the Father" (James 1: 17).

In the strictest sense I cannot give anything to God, because all that I have He gave to me. But I can and do consecrate this life of mine. I do this by a deep, heartfelt recognition that what I have is not my own. I have always been His by right of creation; I now wish to be His by my own free choice. I can and do now accept God's way as my way. As He has freely given all to me, I do now acknowledge His gifts and I desire to give myself to Him.

There is only one thing in this world that God cannot have unless I give it to Him—that is my love. And even this I can scarce withhold when I remember His love for me. I do love Him with all my heart. I do trust Him completely. I do therefore find it easy to say:

> *O God, what offering shall I give to Thee,*
> *The Lord of earth and skies?*
> *My spirit, soul, and flesh receive,*
> *A holy, living sacrifice.*
> *Small as it is, 'tis all my store;*
> *More should'st Thou have if I had more.*
>
> —JOACHIN LANGE, about 1690

**April 18**

READ: Romans 12:1-2

*Dedicate . . . your members to God for the service of righteousness* (Romans 6:13, Moffatt).

## Consecrate Your Abilities

The life of holiness is a life wholly yielded to the Spirit, a life of glad obedience to His leading. Therefore before the Holy Spirit comes in sanctifying power we must yield ourselves entirely to God.

It is not our sins which we consecrate; sins must be confessed, forgiven, and forsaken in conversion. In entire sanctification our personal capacities and possessions are to be consecrated and used. Paul writes, "I plead with you . . . to present all your faculties to Him as a living and holy sacrifice" (Romans 12:1, Weymouth).

God asks, Will you dedicate your whole self to Me? Your eyes to see only holy things? Your ears to hear only what is good? Your hands to do only what is right? Your feet to go only where My Spirit can go with you? Your mind to think only thoughts that I can bless? Your will to choose what Christ approves? Our Lord asks, Will you use your time as I direct? Will you place your talents at My disposal? Will you use and invest your money to further My kingdom? Will you choose your friends so as to honor Me?

In answer to Christ's questions, my glad heart replies, Here is all of me—

> *My feet to run Thine errands, Lord;*
> *My lips to praise or pray;*
> *My hands to lift the fallen ones*
> *And help them on their way;*
> *My every power of mind and heart;*
> *Mine eyes Thy tasks to see.*
> *For any service Thou dost choose,*
> *Lord, here am I; send me.*
>
> —AUTHOR UNKNOWN

READ: Matthew 19:16-22

*Yield yourselves unto God* (Romans 6:13).

## Yield Yourselves

Dr. J. B. Chapman used to tell of an Indian who related his experience in consecration: 'I brought my pony and put him on the altar—but no blessing came. I added my blanket and my tepee—still there was no blessing. Then I added my squaw and my papoose—and there was no blessing yet. But when in addition to all these, I cried, 'And this poor Indian, too, O Lord!' the blessing came."

God can use every *thing* and all the *capacities* that I consecrate to Him, but He is primarily interested in *me*. Jesus would have rejoiced at the relief from human suffering that the consecrated wealth of the rich young ruler might have brought to the poor, but primarily Christ wanted the full allegiance of the man. He asked the young man to give up his wealth only because that wealth represented an unyielded will. The young man's supreme interest in personal possessions put God in second place.

This is the usual experience in our efforts to make a complete consecration. Many specific items can be yielded without a struggle, but God eventually puts His finger on the *one thing* that we prize above all else. It may be our money, a friend, our family, or some personal desire contrary to God's plan for us. The thing itself may be trivial, but it is no small matter when we hold on to it contrary to God's will. It becomes the occasion for the crucial test whether self-will or God's will is to control our lives.

*All to Jesus I surrender;*
*Lord, I give myself to Thee.*
*Fill me with Thy love and power;*
*Let Thy blessing fall on me.*
—J. W. Van Deventer

## April 20

READ: Romans 6: 12-13

*Yield yourselves unto God, as those that are alive from the dead* (Romans 6: 13).

## Yield Yourselves unto God

The essence of consecration is found in the scriptural exhortation, "Yield yourselves *unto God*." Consecration is fundamentally not dedication to God's work, not to the mission field or to the ministry, not to a life of sacrifice nor to lay service in the church; consecration is to God himself. Entire consecration is our willingness and our resolution to accept and to do the whole will of God insofar as it is made known to us.

Such an act of self-dedication offers us the greatest hope for happiness in this life and it is our assurance of seeing God hereafter. In the face of these facts, why do we hesitate? We who have been saved from our sins believe that God is a personal God, that He loves us, and that He has made known His will concerning us. We believe that He is wiser than we, that He is more powerful than all the forces that may oppose Him. We believe that He is more interested in our welfare than we are in ourselves.

If we accept all of this, why should we not dedicate ourselves to His will? Why are we reluctant to consecrate our little all to God in exchange for all of Him? Why should we hesitate to make the supreme acquiescence and say, "Not my will, but Thine, be done"?

### Prayer for today

*Oh, Thou Most High God . . . Glory to Thy holy name! . . . I have nothing to fear. Now, O Father! my God and Savior, I humbly pray Thee so to keep me that all my powers of soul, body, and spirit . . . shall continually, exclusively and eternally glorify Thy holy name through Jesus Christ, my Lord and Savior. Amen and amen.*

—DANIEL SIDNEY WARNER

122

READ: Romans 6: 12-13

*It is God who is at work within you* (Philippians 2:13, Phillips).

## The Wonder of Self-surrender

Christian consecration is rejected by some on psychological grounds. The argument runs as follows: Wholesome personal development requires self-confidence, poise, and a positive self-image. Consecration is a debasing of the self-image and a surrender of man's highest powers of freedom and creativity.

On the surface the argument appears plausible, but accurate thinking goes below the surface. In its truest meaning Christian consecration does not lower man; it exalts God. When I surrender my life to God, I surrender myself, not to be held down, but to be lifted up; not to have freedom and creativity destroyed, but to have them used most effectively. I see how great God is, what a glorious plan He has for my life. I surrender only a stubborn self-centeredness that would otherwise keep me from life's highest development under God.

Fritz Kreisler once sought to buy a rare old violin from an English collector. The collector valued the violin highly as a collector's item and would not sell it.

Kreisler asked permission to play the violin. He took it carefully from the case, tuned the strings, and began to play. The violin sang, and wept, and laughed as only Kreisler could make it do. The collector listened in rapture. He said nothing as Kreisler put the violin carefully back and closed the case. Then he burst out:

"Take it. The violin is yours. I do not own it. It belongs to the man who can make it sing."

I do not have a rare violin, but I have my life to give. It belongs to Christ; therefore I give it to Him.

> *All to Jesus I surrender.*
> *Make me, Saviour, wholly Thine;*
> *Let me feel the holy Spirit,*
> *Truly know that Thou art mine.*
> —J. W. VAN DEVENTER

**April 22**

READ: John 21: 20-22

*What is that to thee? follow thou me* (John 21:22).

## Yield the Future

Jesus asked Peter to follow Him no matter what the future might unfold. This too is a part of entire consecration. When I give myself fully to God, I accept His known will for the present. I also commit myself to accept His as yet unknown will for each decision that the future shall bring.

Can one thus really consecrate to God what he does not yet know? We cannot, of course, live all of life in a moment of time. But we can in a moment of decision resolve to give all of life to God.

This commitment of the future has sometimes been described as placing the "unknown bundle" upon the altar of consecration. As its contents become known to us one by one, the sanctified Christian accepts them. We remind ourselves and God that these things too were included when we said a full yes to the Holy Spirit.

Consecrating the future is like establishing a policy decision in a business firm. Once the policy has been laid down, each employee knows what to do when specific decisions arise that are covered by the policy. Without such policy decisions there are blundering, uncertainty, and struggle.

God's plan is to save us from this kind of spiritual struggle and ineffectiveness. The consecrated Christian does not ask, Will I obey God in this new situation? When a full consecration has been made he only asks, What does God want me to do?

It is great spiritual gain to live where I can sing:

*Many things about tomorrow*
*I don't seem to understand;*
*But I know who holds tomorrow,*
*And I know who holds my hand.**

—IRA STANPHILL

*© Hymntime Publishers. Used by permission.

READ: Matthew 19:16-22

*I beseech you therefore, brethren, by the mercies of God, that ye present your bodies a living sacrifice, holy, acceptable unto God, which is your reasonable service* (Romans 12:1).

## Reasonable Service

Paul called this act of entire consecration a "reasonable service." He knew that God required it; he entreated his fellow Christians to do it; but he insisted that it was what every thoughtful Christian should freely choose to do.

Self-surrender is a reasonable requirement because it is a requirement that every man can meet. If God required talent, some of us would be shut out; if He asked for money, some could not pay. But when God asks for the surrender of myself, He asks for that which is wholly within my power. Jesus did not ask the rich young ruler to sell property belonging to his father, his brother, or his business partner. The requirement concerned only that which was his own: "Go and sell *that thou hast.*" Consecration is reasonable because it is the one condition clearly within my power to meet.

Is it not reasonable also in view of what God has done for me? He gave me life; should I not freely share that life with Him? He gave His only Son to die for my sins; should I not in turn gladly renounce all sin? He offers me eternal life; is it not reasonable that I should accept that offer?

God has made me for himself, and my heart is hungry for Him. There is just one thing that keeps me from my heart's desire—the unwillingness to give myself fully to Him. My mind tells me that resistance is foolish and fatal. My heart bids me take the reasonable route that my mind sees. I take that route.

### Affirmation for today

*Lord, I give myself to Thee. Accept the gift I bring. I am Thine. Today. Tomorrow. Always.*

**April 24**

READ: Romans 12:1-2

*Seek ye first the kingdom of God, and his righteousness; and all these things shall be added unto you* (Matthew 6:33).

## Your Reasonable Service

God wants our lives to be rich and full. Jesus declared: "I am come that they might have life, and that they might have it more abundantly" (John 10:10). How shall we find life's highest happiness?

The psychiatrist answers in two words—personal integration. If we are to be wholesome personalities, life must be organized around some central goal and purpose. The consecrated life is reasonable in view of the requirements for mental health. Consecration demands of us an all-inclusive commitment—and a commitment to life's supreme value. Sooner or later devotion to anything less than God and goodness will fall short of our deepest needs. The highest unification of life and the only permanently successful integration of personality is in the realm of the spirit. Jesus gives us the clue: "Seek ye first the kingdom of God."

The Bible tells us that a "double minded man is unstable in all his ways" (James 1:8). The psychiatrist adds that this instability destroys our happiness. Certainly to live a divided life, to feel pulled apart and at loose ends, to be all at odds with oneself is to be unhappy. On the other hand, as Dr. William H. Shelton says, "Happiness is essentially a state of going somewhere, wholeheartedly, one directionally, without regret or reservation." How else in life can one find such happiness? This radiance of living is made possible by entire consecration. Full devotion to the will of God is our reasonable service, for through consecration comes fullness of life.

*All that I want is in Jesus,*
*He satisfies, joy He supplies;*
*Life would be worthless without Him,*
*All things in Jesus I find.\**

—HARRY DIXON LOES

*© By permission Hope Publishing Co.

READ: Genesis 22: 1-14

*He that loveth son or daughter more than me is not worthy of me* (Matthew 10:37).

## Consecration of Loved Ones

What does entire consecration mean to a devoted parent? Daniel S. Warner gives us a glimpse into God's dealing with him at this point. As a part of his consecration prayer he recorded:

"Levilla Modest, whom we love as a dear child bestowed upon us by Thy infinite goodness, is hereby returned to Thee. If Thou wilt leave us to care for her and teach her . . . we will do the best we can by Thy aid to make her profitable unto Thee. But if Thou deemest us unfit to rear her properly or wouldst have her in Thy more immediate presence, behold, she is Thine, take her. Amen and Amen."

Does God give us these dearest possessions only to take them from us and leave us bereft and broken? No, but in mercy He teaches us how to possess them. If we cannot voluntarily trust our loved ones to God today, in the hour of consecration, our faith in His goodness is not likely to be strong enough to sustain us in the dark hour of bereavement. It is His concern for us that makes Him require the consecration of our loved ones.

The call for this consecration is only a test but it is a real test. God said to Abraham, "Take now thy son, thine only son Isaac, whom thou lovest . . . and offer him . . . for a burnt offering." It is soul-moving to see the tortured father in an agony of obedience for three days. But it is overwhelming to hear God at the crucial moment reverse the order: "Lay not thine hand upon the lad . . . : for now I know that thou fearest God, seeing thou hast not withheld thy son, thine only son from me."

After such a test of devotion God could trust His man— and a man can forever trust God.

**April 26**

READ: Matthew 4:18-22

*Follow me, and I will make you fishers of men* (Matthew 4:19).

## Consecration of a Life's Work

As a young man, eighteen years of age, I knelt one night at an altar in a college chapel. I had found the Lord as a boy. Now I wanted God to sanctify me wholly.

For some time I prayed and tried to follow the instructions of those who were praying with me. At last God whispered to me and said, "Son, would you be willing to preach My gospel?"

My first reply was quick and firm. "No, Lord," I said, "I couldn't do that. I'm going to be a doctor." For more than six years I had dreamed of medicine, and was preparing for it. I couldn't give up those firm plans for my life's work.

But God was speaking to me as clearly as Jesus spoke to the Galilean fishermen. I wanted to give my life entirely to God but I felt powerless to answer His call. He had asked me, "Would you *be willing* to preach?"

In agony I argued, "Lord, how can I say I am willing when I am not willing? How can I be willing when I don't want to preach? When I want to be a doctor?"

The Lord knew that I could not change my desires by a sheer act of will. But He knew that He could change those desires if I would surrender my will to Him. He asked me, "Would you be willing for Me to make you willing to preach?"

From my heart I surrendered. I said, "If You can change my desires so that I can really want to preach, I am willing for You to do it." And a miracle happened. The old desire of six year's standing somehow faded away. God's Holy Spirit filled my soul and I found a real joy in the thought of sharing Christ's message with others. For thirty-eight years that joy has deepened and grown.

READ: Matthew 6: 19-24

*If . . . thine eye be single, thy whole body shall be
full of light* (Matthew 6: 22).

## The Light Within

"Guidance of life by the Light within . . . proceeds in
two opposing directions at once. We are torn loose from
earthly attachments and ambitions—*contemptus mundi*. And
we are quickened to a divine but painful concern for the
world—*amor mundi*. He plucks the world out of our hearts,
loosening the chains of attachment. And He hurls the world
into our hearts, where we and He together carry it in infinitely tender love.

"Such loosing of the chains of attachment is easy, if we
be given times of a sense of unutterable nearness of Himself.
In those moments what would we not leave for Him? For
some persons . . . the work of detachment . . . exists chiefly as
an intellectual obligation. . . . Still others obstruct this detachment, reject it as absurd or unneeded, and cling to mammon
while they seek to cling to God.

"Double-mindedness in this matter is wholly destructive
of the spiritual life. Totalitarian are the claims of Christ. No
vestige of 'our' rights can remain. Straddle arrangements and
compromises between our allegiances to the surface level and
the divine Center cannot endure. Unless the willingness is
present to be stripped of our last earthly dignity and hope,
and yet still praise Him, we have no message. Nor have we
yielded to the monitions of the Inner Instructor.

"But actually completed detachment is vastly harder than
intended detachment. Fugitive islands of secret reservations
elude us. Rationalizations hide them. Intending absolute
honesty, we can only bring ourselves steadfastly into His
presence and pray, 'Cleanse thou me from secret faults.' And
in the X-ray light of Eternity we may be given to see the
dark spots of life, and divine grace may be given to rein-
force our will to complete abandonment in Him. For the
guidance of the Light is critical, acid, sharper than a two-
edged sword. He asks all, but He gives all" (*A Testament of
Devotion,* by Thomas R. Kelly).

**April 28**

READ: Exodus 35: 30-35

*See, the Lord hath called by name Bezaleel . . . and hath filled him with the spirit of God . . . in all manner of workmanship* (Exodus 35: 30-31).

## A Consecrated Life's Work

God calls every man to consecrate his daily task—but He does not call every man to preach. A friend decided that he had been called to the ministry. After serving his first pastorate, he reached a sincere conclusion that he had been mistaken about his call. Though he gave up the ministry he maintained his consecration. Said he, "I decided if I could not make the ministry my business, I would make my business my ministry." And he has done that.

God called Moses by name to be the spiritual leader of Israel. But Moses was not the only one called by name, and spiritual leadership is not the only lifework where our Lord needs consecrated men.

God needed skilled workmen to construct a place of worship. Moses was quick to see the talent of a layman; and he was equally alert to recognize true spiritual consecration in devoted manual skill. He said to the children of Israel: "See, the Lord hath called by name Bezaleel . . . and he hath filled him with the spirit of God, in wisdom, in understanding, and in knowledge, and in all manner of workmanship . . . And he hath put in his heart that he may teach."

Bezaleel was not the only efficient craftsman in Israel but his skill was consecrated. His name means "In the Shadow of God." Every man who performs his daily task in the shadow of God may share in the Bible's testimony to this sainted layman, "The Lord . . . hath filled him with the spirit of God."

> *These hands I give to Thee, my blessed Saviour,*
> *To do Thy will—whatever love demands;*
> *Redeemed and sanctified and in Thy favor,*
> *I gladly yield to Thee this pair of hands.**
>
> —FLOYD HAWKINS

*© 1963 by Lillenas Publishing Co. All rights reserved.

130

READ: Romans 12:1-2

*I appeal to you therefore, brethren, and beg of you in view of all the mercies of God, to make a decisive dedication* (Romans 12:1, *The Amplified New Testament*).

## By the Mercies of God

What are the mercies of God in my life? It takes only a moment of reflection to remind me that all that I am and all that I have came from Him. The food that I eat, the air that I breathe, strength for the day's work, a mind with which to think, the love of family and friends—all of these are mercies of God.

But I am a Christian, and God's mercies to me are still more. My sins have been forgiven. I have the fellowship and help of Christian friends in the church. I know the deep joy of communing with God in prayer. For all of these mercies my heart cries, "Bless the Lord, O my soul, and all that is within me, bless his holy name" (Psalms 103:1).

It is against this background of blessings that Paul pleads with us to make the decisive dedication of our lives. We are asked to consider all that Christ has done for us and all that He died to accomplish in us; then, in view of our love for Christ, to give ourselves wholly to Him.

Is there any good reason why we should hesitate? But hesitate we do! It is the carnal spirit within which draws back from the will of God. This very hesitation is a part of the evil from which we sorely need deliverance. If we have not yet made this full and decisive surrender, let us allow God's servant to speak to our hearts:

> *You have longed for sweet peace,*
> *And for faith to increase,*
> *And have earnestly, fervently prayed;*
> *But you cannot have rest*
> *Or be perfectly blest*
> *Until all on the altar is laid.*
> —ELISHA A. HOFFMAN

**April 30**

READ: Ruth 1: 6-17

*Whither thou goest, I will go; and where thou lodgest,
I will lodge; thy people shall be my people, and thy
God my God; where thou diest will I die, and there
will I be buried* (Ruth 1:16-17).

## The Spirit of Consecration

God is a Person and the best figures of our relationships
to Him are illustrations from personal life. Ruth's pledge of
undying loyalty was made to her mother-in-law, Naomi. But
in this pledge "she speaks the language of one resolved for
God and heaven."

"Whither thou goest, I will go." This is the commitment
a man must make in a changing world. We cannot foresee
the future. We cannot know all the ways that God will lead
us. But we can pledge ourselves to follow.

"Where thou lodgest, I will lodge." We cannot always
choose the place but through consecration we can always
choose the Companion.

"Thy people shall be my people." When we take God,
we take His people for our people. They are not always rich,
or cultured, or wise. But because they are His people they
are good and loving and devoted. I need that kind of companions—His people shall be my people.

Where Thou dost choose, there "will I die, and there
will I be buried." In our consecration we resolve that death
itself shall not separate us from our duty to Christ. Having
done this, we may be sure that even death cannot separate
us from our happiness in Him.

"My God." It is to Him that my consecration is made.

### Prayer for today

*Thou, God, shalt be my God. I love Thee. I wor-
ship Thee. I shall be faithful to Thee so long as life
shall last. This, O God, is my prayer of consecration. I have made my choice forever. I reaffirm it
today. In the name of Jesus. Amen.*

READ: Romans 6:13

*Who then is willing to consecrate his service this day unto the Lord?* (I Chronicles 29:5)

## My Consecration Experience

"I was gloriously saved on Friday afternoon, November 3, 1922. For the next two days I walked on air. Life was new, completely different.

"But on Monday morning, November 6, I felt a hunger for more. I went to the altar in the chapel service. It was hard for me to surrender my will. I fought and struggled. But I found that God wouldn't compromise. There was only one condition, simple but absolute: I must say *yes* to everything.

"I thought I was about through and ready to believe when someone upset the whole affair by asking: 'If God should ask you to preach on the Pullman, would you be willing?'

"What! Preach on a Pullman? I should say not! Well, there I stood, blocked. I hunted in vain for a detour. But there was no other way to victory. Finally, in desperation I said, 'Yes, Lord, I will if it kills me.'

"There was the secret. The proud, self-willed, selfish self had to die. But when I submitted to die in order that Christ might live in me, victory came. At that moment there came the peace of God that passeth all understanding. Quiet, but, oh, how sweet! I knew in my heart that I had said the last yes to all of God's will.

"God has never asked me to preach on a Pullman. But I settled it that day that I would do *whatever* He asked me to do. How glad I am today that as a lad of fifteen, I made a complete consecration of myself to Christ!"—RALPH EARLE.

> *I have made my choice forever*
> *Twixt this world and God's dear Son.*
> *Naught can change my mind, no, never;*
> *He my heart has fully won.*
> —MRS. E. E. WILLIAMS

**May 2**

READ: Romans 6:11-13

*Yield yourselves ... and your members as instruments of righteousness unto God* (Romans 6:13).

## Yield Yourselves unto God

In *The Spirit of Holiness,* Everett Lewis Cattell writes: "In the old days of British rule in India I saw a curious thing at the investiture ceremony where the Maharajah of Chhatarpur received, on coming of age, his ruling powers. . . . It was that moment when the nobles of the court came to pledge their fealty to the British Crown . . . Each one in turn came slowly to the throne, bowed low, and extended his hand draped with a silk handkerchief in which was a quantity of gold.

"It was the right of the Resident on behalf of the Crown to take this gold as a pledge of the loyalty of this Indian nobleman. But instead, he touched it slowly, symbolizing his acceptance of the man's fealty, then withdrew his hand, allowing the man to return to his seat with the gold in his possession. He was free to use that gold in any way he chose so long as it was consistent with his loyalty to the Crown. To use it in any subversive way would be criminal."

In my hour of consecration I pledge my lifelong loyalty to God. He made me what I am, and He gave me all that I have. In my high moment of consecration I come to Him bearing these gifts. God could take them from me but He assures me that He can use them most effectively through me.

### Prayer for today

*All that I am and all that I have, I lay upon the altar of consecration. Thou gavest these gifts to me, and I now return them. If Thou dost take them from me, it is as I freely choose. If Thou dost leave them with me, they shall be as fully Thine. Touch what I bring and it shall henceforth be under Thy control.*

READ: Romans 12:1-2

*Be ye transformed by the renewing of your mind, that ye may prove what is that good, and acceptable, and perfect, will of God* (Romans 12:2).

## Consecration Brings Significant Change

Today's educator defines learning as a change resulting from experience. In these terms we may say that entire sanctification is a significant change that occurs in me as a result of a specific kind of experience with God. What is that change? What kind of experience brings it about?

From the psychological standpoint entire sanctification is having the inner core of myself so changed that I have a maximum openness to the will of God. This is the experience for which Paul prays in our text, "Be ye transformed by the renewing of your mind."

The unrenewed mind chooses its own way in preference to God's way. The transformed mind subordinates itself to God's will. The decisive issue in our walk with God is whether He is to have His way in our lives, *in every area.* Paul urges: "I plead with you . . . to present *all your faculties* to Him as a living and holy sacrifice" (Romans 12:1, Weymouth).

Are there specific area where I resent God's interference in my plans? The reality of my surrender is often measured by the fight that I put up at these points. It is easy to surrender what I don't care about—and that surrender doesn't change me much. It is hard to surrender where I really care—but this is the surrender that counts.

We cannot transform ourselves in this way any more than we can forgive our own sins. But we are able to set the stage so that God can do this for us. Am I ready to offer this prayer?

> *Give me a new, a perfect heart,*
> *From doubt, and fear, and sorrow free;*
> *The mind which was in Christ impart,*
> *And let my spirit cleave to Thee.*
>
> *—Wesley's Hymns*

**May 4**

READ: I Kings 18:21-39

*I will call on the name of the Lord: and the God that answers by fire, let him be God* (I Kings 18:24).

## Sanctification Versus Consecration

Commissioner Samuel Logan Brengle of the Salvation Army cites Elijah's clash with the prophets of Baal as an Old Testament illustration of the distinction between consecration and sanctification. He writes:

"Elijah piled his altar on Mount Carmel, slew his bullock and placed him on the altar, and then poured water over the whole. That was consecration.

"But Baal's priests had done that, with the exception of putting on the water. They had built their altar, they had slain their bullocks, they had spent the day in the most earnest religious devotions, and, so far as men could see, their zeal far exceeded that of Elijah.

"What did Elijah more than they?

"Nothing, except to put a few barrels of water on his sacrifice—a big venture of faith. If he had stopped there, the world would never have heard of him. But he believed for *God* to do something. He expected it, he prayed for it, and God split the heavens and poured down fire to consume his sacrifice, and the stones of his altar, and the very water that lay in the trenches. That was sanctification!

"God wants sanctified men. Of course, men must be consecrated—that is, given up to God—in order to be sanctified. But when once they have yielded themselves to Him ... then they must wait on God and cry to Him with a humble, yet bold, persistent faith till He baptizes them with the Holy Ghost and fire. He promised to do it and He will do it, but men must expect it, look for it, pray for it, and if it tarry, wait for it" (*Helps to Holiness*).

> Come, Father, Son, and Holy Ghost,
>   And seal me Thine abode!
> Let all I am in Thee be lost;
>   Let all be lost in God.
>
> —*Wesley's Hymns*

May 5  7

READ: Acts 26:16-18

*I send you . . . that they may receive forgiveness of sins and a place among those who are sanctified by faith in me* (Acts 26:17-18, R.S.V.).

## Sanctification Is by Faith

When we have completed our consecration to God, we have almost finished with all that human endeavor can do to obtain the blessing of entire sanctification. Almost but not quite. When consecration is complete, we rest the case with God and by *faith* we receive the promised gift.

There is a sense in which faith is the only condition for receiving the Holy Spirit. Desire and consecration are necessary but they are foundations for our faith. They are necessary because without them faith does not function. But one may have both desire and consecration and yet not receive the blessing if faith be lacking. On the other hand, faith is the one condition that is never absent when the blessing comes, and the one condition that can never be met without the blessing following.

It is often the presence or absence of faith which accounts for the differences we see in those who seek to be sanctified. Occasionally a seeker weeps, prays, agonizes, and exhausts himself in a search which extends into weeks. In these cases the struggle seems necessary to help the seeker reach a place of faith. Others meet God's conditions and exercise faith almost without conscious effort. Dr. J. B. Chapman, sanctified the next night after his conversion, writes: "I was not really conscious of holding anything back from God. I did answer *yes* to every suggestion. After an hour of prayer and searching the heart, I was able to trust for the sanctifying fullness of the Holy Spirit."

### Affirmation for today

*I believe the Bible teaches that God wants to sanctify converted Christians. I ask Him to cleanse and fill me. I do now open my heart to the Holy Spirit and trust His promise to sanctify my soul.*

**May 6**

READ: Hebrews 11:1-6

*Without faith it is impossible to please him: for he that cometh to God must believe that he is, and that he is a rewarder of them that diligently seek him* (Hebrews 11:6).

## Faith—Open Door to God's Gifts

"A few years since, a college friend . . . was bowing with many others as a seeker of full salvation. . . . As I knelt by him to encourage and instruct him, he said: 'O give me a promise, give me a promise!'

"I repeated in his ear, 'Wherefore he is able also to save them to the uttermost that come unto God by him' (Heb. 7:25). The words were scarcely off my lips before he exclaimed: 'That is what I wanted; I believe it; praise the Lord, O my soul, I am fully saved' " (S. A. Keen, *Faith Papers*).

Why must we have faith in order to be sanctified wholly? In our scripture for today God's Word gives us the answer. We are reminded that faith is the open door to all of His gifts of grace—"He that cometh to God must believe."

Paul tells us, "For by grace are ye *saved through faith*." It is true also of entire sanctification. Peter declares, "God, which knoweth the hearts . . . put no difference between us and them, *purifying their hearts by faith*." Of this gracious, cleansing experience we must say, it is "by grace . . . through faith" (Ephesians 2:8-9). Our Lord settled that issue as clearly as words can state it when He sent Paul to the gentiles to "open their eyes, and turn them from darkness to light, and from the power of Satan unto God, that they may receive forgiveness of sins, and inheritance among them which are *sanctified by faith that is in me*" (Acts 26:18).

> *Faith, mighty faith, the promise sees,*
> *And looks to that alone;*
> *Laughs at impossibilities,*
> *And cries, "It shall be done!"*
>
> —CHARLES WESLEY

138

READ: Hebrews 7: 23-28

*Wherefore he is able also to save them to the uttermost that come unto God by him* (Hebrews 7:25).

## Able to Save to the Uttermost

We saw yesterday how our text for today kindled faith in a man's soul for entire sanctification. What does it mean to be saved "to the uttermost"? Verses 23 and 24 clearly indicate the idea of duration. Earthly priests could help only for a short time because human life is limited. But Christ "ever liveth to make intercession." This is a glorious truth, but there is more.

Christ is a better High Priest not only because He has a longer ministry; He also has a better one. The system of the former priests "made nothing perfect" (v. 19). By implication these priests were unholy, defiled, and sinners by nature (v. 26). They could offer nothing better than they had. But Christ is different. He offers us freedom from all sin. Weymouth translates verse 26, "Such a High Priest as this was exactly suited to our need—holy, guileless, undefiled."

The Greek word for *uttermost* is used only one other time in the New Testament (Luke 13:11). It means *wholly* or *completely*. When the author of Hebrews declares that Christ is able to save to the uttermost, he means that Christ has the power to save us completely and perfectly. He can save us not only from the guilt and punishment of sin, but also from its nature and power. In another passage the author says of Jesus: "He that sanctifieth and they who are sanctified are all of one: for which cause he is not ashamed to call them brethren" (Hebrews 2:11). This sanctification in its wider meaning includes cleansing from all sin and the indwelling Holy Spirit. It is received by faith.

It is this complete salvation of which we sing:

*Saved to the uttermost! Cheerfully sing*
*Loud hallelujahs to Jesus, my King.*
*Ransomed and pardoned, redeemed by His blood,*
*Cleansed from unrighteousness—glory to God!*
—W. J. KIRKPATRICK

**May 8**

READ: Luke 11:9-13

*I say unto you, Ask, and it shall be given you* (Luke 11:9).

## Ask, and It Shall Be Given You

"The [crucial] step toward obtaining the blessing is faith. Faith for this particular thing. Here you have come as a justified Christian, assured by the inner witness of the Holy Spirit that you are a child of God. You have found by reading the Bible and searching your own heart that God commands you to be holy and that He has provided the means for making you so. You have now brought your all to the altar of God in consecration. You have dedicated yourself and all you are and all you ever expect to be to God.

"You believe He is willing and able to make you holy, and that He is ready to do it this very hour. There is nothing more that God can do in promising. There is nothing more that you can do in meeting the conditions of His promises. To hesitate is to doubt and indicate your uncertainty as to whether He will do what He has said. So without fear and without hesitation, you step right out on the promise and announce to three worlds, 'I believe that Jesus Christ sanctifies me now.'

"The steps have been taken. . . . The only thing left is . . . the blessing that God has promised. Will it fail? Will He fail? To ask is to answer. He will not fail. He will come in sanctifying fullness and make your heart His throne. He will purge out the dross of inbred sin and make you clean. . . . I join you in praise. I sing hallelujah, 'the Comforter has come!'" (J. B. Chapman).

> *I want Thy life, Thy purity,*
> *Thy righteousness, brought in;*
> *I ask, desire, and trust in Thee,*
> *To be redeemed from sin.*
>
> —*Wesley's Hymns*

READ: Mark 11: 22-24

*What things soever ye desire, when ye pray, believe that ye receive them, and ye shall have them* (Mark 11: 24).

## My Faith Must Be Definite

W. W. Clay testifies: "Many years ago I sought the baptism with the Holy Ghost. I gladly accepted His will, but there was no sign of the Spirit's infilling. Then Someone seemed to say, 'What things soever ye desire, when ye pray, believe that ye receive them, and ye shall have them.' I was afraid I would be mistaken about the experience, and I told the Holy Spirit so. Again came the verse of scripture to me, and I seemed to hear a whisper, 'If you believe that He has given you what you have asked for, why remain longer on your knees?' I arose, and there came into my heart such a peace and sweet rest! I knew He had come."

Faith for entire sanctification is simply believing God's Word concerning heart holiness. When John Wesley was asked, "What is that faith whereby we are sanctified?" he answered: "First believe that God has *promised* to save you from all sin, and to fill you with all holiness; secondly, believe that He is *able* thus to save to the uttermost all that come unto God through him; thirdly, believe that He is *willing*, as well as able, to save *you* to the uttermost; to purify you from all sin, and fill up all your heart with love. Believe fourthly, that He is not only able, but willing to do it *now!* Not when you come to die; not at any distant time; not tomorrow, but *today*. He will then enable you to believe, *it is done*, according to His Word."

> 'Tis done: Thou dost this moment save,
> With full salvation bless;
> Redemption through Thy blood I have,
> And spotless love and peace.
>
> —Wesley's Hymns

**May 10**

READ: John 14: 13-17

*I will pray the Father, and he shall give you another Comforter, that he may abide with you for ever* (John 14: 16).

## My Faith Must Be Personal

The third point in Wesley's explanation of yesterday is our truth for today: "Believe that He is willing, as well as able, to save *you* to the uttermost; to purify *you* from all sin, and fill up all *your heart* with love."

God has given us great and precious promises regarding entire sanctification but we must appropriate them for our personal need. It is not enough to believe the doctrine, nor even to gladly acknowledge that others have found the experience. We must believe with the heart that our Lord's promise of the Holy Spirit is meant for us.

All of the soul's conscious dealings with God have this deeply personal quality. Therefore the promise of holiness is personal. We are assured, "If *ye* shall ask any thing in my name, I will do it." In the light of this great promise, our Lord declares, "I will pray the Father, and he shall give *you* another Comforter." Paul's prayer for new Christians was personal: "The very God of peace sanctify *you* wholly; and I pray God *your* whole spirit and soul and body be preserved blameless unto the coming of our Lord Jesus Christ. Faithful is he that calleth *you*, who also will do it" (I Thessalonians 5: 23-24).

When I have made a complete personal surrender to God, I may ask in faith for the baptism with the Holy Spirit. This I know is according to His will. On the authority of our Lord's promise I may believe that He has filled me with His Holy Spirit.

> *When Jesus makes my heart His home,*
> *My sin shall all depart;*
> *And lo! He saith, I quickly come,*
> *To fill and rule thy heart.*
>
> —*The Salvation Army Tune Book*

142

READ: I John 1: 5-7

*If we walk in the light . . . the blood of Jesus Christ his Son cleanseth us from all sin* (I John 1: 7).

## William Booth's Testimony

William Booth, founder of the Salvation Army, affirms that when we meet the conditions of consecration we may rightfully, as the General himself did, accept entire sanctification by faith. He says:

"What is the faith that sanctifies? It is that act of simple trust which, on the authority of Christ's word, says, 'The blood of Jesus Christ does *now* cleanse me from all inward sin, and makes me pure in heart before Him; and I do here and now commit myself to Him, believing that He receives me, and that He will evermore keep me holy while I thus trust Him.'

"When a soul thus trusts God, will he be, in every sense, made clean? Yes, *always*—that is, if having the assurance that he does fully renounce all known and doubtful wrong doing, and gives himself up to the doing of the will of God in all things, he thus trusts God for full cleansing.

"Such a soul has the authority of God's Word for believing that the work is done, no matter how he feels; and he must hold on to this faith till the feeling comes. If we confess our sins, He is *faithful* (to His own promise) and *just* (to the suffering and agony of His Son, which purchased the blessing) to cleanse us from all unrighteousness."

*The blessing by faith I receive from above.*
*Oh, glory! My soul is made perfect in love;*
*My prayer has prevailed; and this moment I know*
*The Blood is applied, I am whiter than snow.*
—JAMES NICHOLSON

**May 12**

READ: I John 3: 21-22

*Beloved, if our heart condemn us not, then have we confidence toward God* (I John 3: 21).

## When Faith Comes Easily

Dr. S. S. White testifies, and multiplied thousands could join him when he writes: "It was not difficult for me to believe after I had placed everything on the altar for time and for eternity."

There are many such cases in which the witness of the Spirit follows full consecration so immediately that there seems to be no conscious exercise of faith. This does not mean that faith is lacking, but only that it has been operating all the while.

When we start to seek holiness, that in itself is an expression of our faith that God will give us His Holy Spirit. When, in obedience to light received, we consecrate ourselves wholly to God, that too is an act of faith. Every act of obedience to any suggestion of the Spirit is an expression of our faith that when we have obeyed *all* of His will we shall receive the blessing. Such seeking and obedience can be so wholehearted and trustful that we finally believe for the blessing without consciously trying to exercise faith.

Ordinarily our faith is thus almost an automatic experience. It is easy to accept the promises of God when we have sincerely done our best to meet the conditions of those promises. It is natural to trust God when we love Him. The Bible teaches us that our faith is "faith which worketh by love" (Galatians 5: 6).

When we have sincerely said, "All to Jesus I surrender, all to Him I freely give," it is perfectly natural to add,

> "I will ever love and trust Him,
> In His presence daily live."
> —J. W. VAN DEVENTER

144

READ: Mark 9:17-24

*Lord, I believe; help thou mine unbelief* (Mark 9:24).

## When Faith Is Difficult

We saw yesterday that effective faith appears to be almost automatic with many seekers after Christian holiness. But there are others who must take this step by sheer determination and in the face of powerful spiritual opposition.

There are no easy victories in the spiritual life. Especially does the devil hate to see God's children sanctified wholly. In general, where consecration has occasioned a severe struggle, once the place of surrender is reached, the step of faith seems to be taken easily. On the other hand, if consecration has not been a serious problem, the exercise of faith may present a real challenge. It is only the mercy of God, which will not allow us to be tested beyond what we are able to bear, that keeps the enemy from giving maximum opposition to our progress at every point.

Our scripture for today reminds us that God is deeply concerned with every experience which concerns us deeply. Jesus was concerned to help a father with a demon-possessed child. God will not fail us when our need is for a clean heart.

How wonderful our Heavenly Father is! He saves us from our sins. He reveals to us the way of holiness in the Scriptures. He sends the Holy Spirit to convict us of our need. He draws us on by making our hearts hungry for the grace of full salvation. And then, when we falter in the small thing that we ourselves must do—in the act of faith—He even helps us to believe. All the way along He helps us. So,

> [I'll] keep on believing; Jesus is near.
> [I'll] keep on believing; there's nothing to fear.
> [I'll] keep on believing; this is the way;
> Faith in the nighttime as well as the day.
> —C. S. BULLOCK

**May 14**

READ: Philippians 3:12-15

*Forgetting those things which are behind, and reaching forth unto those things which are before, I press toward the mark for the prize of the high calling of God in Christ Jesus* (Philippians 3:13-14).

## When Faith Is Hindered by Former Failures

If we have sought several times to be sanctified and for any reason have been disappointed in our search, we may expect a struggle at the point of faith. If we have backslidden through failure to walk in the light, faith for restoration is usually more difficult than when we first sought for holiness.

If we have formerly sought the blessing but, not receiving the witness of the Spirit, have relaxed our seeking and settled back resigned to a life without being sanctified wholly, we may expect the exercise of faith to require determined effort.

Sometimes the struggle to believe comes as a result of disillusionment. Because of faulty teaching we expected God to do for us at an altar and in a moment of time what He plans to do for us by the process of growth in grace. Failing to see the dramatic changes which we had expected, we assume that we were mistaken in our faith and inwardly resolve not to be caught that way again—we will believe when we see! This situation is near tragic, for it adds error to error. We are mistaken in our knowledge of what God proposes to do for us in the crisis experience, and we err again in refusing to accept God's promise of entire sanctification *by faith.*

Whatever the past may be, we are confronted anew by God's promises today. Let us bring our need to Him and cast ourselves upon the assurance, "Him that cometh to me I will in no wise cast out" (John 6:37).

> *I mean to keep believing when it seems I'm not receiving;*
> *I mean to keep on trusting in His name.*
> *I know He'll not forsake me; whatever should o'ertake me,*
> *I mean to keep believing just the same.**

—HERBERT BUFFUM

*© John T. Benson, Jr. Used by permission.

146

READ: John 11: 38-44

*Said I not unto thee, that, if thou wouldest believe, thou shouldest see the glory of God?* (John 11: 40)

## I Will Believe God for Heart Cleansing

Dr. S. A. Keen tells of a man who testified, "For twenty years I asked God to give me faith for entire sanctification but I did not get the blessing. Then one day God said to me, 'I want *you* to give me *your* faith.' I did it, and in twenty minutes the blessing came!"

But can I deliberately will to believe God for a clean heart? The answer is, *Yes.* Because faith is so often spontaneous we seldom think of it as being subject to our own will, but it is. J. A. Wood writes: "God gives the *truth* . . . and the *power* to believe; but He believes for no one. While He *helps* the believer, the *act of believing* is purely the believer's, and is *voluntary.*" We can believe if we will believe. Not easily of course, but then many possible choices are not easy choices.

Our failure at the point of faith is often considered less serious than failure in consecration. But in this attitude we are mistaken. Persistent failure to trust God is as serious as refusing to give Him first place in our lives. Either failure will keep us out of the experience of entire sanctification.

Dr. Kenneth Grider describes faith as a kind of exercise in which the human spirit stretches itself, believing God for what has not yet come to pass. It is this decision that God asks of us—the decision to stretch our spirits toward Him. Is the step of faith difficult for me? Then I must be as determined and as diligent in believing God's promise as I have been in making a full consecration to Him. With the song writer I affirm:

> *I can, I will, I do believe,*
> *I can, I will, I do believe,*
> *I can, I will, I do believe,*
> *That Jesus sanctifies.*
> —AUTHOR UNKNOWN

**May 16**

READ: Romans 7:18-25

*Take heed, brethren, lest there be in any of you an evil heart of unbelief* (Hebrews 3:12).

## Unbelief and Carnality

We need unrelenting prayer and continued persistence when we fail to find victory because we have failed to trust God. The need is emphasized by A. Paget Wilkes when he points out that this very unbelief is a part of the carnal mind from which we seek deliverance.

"Unbelief . . . does not necessarily lie in the will. It is not so much that we are unbelieving, as that in us . . . there is 'an evil heart of unbelief.' It is as St. Paul declares, 'not I, but sin that dwelleth in me,' . . . We have to take sides with God and our own regenerate nature against it, recognizing that it is abnormal, an intrusion, a parasite, a disease of the soul that should not and need not be there. When we understand and see this we are halfway to victory."

Our serious situation is that we seek to be rid of the carnal mind, and we must have faith in order to be free. But the very presence of the carnal mind makes faith well-nigh impossible. If we are caught in this dilemma of the spirit, God will graciously help. We may be compelled to join the distraught father who "cried out, and said with tears, Lord, I believe; help thou mine unbelief" (Mark 9:24). But if we thus seek for Christian holiness we shall be filled, for the Holy Spirit comes to the sincerely seeking soul.

> *I would, but Thou must give the power;*
> *My heart from every sin release;*
> *Bring near, bring near, the joyful hour.*
> *And fill me with Thy perfect peace.*
>
> —*Wesley's Hymns*

A Gift of Faith

READ: Acts 1: 4-5; 2: 1-4

*Wait for the promise of the Father [and] . . . ye shall be baptized with the Holy Ghost not many days hence* (Acts 1: 4-5).

## When I Must Wait for the Promise

Our Lord promised His followers that if they would tarry they would receive the Holy Ghost "not many days hence." Jesus himself knew that the blessing would come to them on the Day of Pentecost, but the disciples were not told this. They knew it was to be soon; it therefore might be any day or any moment. They were to be in a continuous state of expectancy. Their part was to act in faith upon the word of their Lord. This faith was to be expressed by continued tarrying—not for fifteen minutes, not for an hour, not for a day or for a week—not for any specified time, but "until ye be endued with power from on high" (Luke 24: 49).

We also are to tarry for the Holy Spirit until He comes—even when His coming seems long delayed. Sometimes this delay in receiving the Holy Spirit is God's way of making our experience with Him richer and deeper when He comes.

Too often we expect to come to an altar, make a full consecration, exercise sanctifying faith, and receive the fullness of the Holy Spirit in fifteen minutes. It can happen this way, but we should not count on it as a normal procedure. Only God knows when our human hearts are fully ready to be filled with the Holy Spirit, and He will fill us the moment we are really ready. Our own eager expectation and firm faith are always essential, and we must therefore be careful to maintain that expectation and that faith even though they are not rewarded immediately. In this attitude of faith and eager anticipation we offer our prayer today:

> *Father, Son, and Spirit, come*
> *And with Thine own abide.*
> *Holy Ghost, to make Thee room,*
> *Our hearts we open wide.*
>
> —*Wesley's Hymns*

**May 18**

READ: Luke 24: 45-49

*And, behold, I send the promise of my Father upon you: but tarry ye in the city of Jerusalem, until ye be endued with power from on high* (Luke 24: 49).

## The Promise of My Father

This promise that Jesus gave on the mount of ascension was fulfilled ten days later. "And when the day of Pentecost was fully come . . . they were all filled with the Holy Ghost" (Acts 2: 1, 4). But the promise and its fulfillment were not for the disciples only. In the Garden of Gethsemane Jesus said, "Neither pray I for these alone, but for them also [all of them] which shall believe on me" (John 17: 20). If the coming of the Holy Spirit seems delayed, let us remember that He is promised to us also, and the promise is that we shall receive Him "not many days hence."

If I do not now enjoy the experience of heart holiness, is not that gracious gift of God my deepest need? The baptism with the Holy Spirit was important enough that the disciples tarried ten days for His coming. Is the presence of God's Holy Spirit not important enough for me to give major attention to prepare my life for His coming—whether it takes ten days, or less, or longer?

Our part is to keep an open ear to God's voice and an open heart to His will, to maintain an attitude of expectancy, to keep pressing our claim and to keep trusting God's promise. This trust in God's promise is the one condition which can never be met without the blessing following. Since God has promised to give me His Holy Spirit, I yearn to be ready for His coming. I sincerely pray:

> *Give me thyself; from every boast,*
> *From every wish set free.*
> *Let all I am in Thee be lost;*
> *But give thyself to me.*
>
> *—Wesley's Hymns*

READ: Psalms 119:10-12

*The apostles said unto the Lord, Increase our faith* (Luke 17:5).

## Faith Cometh by Hearing

I am hungry for the fullness of the Holy Spirit. I remember that "faith cometh by hearing, and hearing by the Word of God" (Romans 10:17), so I open my heart to hear what God would say to me from His Word.

"Then will I sprinkle clean water upon you, and ye shall be clean . . . A new heart also will I give you . . . and I will take away the stony heart out of your flesh . . . And I will put my Spirit within you, and cause you to walk in my statutes, and ye shall keep my judgments, and do them" (Ezekiel 36:25-27).

"And I say unto you, Ask, and it shall be given you; seek, and ye shall find; knock, and it shall be opened unto you. For every one that asketh receiveth; and he that seeketh findeth; and to him that knocketh it shall be opened. If ye then, being evil, know how to give good gifts unto your children: how much more shall your heavenly Father give the Holy Spirit to them that ask him?" (Luke 11:9-10, 13)

"And the very God of peace sanctify you wholly; and I pray God your whole spirit and soul and body be preserved blameless unto the coming of our Lord Jesus Christ. Faithful is he that calleth you, who also will do it" (I Thessalonians 5:23-24).

My glad heart can only sing, Thank You, Lord, for these "exceeding great and precious promises." My faith takes hold. By Thy grace I have become a partaker of the divine nature (II Peter 1:4). "Thanks be unto God for his unspeakable gift" (II Corinthians 9:15).

*All to Jesus I surrender;*
*Now I feel the sacred flame.*
*Oh, the joy of full salvation!*
*Glory, glory to His name!*
—J. W. VAN DEVENTER

READ: I Corinthians 2: 9-12

*God hath revealed them unto us by his Spirit . . . that
we might know the things that are freely given to us
of God* (I Corinthians 2: 10, 12).

## We Need to Be Sure

A Christian woman serving God as best she knew how
came to her pastor and asked, "How can I be sure that I am
among God's elect?" The pastor replied, "I feel sure for
myself but I cannot tell you that you can be sure." This
sincere Christian deserved a better answer than that from her
spiritual guide.

God knows that we need to be sure of our standing before
Him. When we are uncertain we are troubled and therefore
easily swerved from our course. On the other hand certainty
brings to us rest and stability. In a matter so vital as our
entire sanctification we need to be sure. Since God's requirements are specific and definite, we need to know that
His requirements have been met and that our lives are
pleasing to Him.

We not only long to know that we are sanctified but it
is reasonable that we should be assured. We can stub our
toes and know it. When we fall in love we know it. We can
feel the stirring of carnality and know it. When our hearts
are hungry for entire sanctification, we know it. Is it not
therefore reasonable that when the Holy Spirit fills our hearts
we should also know it?

God has never disappointed a deep human hunger. For
thirst He has given water; for hearing He has provided music;
for seeing He has filled the world with beauty; for spiritual
hunger He has provided fellowship with himself. Our hungers are real. Are these hungers not intimations of God's
satisfactions?

> *I want the witness, Lord,*
> *That all I do is right,*
> *According to Thy will and Word,*
> *Well-pleasing in Thy sight.*
>
> *—Wesley's Hymns*

READ: Romans 8:14-17

*The Spirit itself beareth witness with our spirit, that we are the children of God* (Romans 8:16).

## God Gives Us Assurance

The Christian yearns to be sure that his life is pleasing to God. Holiness people believe that he can be sure. We believe that "entire sanctification is provided by the blood of Jesus, is wrought instantaneously by faith, preceded by entire consecration; *and to this work and state of grace the Holy Spirit bears witness.*" This inner illumination by the Holy Spirit brings with it a deep sense of personal assurance.

The doctrine of the witness of the Spirit has been a distinctive emphasis of the Wesleyan teaching because it is so clearly taught in the Bible. John testifies, "Hereby know we that we dwell in him, and he in us, because he hath given us of his spirit" (I John 4:13). Paul confirms the truth thus: "The Spirit itself beareth witness with our spirit, that we are the children of God" (Romans 8:16). Peter describes this assuring work of God in the soul when he reports the experience at the house of Cornelius: "And God, which knoweth the hearts, bare them witness, giving them the Holy Ghost, even as he did unto us" (Acts 15:8).

Based on this clear scriptural teaching we rejoice in the doctrine of assurance. J. A. Wood has written, "Christian holiness is a matter of *positive conscious experience* within the reach of all believers." John Wesley said, "None therefore, ought to believe that the work is done till there is added the testimony of the Spirit, witnessing his entire sanctification as clearly as his justification." With glad hearts we may sing:

*Blessed assurance, Jesus is mine!*
*Oh, what a foretaste of glory divine!*
*Heir of salvation, purchased of God,*
*Born of His Spirit, washed in His blood!*
—FANNY J. CROSBY

**May 22**

READ: Acts 2:1-4

*And they were all filled with the Holy Ghost* (Acts 2:4).

## Christians Were Sure at Pentecost

Christian men and women knew that they were filled with the Holy Spirit on the Day of Pentecost. That day made a difference in their lives. Something happened that was different from the preceding days of tarrying.

*Suddenly* they heard a sound like the rushing of a violent wind. At first it seemed to be above them. Then it came closer and grew louder until the roar filled the whole building. These men were aware of something unusual—as aware as we are when a jet plane takes off while we duck our heads and put our hands over our ears.

On the Day of Pentecost men saw as well as heard something out of the ordinary. Each one saw something like flames of fire resting on the heads of his brethren. From the amazed glances turned in his direction, each knew that a similar flame rested on himself. And was there the added confirmation of a tingling sensation like fire running through the veins? A fire that consumed carnality, thrilled the soul, and exhilarated the body? It must have been so.

They were all filled with the Holy Ghost and they knew it—knew it because they were conscious of a power in them that was more than their own. They began to glorify God in languages that were not known to them.

And is God a respecter of persons that He should make himself known at Pentecost but conceal himself at present? The testimony of experience shouts a glad *No*. Many of us can join in the radiant witness:

> *Oh, I never shall forget how the fire fell,*
> *How the fire fell, how the fire fell!*
> *Oh, I never shall forget how the fire fell*
> *When the Lord sanctified me!*
> —JOHNSON OATMAN, JR.

154

READ: Acts 15: 7-9

*And God, which knoweth the hearts, bare them witness, giving them the Holy Ghost, even as he did unto us* (Acts 15: 8).

## God Witnessed to the Gentiles

The 120 disciples were sure that the Holy Spirit was given to them on the Day of Pentecost. In our scripture for today Peter reminds his brethren that God gave the assuring presence of the Holy Spirit to gentiles, "even as he did unto us." The Revised Standard Version makes this central meaning clear: "And God who knows the heart *bore witness to them,* giving them the Holy Spirit just as he did to us."

The witness of the Spirit is not always conveyed in the same manner, but the assurance is always present. At this gentile Pentecost we read of no rushing wind or tongues of fire, but *God bore witness to them.* Thus it was in the life of a young man, David Hall, who testifies today: "I was converted in a Sunday night church service. . . . The night after my conversion, a revival campaign began. After going to the altar for sanctification, I believed, through intellectual assent, that God had done the work for me. However, in reality, I did not receive the experience at this time. After going to the altar for heart cleansing, I still felt the need of God's power in my life.

"I determined to find the experience one night, and after one full hour of prayer, I told God that if He would not bless me I would serve Him regardless. The next morning while playing a hymn at the piano God definitely and wonderfully sanctified me. The name of the hymn, significantly, was 'The Unveiled Christ.' There was no doubt then. After six months of diligent seeking both intellectually and spiritually the work was done." With Charles Wesley we may all bear glad witness:

> *Our nature's turned, our mind*
> *Transformed in all its powers;*
> *And both the witnesses are joined,*
> *The Spirit of God with ours.*
> —*Wesley's Hymns*

**May 24**

READ: I John 3:18-22

*Beloved, if our heart condemn us not, then have we confidence toward God* (I John 3:21).

## The Witness of Sincerity

The assurance of full salvation is like a river with four tributary streams flowing into it: (1) the witness of our own honesty before God, (2) the witness of God's promises, (3) the witness of the Holy Spirit, and (4) the testimony of a changed life.

The first source of assurance arises in our own spirits as we complete our consecration. A young man testified: "At that moment there came the peace of God that passeth all understanding. Quiet, but, oh, how sweet! I knew in my heart that I had said the last yes to all of God's will."

It is this experience—I knew in my heart that I had said the last yes"—that may be called the witness of sincerity. In this moment we have the witness of our hearts that every condition of consecration has been met. It is a long step toward assurance when with utter sincerity we can say, "I have met God's requirements."

An ignorant sincerity is not enough to fully satisfy God, but sincere obedience to the divine will is pleasing to Him. John tells us, "Beloved, if our heart condemn us not, then have we confidence toward God." This certainty within our own spirits is a prelude to and joins with the witness of the Holy Spirit. Paul declares, "And when we cry, 'Abba! Father!' it is this Spirit testifying along with our own spirit that we are children of God" (Romans 8:16, Moffatt). When we are fully consecrated we can sing with Fanny Crosby:

> *Perfect submission, all is at rest.*
> *I in my Saviour am happy and blest;*
> *Watching and waiting, looking above,*
> *Filled with His goodness, lost in His love.*

READ: I John 1: 5-7

*If we walk in the light as he is in the light . . . the blood of Jesus Christ his Son cleanseth us from all sin* (I John 1: 7).

## The Witness of the Word

Dr. Orval J. Nease tells of his mother's experience as she sought to be sanctified wholly. He says: "Mary Storey, wise altar worker that she was, began to quote scripture to aid Mother's faith. Putting an Old Testament portion with a New Testament selection, she quoted, 'Whatsoever toucheth the altar is holy . . . the altar . . . sanctifieth the gift.' It was the avenue of assurance Mother needed, and with firm confidence she said, 'That being true, on the authority of God's Word, I am sanctified.' "

This authority of God's Word is a second tributary to our stream of assurance. We always do business with God upon the basis of our faith in His promises. One of these promises is our text: "If we walk in the light, as he is in the light, we [God and I] have fellowship one with another, and the blood of Jesus Christ his Son cleanseth us from all sin."

To walk in the light means to be fully obedient to all of God's known will for us. When we do this, God has promised to sanctify wholly to cleanse us from all sin. Our assurance of sanctification is in proportion to our faith in God's promise. If we are inclined to be doubtful and hesitant, we have little assurance. When we boldly claim the promise and assert our faith, we have the witness of God's Word that the work has been accomplished in the soul. There can be no more reliable evidence than the promise of God; when conditions are fully met, the work is done.

*How firm a foundation, ye saints of the Lord,*
*Is laid for your faith in His excellent Word!*
*What more can He say than to you he hath said,*
*To you who for refuge to Jesus have fled?*
—GEORGE KEITH

**May 26**

READ: I John 5: 9-10

*He that believeth on the Son of God hath the witness
in himself* (I John 5:10).

## The Witness of the Spirit

John Wesley once wrote: "By the testimony of the Spirit,
I mean an inward impression on the soul, whereby the Spirit
of God immediately and directly witnesses to my spirit that
I am a child of God." This is ultimate assurance.

This witness of God's Spirit is confirmation of a *fact*.
In consecration we give ourselves as a living sacrifice to
God; the Spirit of God then assures us of our acceptance and
cleansing in sanctification. As we sincerely seek to be sure
of the facts, God's Holy Spirit gives us the witness that our
hearts seek.

The baptism with the Holy Spirit takes place in the
human spirit and is thus a deeply personal experience. The
supreme witness that we are wholly sanctified must therefore
be an inner assurance. Such witness may come suddenly with
overwhelming power and a surge of uncontrollable joy; it
may come suddenly with a deep sense of inner cleanliness
and peace; it may come gradually as a deepening consciousness that we are wholly the Lord's.

There is thus no uniform way that the Holy Spirit witnesses to His coming. God is a God of variety, and men
differ greatly in temperament. God therefore adapts the
revelation of himself to our individual needs. But there is
one thing that we may depend upon. To every sincerely
seeking soul the Holy Spirit comes with an inner witness
that is wholly satisfying to that heart. When He has come
we exult with the poet:

> *He makes me clean, He makes me clean!*
> *Mine eyes the glorious King have seen.*
> *Just now I feel the sacred flame.*
> *Oh, glory to His precious name!*\*
>
> —GEORGE BENNARD

\*© 1940, renewal, The Rodeheaver Co. Used by permission.

READ: Galatians 5: 22-25

*The fruit of the Spirit is love* (Galatians 5: 22).

## The Confirming Witness

We know that we have been sanctified wholly when, in answer to our prayer, the Holy Spirit reveals himself directly to our consciousness. Wesley writes that the child of God can no more doubt this evidence "than he can doubt of the shining of the sun, while he stands in the full blaze of its beams."

But there is also a confirming witness—the witness of a changed nature. The crisis of entire sanctification makes a difference in human experience. When our lives are filled with God's Holy Spirit we rightfully expect some fruit of the Spirit. This fruit, Paul reminds us, is "love, joy, peace, patience, kindness, generosity, fidelity, adaptability and self-control" (Galatians 5: 22-23, Phillips).

When the Holy Spirit comes in sanctifying power He so cleanses the soul that our attitudes, impulses, and thoughts are all motivated by love. It is a change in the depths of our nature which lies beyond our deliberate control. And yet its effects are felt in our conscious experience.

It was this confirming witness of a changed attitude to which a young lady testified. She rose from the altar with a radiant face and exclaimed, "Oh, I love everybody!"

Always our unshakable confidence is in the assurance of God's own witness to us. When God has cleansed our hearts and witnessed to our spirits, we ought never to doubt that work of grace because of our changing moods or personal shortcomings. But it is a source of indirect and secondary assurance to be able to sing to the glory of God that we have experienced:

> *A rest where all our soul's desire*
> *Is fix'd on things above;*
> *Where doubt and pain and fear expire,*
> *Cast out by perfect love.*

> —*Wesley's Hymns*

**May 28**

READ: Acts 1: 1-5

*Before many days you shall be baptized with the Holy Spirit* (Acts 1: 5, R.S.V.).

## Tarry Until Ye Be Endued

Ordinarily we may expect the witness of the Spirit to follow almost immediately after entire consecration and the exercise of our faith. Normally we may expect immediate assurance of faith—but not always.

Jesus promised His followers that they should receive the Holy Spirit, but He did not tell them when. He told them only to begin seeking and not to give up until they had received: "Tarry ye in the city of Jerusalem, until ye be endued with power from on high" (Luke 24: 49). In Acts we see that Jesus let His disciples know that there would be some days of seeking: "Wait for the promise of the Father . . . but *before many days* you shall be baptized with the Holy Spirit" (Acts 1: 4-5, R.S.V.). We know that these first disciples tarried for ten days. But the blessing was worth the waiting.

In Samaria (Acts 8: 14-17) and in Ephesus (Acts 19: 1-6) the Holy Spirit came to seeking Christians with no delay. Why does the blessing come to some immediately, while others must tarry for a time? We do not know all of the answer but we can be sure that the delay is not due to any unwillingness on God's part. Jesus tells us: "If ye then, being evil, know how to give good gifts to your children: how much more shall your heavenly Father give the Holy Spirit to them that ask him?" (Luke 11: 13) We know also that, if the Gift is delayed, it is no new experience to Christians. Others have known this delay and at its end they have found their hearts' desire. We need only to tarry until He comes.

> *I wait, till He shall touch me clean,*
> *Shall life and power impart,*
> *Give me the faith that casts out sin,*
> *And purifies the heart.*
>
> —*Wesley's Hymns*

READ: Genesis 15: 1-11, 17-18

*Abraham believed God, and it was accounted to him for righteousness* (Galatians 3: 6).

## The Assurance of Active Faith

During the altar service Sunday night my pastor was praying with a young woman who was seeking to be sanctified wholly. She had prayed earnestly, consecrated fully, and placed her confidence in the promises of God, but she still lacked the witness of the Spirit for which her heart yearned. The pastor gave her this advice: "Before you go to bed tonight, thank God for sanctifying your soul. In the morning, thank God for the gift of His Holy Spirit. Tell someone tomorrow that God has cleansed your heart." This was sound spiritual counsel. Assurance comes with affirmation and the deliberate exercise of faith in the promises of God.

In our scripture for today God had a great blessing for Abram. To a man who was childless God promised descendants like the stars in the heavens; to him who was homeless God promised the whole land of Canaan. When Abram asked for some assurance of these divine promises God instructed him to prepare a sacrifice. The Lord planned to touch this offering with holy fire as evidence of His sure promises, but God's man was tested before God's confirming witness came.

Abram did what God told him to do. He erected an altar; he prepared the sacrifice exactly as he had been told. But no fire came from heaven; only buzzards gathered to annoy the seeker and to mock a man's faith. But Abram drove off the birds and guarded his offering until the sun went down. Then, in answer to his faith, God gave him the assurance that he sought. When darkness fell, the fire of God ran through the sacrifice and assurance came to Abram's heart. God always rewards active faith with glowing assurance.

### Affirmation for today

*I will continue to obey God; I will trust Him for assurance and actively believe His promise until the witness is given.*

**May 30**

READ: Psalms 37: 3-7

*Rest in the Lord, and wait patiently for him* (Psalms 37: 7).

## When the Witness Is Delayed

If the witness of the Spirit is delayed, we must never give up without being satisfied. It does not indicate a lack of faith to keep on seeking until we are assured. In fact, a continuing, persistent pressing of our claim is proof of our faith in God's promise. If we do not find clear assurance in our first trip to the altar, we need not be embarrassed. We ought not feel frustrated, and above all we dare not surrender to discouragement. It is far better to do more extended seeking than to hurry through to an unsatisfactory experience.

If after earnest prayer and honest efforts to consecrate and to believe, we do not yet have inner assurance, we may leave the altar without spiritual defeat. We are never defeated while we continue our search.

If we do thus leave the altar we must be sure that we are not stopping—only changing the location of our tarrying. If we are thus sure that we do not consider leaving the altar as a stopping point, we can go without discouragement to ourselves and to those who are praying for us.

It will be helpful to us and to them if we put ourselves on record to the effect that we are seeking, that as far as we know our consecration is complete, that we are believing the promises of God, but that we do not yet have the assurance of the Spirit. Let us then commit ourselves to seek privately and publicly until that assurance comes.

### Prayer for today

*How long, O Lord? Wilt thou forget me for ever?*
*How long wilt thou hide thy face from me?*
*But I have trusted in thy steadfast love;*
*my heart shall rejoice in thy salvation.*
*I will sing to the Lord*
*because he has dealt bountifully with me.*

(Psalms 13: 1-2, 5-6, R.S.V.)

READ: Luke 11:9-13

*Ask, and it shall be given you; seek, and ye shall find; knock, and it shall be opened unto you* (Luke 11:9).

## The Witness Will Come

Yesterday we saw that, when the witness of the Holy Spirit is delayed, we must persist in our seeking. God will honor a faith that is attested by our willingness to thus tarry. And His tarrying is never arbitrary. In time we shall see that it was best for us.

As we wait in His presence, in private or in public services, God may reveal to us new depths of consecration which we had not yet reached. He may teach us precious lessons of persistent prayer. He may desire to strengthen our faith for the days ahead when we shall face other delayed answers to our agonizing prayers.

If, however, our tarrying is to be pleasing to God, we must continue active seeking, and our waiting must be in a spirit of trust. Any disposition to quit seeking must be overcome, and any spirit of rebellion against delay must be regarded as a manifestation of the carnality from which we seek deliverance. We must persistently tell God of our hunger for holiness, remind Him of His promises, and ask Him to reveal any further work needed on our part.

If we thus tarry, God will keep His promise. The Holy Spirit will come. He will come in His fullness; He will come with cleansing power; He will come with deep, soul-satisfying, inner illumination and the personal assurance that we are now sanctified wholly. We too may sing from glad hearts.

*Peace, perfect peace! Love, perfect love!*
*Sweeping o'er my soul in heav'nly tides!*
*Rest, perfect rest! Joy, perfect joy!*
*Is mine since the Holy Ghost abides.*
—F. E. HILL

**June 1**

READ: Acts 2:1-4

*And when the day of Pentecost was fully come . . .
they were all filled with the Holy Ghost* (Acts 2:1, 4).

## The Fourth Great Day

"Almost everyone is acquainted with three of Christianity's great days: Christmas, Good Friday, and Easter. But Christianity has four. The fourth is Pentecost, the day when the Holy Spirit was given to the Church, and through the Church to the world.

"What is the promise of Pentecost for the ordinary man of today? Simply that the redeeming power of Jesus Christ is available right now, in both the forgiveness of his sins and the sanctification of his nature.

"It means that no man needs to feel alone. In his heart can dwell constantly a divine Friend who is quite capable of giving power in temptation, solutions to problems, joy in spite of the buffetings of life.

"It means that no life need be barren or aimless. There is a plan for everyone; and the Holy Spirit is able to lead us every day toward the fulfillment of that design.

"It means that the struggle for righteousness need not be futile and hopeless. A power for goodness may be ours. The Holy Spirit can break the chains of our vices. He can cleanse us from our pollutions. He can wash away our bitterness. He can take away our hardness. He can turn us upward toward God, and outward toward people, and forward toward the future. He can make it as natural to live joyously in the realm of the Spirit as before it was natural to live in the realm of the flesh.

"Pentecost is our need. Pentecost the Church must have. Pentecost is ours for the asking. Do we dare enter into this great adventure?" (RICHARD S. TAYLOR)

**Prayer for today**

*Our Father, save us from having a form of godliness, while denying the power thereof; may we tarry for a new baptism with Thy Spirit, that we may be equipped for the demands of our day. In Jesus' name. Amen.*

READ: John 16: 12-15

*When he, the Spirit of truth, is come, he will guide you into all truth* (John 16: 13).

## When He Is Come

For the past several weeks we have been thinking of the steps by which we enter the sanctified life. We are now to consider what God does for us in this experience.

But first, let us pause a moment to reflect that entire sanctification is a work of God. There is a sense in which we ought never to impose our human tests upon this miracle of grace. When we apply tests and our lives do not measure up fully, we are tempted to wonder if we were really sanctified. To wonder is to move in the direction of doubt; to doubt the work of God is to lose our assurance.

Nevertheless, with our eyes wide open to this hazard we go forward confident that God can guide us past the hazard to a wider plain of understanding. We boldly ask, What differences shall I expect in my life as a result of the baptism with the Holy Spirit?

Jesus promised that when the Holy Spirit came He would guide us into all truth—He would make us the kind of persons that God wanted us to be and lead us in all the ways that God wanted us to go. "When he is come," life grows richer and fuller. We shall examine our spiritual needs to discover how God has planned to help us. We shall listen to the testimonies of those who have been sanctified in order to learn what are the possibilities of this grace. As we listen, our faith will be kindled.

### Thought for today

*If Satan can make a perfect sinner, God can make a perfect saint.*—C. W. RUTH.

**June 3**

READ: Hebrews 2:11-12

*Both he that sanctifieth and they who are sanctified are all of one: for which cause he is not ashamed to call them brethren* (Hebrews 2:11).

## Jesus Calls Me His Brother

In what sense are He who sanctifies and they who are sanctified "all of one"? The Revised Standard Version makes this clear. "He who sanctifies and those who are sanctified have all one origin"—both have come from God himself. I am awed when I remember that my Lord and I have this same spiritual heritage. Paul reminds us that "God was in Christ" (II Corinthians 5:19). And now this same God, the Holy Spirit, fills my sanctified heart.

Because of this oneness I may expect my desires and impulses to be like my Lord's. This was not true in the past. When I was filled with the carnal mind there was antagonism to the things of Christ; I did not want what Jesus wanted; my desires were different from His. The great transformation of heart holiness is that it makes us like Jesus in our responses to good and evil. The Holy Spirit draws us on to be like the Master in all our attitudes toward God and men. Paul exhorts us, "Let this mind be in you, which was also in Christ Jesus." Peter declares that this is the precise reason for our being sanctified. We are "chosen . . . by God the Father and sanctified by the Spirit *for obedience to Jesus Christ*" (II Peter 1:2, R.S.V.).

The love of God shed abroad in our hearts makes us long to be like our Lord. When we are filled with God's Holy Spirit we want what He wants, and because of this likeness, Christ is not ashamed to call us brethren.

> *My desire, to be like Jesus;*
> *My desire, to be like Him.*
> *His Spirit fill me, His love o'erwhelm me—*
> *In deed and word to be like Him.**
> —LILLIAN PLANKENHORN

*© Lillian Plankenhorn. Used by permission.

166

READ: Ephesians 4: 22-24

*Put on the new nature, created after the likeness of God in true righteousness and holiness* (Ephesians 4: 24, R.S.V.).

## The New Nature

In our scripture for today God's Word speaks of "putting on the new man." Literally it means to put on a new nature. When the Holy Spirit comes in His fullness this new nature is reflected in the fruits of the Spirit. Paul lists them as "love, joy, peace, longsuffering, gentleness, goodness, faith, meekness, temperance." When we are sanctified wholly we experience all of these Christlike attitudes in some measure, but usually one of them will be more prominent than others.

It is this fact which J. A. Wood points out when he writes: "One person realizes principally a marked increase of faith, and he calls it 'the rest of faith.' . . . Another is permeated with a sense of the divine presence . . . and calls it 'the fullness of God.' Another feels his heart subdued, melted, refined, and filled with God, and calls it 'holiness.' [One man] realizes principally a river of sweet, holy love flowing through the soul, and he calls it 'perfect love.' Another is prostrated under the power of the refining and sin-killing Spirit, and calls it 'the baptism of the Holy Ghost.' And another realizes . . . complete submission to God; he calls it 'entire sanctification.' Still another may feel . . . complete conformity to all the will of God, and calls it 'Christian perfection.' "

Call it what we please, this gift of God is a transformation of my spiritual nature. I am given a spirit "created after the likeness of God." It makes me a new man, truly righteous and holy.

*Love brings the glorious fullness in,*
*And to His saints makes known*
*The blessed rest from inbred sin,*
*Through faith in Christ alone.*

—*The Salvation Army Tune Book*

167

READ: Philippians 2:12-15

*It is God Himself who is at work in you to help you to desire it as well as do it* (Philippians 2:13, Williams).

## Different Desires

We shall still be tempted through the channel of our natural desires even after we have been sanctified wholly. But we must not assume that the desires of the sanctified Christian are no different from what they were before his heart was cleansed. It is in this fountainhead of human life, in the deepest motivations of the soul, that the Spirit of God performs His cleansing work. What difference, then, does sanctification make in my desires?

The sanctified man feels no real approval for any impulse that he knows to be wrong. If in my experience of temptation I become aware of any desire contrary to the will of God, I know that this impulse does not represent the real attitude of my spirit. In the hour of testing I may have some temporary desire for the object of temptation, but I know a deeper and more permanent desire to love and serve God.

What has the Holy Spirit done for me in answer to my prayer for a holy heart? He has given me a very great love for God. Because I love God with all my heart, that love keeps me faithful in the hour of temptation. God's Holy Spirit also gives me a sincere love for men. There is within me a positive desire to share another's load. When I see someone in need, it is the indwelling Holy Spirit who makes me want to be helpful.

### Affirmation for today

*The sanctifying Spirit of God has made a difference in my life. He made me different the day I invited Him to come in. He has often helped me to be more like Jesus than I could have been even when I honestly tried. I promise anew today to keep my life wide open to the sanctifying power of God's Holy Spirit, who has come to live in me.*

READ: Acts 1: 4-8

*Ye shall receive power, after that the Holy Ghost is come upon you: and ye shall be witnesses unto me (Acts 1: 8).*

## Her Husband Saw a Difference

Mrs. —— was having a hard time trying to be a Christian. She had been saved from her sins but had been back at the altar a number of times. Life with an unsaved, unsympathetic husband was not easy. She wanted to resign from her lodge, but he objected and they quarreled about it. When she spent time with her Sunday school class he criticized her and she often retorted angrily. Home life was nearly unbearable and her efforts to serve God seemed to be the chief cause of the conflict.

One Sunday evening at the altar God came to her in heart-cleansing power. She testified to the pastor: "As I prayed, it dawned on me that by God's help I did not have to react in resentment and in anger. I asked God for grace enough to control my temper, but He did more than that for me. To my surprise I found that *I did not feel angry.* My home life was still unpleasant but my heart was filled with love for God and love for my unsaved husband."

The change in Mrs. ——'s life was a powerful witness for Christ. In a few weeks the husband stopped fussing about her church activities; he now saw that she was a better companion because of what God was doing for her. She again proposed quitting the lodge. To her surprise he replied, "Go ahead if you want to." I heard the story at the close of a Sunday school teachers' dinner where her husband had attended with her. Do I need that kind of help from God? Could He do it for me too?

> His pow'r can make you what you ought to be;
> His blood can cleanse your heart and make you free;
> His love can fill your soul, and you will see
> 'Twas best for Him to have His way with thee.
> —CYRUS S. NUSBAUM

**June 7**

READ: Acts 4:31-35

*They were all filled with the Holy Ghost, and they ... were of one heart and one soul: neither said any of them that ought of the things which he possessed was his own; but they had all things common* (Acts 4: 31-32).

## Concern for the Needs of Others

Our scripture for today describes the continuing work of God in the lives of His people. This outpouring of the Spirit was not the baptism with the Holy Spirit in the same sense that it had occurred on the Day of Pentecost. It was rather a fresh anointing, and with it came a fresh realization of what it meant to live the Spirit-filled life.

When I am filled with the Holy Spirit, will I sell my property and give the money to the poor? Maybe yes, maybe no. Let us ask the question in another way. If my child whom I love needs an education would I mortgage my home to make it possible? If my wife needs an expensive operation to save her life, would I sell the house to save her? The answers are clearly *Yes.* The needs of those whom I love mean more to me than money in the bank.

Can God help me always to live so that the needs of people and the concerns of His work are more important than my bank balance? This is the spirit that took possession of these Christians in Jerusalem. This is the urge that moved a friend to forego a new car in order to do his part on a new church building. This is the spirit of the Holy Spirit. When we are sanctified, self-seeking gives place to concern for others. Not because of our own goodness, but because "the love of Christ constraineth us."

**Thought for today**

*Bible holiness will make us dead to our property; it puts it on God's altar.*—M. W. KNAPP.

READ: II Corinthians 8: 7-9

*For ye know the grace of our Lord Jesus Christ, that,
though he was rich, yet for your sakes, he became
poor, that ye through his poverty might be rich* (II Corinthians 8:9).

## Christian Simplicity

We saw yesterday that Spirit-filled persons are concerned
with the needs of others. This deep concern is one of the
spiritual roots from which the grace of Christian simplicity
grows. How can I be lavish with me and mine when there
are men around me who suffer from want?

On September 9, 1776, John Wesley wrote to His Majesty's officer of Excise, Bristol:

"Sir,—I have two silver spoons at London and two at
Bristol. This is all the plate which I have at present, and I
shall not buy more while so many around me want bread."

Am I concerned enough for spiritual values and for people
around me that I limit my personal expenditures? Can I,
a Christian in the homeland, wear a diamond ring—granted
its beauty and sentimental value—when that bit of personal
indulgence represents from one to six months' living for
my missionary friend who is working for God on a foreign
field? Can we who name the name of Christ spend freely
for personal adornment and pleasure when men are dying
for the message of salvation that our gifts could help send?

Is the appeal of verse 7 God's personal appeal to me:
"As ye abound in everything, in faith, and utterance, and
knowledge . . . see that ye abound in this grace also"? What
does the Holy Spirit say to me today through the example of
Jesus, who, "though he was rich, yet for your sakes he
became poor"? Do I not move closer to the spirit of my
Master as I follow the ideal of Christian simplicity in all
personal expenditures?

> *Make me more like Thee, Saviour,*
> *Make me more like Thee,*
> *That others in my conduct*
> *Thine image they may see.*
> —*Waves of Glory, No. 2*

**June 9**

READ: Romans 5: 1-5

*We have access by faith into this grace wherein we stand, and rejoice in hope of the glory of God* (Romans 5: 2).

## Christian Stability

Dr. Clyde W. Meredith testifies to the desire of many an unsanctified Christian when he writes: "Not many months after my conversion, I, too, knelt at the altar again, deploring my weakness, my failures, my inner struggle, my defeats that had often driven me to the secret chamber for a fresh application of the Blood for the restoration of divine favor. *I wanted an establishing grace*" (*Flames of Living Fire*, Beacon Hill Press).

Is such grace from God available for me? In our text Paul testifies that it is. "We have access by faith *into this grace wherein we stand*." Sanctifying grace is a stabilizing experience. With the inner foe of carnality destroyed we find it easier to withstand victoriously the attacks of Satan. Because our minds are fixed on Christ, the temptations of the world have less pull upon our souls. When we have the Holy Spirit within and rely wholly upon God, there is no power on earth or from hell that can defeat us.

This grace for victorious and joyful living is available through the power of the Holy Spirit in entire sanctification. If we have been up-and-down in our Christian experience, we may confidently expect heart holiness to give more constant victory. As newly converted Christians, we may count on more rapid and steady spiritual growth if we seek to enter into the experience of holiness early in the Christian life.

### Assurance for the sanctified

*I am persuaded, that neither death, nor life, nor angels, nor principalities, nor powers, nor things present, nor things to come, nor height, nor depth, nor any other creature, shall be able to separate us from the love of God, which is in Christ Jesus our Lord* (Romans 8: 38-39).

READ: Ephesians 4:30-32

*Let all bitterness, and wrath, and anger . . . be put away from you, with all malice* (Ephesians 4:31).

## Delivered from Unholy Anger

Dr. D. I. Vanderpool testifies: "I had been converted only a few days when a fellow with whom I had had trouble insulted me. My first impulse was to fight. For a full minute the war was on in my heart. I was filled with fear when I considered how near I came to doing something which I would have always regretted.

"An elderly lady who heard of my conversion spoke to me one day and inquired how I was getting along spiritually. I said, 'Oh, fine! I only wish I could get victory over my quick temper.'

"Then she said, 'Well, Son, you do not have all the Lord has for you.' My next question was, 'Do you mean I can get rid of that inward uprising?' She quickly replied, 'Yes, and you ought not to put it off.'

"A few days afterwards I sent word to a man who was having a cottage prayer meeting that I wanted him to make an altar call the next Tuesday night, for I wanted to be sanctified. The man gave a little talk at the prayer meeting and finally set out a chair and said, 'I understand there is a fellow here that wants special prayer.' I quickly knelt at the chair and began to pray for God to sanctify me. A fellow who knew the way came and knelt by me and began to probe my consecration. He further instructed me that the same Christ that gave me pardon also purchased my cleansing. My faith reached up; I trusted Him to sanctify. A quiet assurance came into my heart that Christ was faithful and that the work of cleansing had been wrought in my heart.

"I have thanked God a thousand times that I met the little old lady who said, 'You do not have all the Lord has for you' " (*Flames of Living Fire,* Beacon Hill Press).

**June 11**

READ: Ephesians 3:14-19

*Christ liveth in me: and the life which I now live in the flesh I live by the faith of the Son of God* (Galatians 2:20).

## Deepened Fellowship with God

The hunger for holiness is a hunger for God. Pascal prayed, "All that is not God cannot satisfy my yearning. It is God himself whom I seek and for whom I pray." As our hunger is for more of God, so our satisfaction is in finding that "more."

To be filled with the Holy Spirit is to keep every room of my soul opened wide to Him; to have Him move freely about the entire premises; to know the divine fellowship in every aspect of my life. To be filled with the Spirit of God is to know the comfort of His presence in my sorrows, the guidance of His wise correction in my mistakes, the glad sharing of His love in my joys, the inspiration of His mind in the new tasks that I undertake.

This deepened fellowship with God comes to us with something akin to the deepened human fellowship that we felt on our wedding day.

J. A. Wood writes of his experience of entire sanctification: "I felt an indescribable sweetness permeating my entire being. I was conscious that Jesus had me and that the Heaven of heavens was streaming through and through my soul. From that hour the deep and solid communion of my soul with God, and the rich baptisms of love and power, have been 'unspeakable and full of glory.' There was a divine fragrance and sweetness imparted to my soul when the Saviour cleansed and filled it with pure love. It has ever remained with me, and I trust it ever will."

> *The closer I walk, the sweeter He seems.*
> *Much fairer is He than all of my dreams.*
> *His love lights my way when pathways are dim,*
> *The closer I walk to Him.*
> —HALDOR LILLENAS

READ: Matthew 19:16-21

*If thou wilt be perfect . . . come and follow me*
(Matthew 19:21).

## Glad Acceptance of God's Plan

In *Flames of Living Fire,* Louise Robinson Chapman writes: "I sought heart holiness, publicly and privately for two years. Three things troubled me: I still wanted to follow the plans I had made for my own life; I was afraid God wanted me to preach; and I was afraid that God was going to send me to Africa as a missionary. One noon hour I told the Lord that I did not intend to leave until this question was settled forever. I began with my life plans. I promised God that I would work no more on them unless I had direct orders from the Almighty to do so. Preach? I would try.

"Then Africa loomed up. I saw myself away out in the jungle. I was dressed in a hideous black dress. All my teeth except two or three were gone. I sat on an old soap box by the side of a grass hut while a few naked children played at my feet. I started up in fear, and then I heard myself saying, 'Lord God Almighty, You have a little old woman on Your hands from this very moment, now, and throughout eternity.'

"I jumped to my feet, feeling light as a feather. The room seemed to be on fire with the presence of God. Fear and hunger had gone, and I was free and satisfied. My heart was aflame with the love of God. I loved His will for me. I was ready to start immediately for Africa. I had not only settled my call but had been baptized with the Holy Ghost!"

*I'll go where You want me to go, dear Lord,*
*Over mountain, or plain, or sea;*
*I'll say what You want me to say, dear Lord;*
*I'll be what You want me to be.*
—MARY BROWN

**June 13**

READ: I John 4: 7-11

*You must love the Lord your God with your whole heart. . . . You must love your neighbor as you do yourself. No other commandment is greater than these* (Mark 12: 30-31, Williams).

## No Attitude Contrary to Love

Early in the life of His people God revealed His supreme will for man: "Thou shalt love the Lord thy God with all thine heart" (Deuteronomy 6: 5). The same revelation was given to John: "Love is of God; and every one that loveth is born of God, and knoweth God" (I John 4: 7). Paul declares: "The fruit of the Spirit is love" (Galatians 5: 22). Jesus himself tells us His Father's will for us: "Thou shalt love the Lord thy God with all thy heart . . . and thy neighbour as thyself" (Luke 10: 27).

Is it any wonder that John Wesley declared of the doctrine of perfect love: "I tell you, as plain as I can speak, where and when I found this. I found it in the oracles of God, in the Old and New Testaments, when I read them with no other view or desire but to save my own soul"?

In answer to the question, "What is Christian perfection?" Wesley replied: "Pure love, reigning alone in the heart and life, this is the whole of scriptural perfection . . . The loving God with all our heart, mind, soul, and strength. This implies that *no wrong* [attitude], *none contrary to love*, remains in the soul; and that all the thoughts, words, and actions are governed by pure love." When asked, "Is there no danger of a man being deceived about being sanctified?" Wesley answered: "So long as he feels nothing but love animating all his thoughts and words and actions he is in no danger."

*More love to Thee, O Christ, more love to Thee!*
*Hear Thou the prayer I make on bended knee;*
*This is my earnest plea: More love, O Christ, to Thee;*
*More love to Thee, more love to Thee!*

—ELIZABETH PRENTISS

READ: Galatians 5: 22-25

*The love of God is shed abroad in our hearts by the Holy Ghost which is given unto us* (Romans 5: 5).

## The Fruit of the Spirit Is Love

When God fills us with His Holy Spirit, He seeks to make us like himself in love. The Bible tells us that "the fruit of the Spirit is love."

Our English word is a term of many meanings—someone has said that love covers everything "from Heaven to Hollywood." But the New Testament uses the specific word *agape* to tell us of God's love. It means *caring*—caring till it hurts.

In *The Call to Holiness*, Frederick L. Coutts tells the story of a Bible translator working among the Bantu of the Congo basin. He was searching for the native equivalent of the love of God when he heard a mother crooning over her child. When asked to explain the meaning of the word she was using the mother replied: "White man, that word means that when I think of what will befall my baby girl when she grows up, it hurts me." The translator had his word. That is how God cares for us.

God loved so much that He gave. Dr. E. Stanley Jones has reminded us that we may understand this love by writing our own names into John 3: 16. "God so loved Albert Harper, that he gave his only begotten Son, that if Albert Harper believeth in him, he should not perish, but have everlasting life."

But can it be that this is the love of God that is shed abroad in *our hearts* by the Holy Ghost? Only in our Lord do we see that love perfectly, but to us also God gives this gift of heaven, this first fruit of the Spirit. It is incredible but true.

> *My soul breaks out in strong desire*
> *The perfect bliss to prove;*
> *My longing heart is all on fire*
> *To be dissolved in love.*
> —*Wesley's Hymns*

**June 15**

READ: Philippians 4: 4-7

*Rejoice in the Lord alway: and again I say, Rejoice* (Philippians 4: 4).

## The Fruit of the Spirit Is Joy

W. E. Sangster tells how Dr. Farmer, organist at Harrow, pleaded with the Salvation Army drummer not to hit the drum so hard. To which the beaming bandsman replied: "Lor' bless you, sir, since I've been converted I'm so 'appy, I could bust the blooming drum."

"The fruit of the Spirit is . . . joy," and they who are filled with the Spirit may rightfully expect a large harvest. In the Psalms, God says of Jerusalem, "I will satisfy her poor with bread. I will clothe her priests with salvation: and *her saints shall shout aloud for joy*" (132: 15-16). Isaiah reminds us that it is those who travel "the way of holiness" who shall "come to Zion with songs and everlasting joy upon their heads" (35: 8, 10).

The truth that is hinted in the Old Testament is made explicit in the New. It was in the opening of His earnest petition for the sanctification of the disciples that Jesus prayed: "And now come I to thee . . . that they might have my joy fulfilled in themselves" (John 17: 13). Paul reminds us that our joy in the kingdom of God is "joy in the Holy Ghost" (Romans 14: 17).

The fountain of Christian gladness has its source in God. It is when we are most sure of Him that this fountain bubbles up in utter contentment. I am glad today that I have given myself wholly to God. Even now I feel the joy of His presence. I join with Floyd Hawkins in his glad testimony:

> Oh, I have found it, the Crystal Fountain
>> Where all my soul's deep needs have been supplied,
> So freely flowing from Calv'ry's mountain,
>> And now my soul is fully satisfied.*

—FLOYD HAWKINS

*© 1952 by Lillenas Publishing Co. International copyright.

178

READ: Philippians 4: 4-7

*Thou wilt keep him in perfect peace, whose mind is stayed on thee* (Isaiah 26: 3).

## The Fruit of the Spirit Is Peace

Peace of mind has its roots in peace with God. The peace of the Christian is not the placid life of the slothful who never tackles a hard job. Nor is the peace which is the fruit of the Spirit the undisturbed tempo of a life upon which fortune smiles and everything seems to turn out just right. Our peace is not due to indifference or lack of problems; it is peace in the midst of pressures. It is a calm spirit even when we ride in a storm-tossed vessel. Paul gives us the secret: "Sirs, be of good cheer: *for I believe God*" (Acts 27: 25).

As I pray and affirm my faith in God, I find that my worries no longer worry me. The wonder of God's promise becomes real: "And the peace of God, which passeth all understanding, shall keep your hearts and minds through Christ Jesus" (Philippians 4: 7).

In *Helps to Holiness*, Samuel Logan Brengle testifies: "The Lord has been allowing me to pass through a series of the most troublesome little times, just calculated to annoy me to the uttermost. But while waiting on Him in prayer, He showed me that if I had more confidence *in Him* in my difficulties, I would keep on rejoicing . . . and so I proved it to be. Bless His holy name! I did rejoice, and one trial after another vanished away. Only the sweetness of my Lord's presence and blessing remained, and my heart has been kept in perfect peace since."

> Peace, perfect peace! Love, perfect love!
> Sweeping o'er my soul in heav'nly tides!
> Rest, perfect rest! Joy, perfect joy!
> Is mine since the Holy Ghost abides.
> —F. E. HILL

**June 17**

READ: Colossians 1: 9-12

*The fruit of the Spirit is . . . longsuffering* (Galatians 5: 22).

## The Fruit of Patience

There is no English word that gives the full meaning of our text. It was Coverdale who first used the term *long-suffering*. The central thought is patience, the grace to keep good-tempered under provocation. Here is certainly a widespread human need, and just as certainly, here is an available grace from God. No life can be free from provocation but God gives grace to face the pressures in the spirit of Jesus.

The Holy Spirit enables me (1) to suffer without growing bitter. Though sanctified wholly, I can be deeply hurt; but the love of God in my life saves me from bitterness—and that is a very great salvation. I may be mistreated by another, but God's Spirit (2) preserves me from resentment. This acid cannot corrode my spirit when I remember that God's wisdom and love are over both me and him who has wronged me. When the Holy Spirit keeps me free from resentment He thus (3) saves me from a spirit of revenge. It is the love of God in my heart that produces this fruit of the Spirit.

George Fox, the saintly Quaker, testifies: "I knew Jesus and He was very precious to my soul, but I found something within me that would not keep patient and sweet and kind. I did all that I could to keep it down, but it was still there. I besought Jesus to do something for me and I gave Him my will. He came into my heart and took out all that would not be kind and sweet and patient and shut the door and shut himself in."

> *Oh, how patient Thou hast been*
> *With my pride and inbred sin.*
> *Make my heart just like Thine own;*
> *Come, Lord, take Thy throne.*
>
> —ADELAIDE A. POLLARD

READ: Romans 12:9-10

*The fruit of the Spirit is . . . kindness* (Galatians 5: 22).

## Gentleness

The word that we read as *gentleness* in the Authorized Version is more often translated *kindness*. The nature of this fruit reminds us that the Spirit's presence is not to be seen only in the unusual—tongues of fire and the rushing mighty wind. Kindness is the spirit of love manifested in small things. To be kind is to be loving in the little contacts of life.

This fruit is a variety that does not blossom and grow without some cultivation. W. E. Sangster comments: "Indeed, some eminent saints have not been as eminent in this fruit of the Spirit as in others, and have worn their halo a little askew."

Dr. S. A. Keen once wrote to his wife: "I have no doubt as to being saved, and filled with the Spirit. . . . Yet there are some . . . touches of Christlikeness that I want. I seem to have more of the dynamics of the Spirit's presence than of His assimilating powers. I have blessedly the power of Christ, but not so fully developed the mind of Christ." Here is a confession and a prayer in which perhaps all of us should join from time to time.

Dr. Hardy C. Powers reminds us that most of the things that we do to advance the cause of Christ are the little, unnoticed things. Therefore I ask, Does the fruit of the Spirit appear in the routine contacts of my life? I seldom have opportunity to express my love in great acts of self-renunciation. But today there will be opportunities to be kind.

### Prayer for today

*Dear Lord, I do not know all who shall cross my path in these twelve hours, but at evening may someone have cause to remember, A sanctified Christian was kind to me today. Amen.*

**June 19**

READ: John 15: 1-5

*The fruit of the Spirit is . . . goodness* (Galatians 5: 22).

## Goodness

My church asks that I give evidence of God's grace in my life by: "Seeking to do good to the bodies and souls of men; feeding the hungry, clothing the naked, visiting the sick and imprisoned, and ministering to the needy, as opportunity and ability are given." The Bible says, "The fruit of the Spirit is . . . goodness." My heart yearns for more of that fruit.

Goodness is difficult to define in any simple terms. Perhaps it will help to call it kindness in action. Goodness is love that has put on its overalls. The *good shepherd* went out to find the lost sheep. The *good Samaritan* bandaged a man's wounds and cared for him. Though this quality of life is not easy to define, I have no trouble recognizing it; and instinctively I know that it is right. Tennyson speaks to hearts everywhere:

> *Howe'er it be, it seems to me*
> *'Tis only noble to be good.*

But this goodness is a fragile fruit. If I examine it too closely, a worm starts to hatch at its core and may eventually spoil the whole. When I feel satisfied with the size of this fruit, it withers. Any self-congratulation destroys it because goodness is not mine. If it is present in me, it is the fruit of the Spirit, who is my Life. I gladly acknowledge the words of my Lord: "The branch cannot bear fruit of itself, except it abide in the vine."

### Affirmation for today

*I now yield myself anew to the pruning of the Heavenly Father to be as good a man as I ought to be, to be the fruitful branch that He desires.*

READ: John 15: 7-9

*What the Spirit produces is . . . faithfulness* (Galatians 5: 22, Goodspeed).

## The Fruit of the Spirit Is Faith

Perhaps this modern translation of the text will give a cutting edge to a word grown dull through long use. The fruit of which Paul here speaks is *fidelity,* or as Goodspeed translates it, *faithfulness.* It is the grace to keep walking with God when others have quit.

Just to continue faithfully in the Christian life does not seem to be a scintillating virtue but it is what we need to see us through to the end of our journey. In dozens of daily decisions we do not need new light—just grace to be faithful to the truth that we already know. We need courage to do what is right. We need determination to try again when we have failed.

The Christian race is from here to heaven—and we need to keep running as long as we are here. The spectator can quit and go home if this marathon wearies him, but he who wins the race must keep picking up his feet and putting them down until he crosses the finish line.

We who have been sanctified wholly must confess that a hundred times we have been ready to quit. But the indwelling Holy Spirit has given us courage to jog on. Sometimes the running has been sheer dogged endurance; but ever and again He has so filled us with a sense of His presence that we have run and not been weary. In both instances He has given us grace to keep going. Paul too must have known those moments of strength. We join his glad testimony to the Galatians: "What the Spirit produces is . . . faithfulness."

### A personal testimony

*I know not how others would testify, but as for me, the grace of keeping on—the Spirit's encouragement to try yet again—more than any other grace has brought me to this point in my Christian life.*

June 21

READ: I Corinthians 9:19-22

*The Spirit . . . produces in human life fruits such as
. . . adaptability* (Galatians 5:22, Phillips).

## The Fruit of the Spirit Is Meekness

The meekness that the Spirit gives is not mousiness. To
a "Mr. Milquetoast," the Holy Spirit is more likely to give
courage. God always seeks to bring wholeness and balance
to our lives.

The meekness which is the fruit of the Spirit is a disposition to adapt myself to other persons for the sake of the
gospel. The last phrase is important. I may adapt because
I am afraid to cross another person, or because I have no
principles for which I would give my life. Christian meekness is the will to let the other fellow have his way if I can
thereby avoid un-Christlike tensions.

Most of my own occasions for Spirit-nurtured meekness
come at the point of differences with good men; we are both
trying to do God's work but differences in temperament and
training incline us to follow different paths. Christian adaptability may lead me to go my brother's way. Or it may con-
strain me to help him with his labors even while I continue
to do the work of God according to my own best judgment.

Sometimes in the spirit of Jesus we must adjust to the
ignorance of others—and do so without a feeling of superior-
ity. Jesus prayed, "Father, forgive them; for they know not
what they do" (Luke 23:34). At other times meekness is
accepting the unfairness of evil men, "if God peradventure
will give them repentance to the acknowledging of the truth"
(II Timothy 2:25).

Paul could testify, "I am made all things to all men,
that I might by all means save some." Waiving personal
rights was Paul's daily Christian practice. How often is it
mine?

**Prayer for today**

*Dear Lord, give me more of this grace today.
Let the fruit of meekness be nurtured in me by Thy
Holy Spirit. Amen.*

READ: I Corinthians 9: 25-27

*I discipline my body and make it serve me* (I Corinthians 9: 27, *Berkeley Version*).

## The Fruit of the Spirit Is Temperance

Perhaps Paul listed this fruit last because it is the most difficult to cultivate. Temperance is self-control. In the unsaved person it rises no higher than control of the self by the will and in the interest of self-chosen goals. But in the sanctified life temperance is the control of self by the Holy Spirit, and this discipline is exercised in order to achieve spiritual goals.

John Wesley's mother reminded her son of the need for Christian discipline when she wrote to him, "Whatever weakens your reason, impairs the tenderness of your conscience, obscures your sense of God, or takes off the relish of spiritual things, whatever increases the authority of your body over mind, that thing for you is sin."

The battle is not only against evil; it is often against the lesser goods as well. For us who seek to live disciplined lives in the Spirit there is, as David Hill puts it, "an altar of sacrifice, unseen, but real and present . . . there is some physical self-sacrifice, the abandonment of some bodily indulgence . . . It may be less sleep . . . or less food, or less sexual intercourse, or less ease, or more work, or greater effort, or more unpleasant work, or more dangerous and self-denying service. But, whatever it may be (there is) a giving up which costs something, a sacrifice which implies the surrender of one's own pleasure, ease, comfort, will."

This readiness to discipline myself in order to better serve God is the fruit of the Spirit. We call it temperance.

### Affirmation for today

*My redeemed spirit yearns for the fellowship of God more than anything else. I yield myself to the discipline of His Holy Spirit in order that I may the better know Him. That knowledge is worth more than all.*

**June 23**

READ: Colossians 1: 9-12

*Walk worthy of the Lord . . . being fruitful in every good work, and increasing in the knowledge of God* (Colossians 1: 10).

## Holiness Is Wholeness

We have come to the end of Paul's Galatian list of the fruits of the Spirit. It is not a complete list because the Apostle here points out chiefly aspects of a holy life in relation to our fellow men. He does not discuss our sonship to God.

We have looked at these fruits one by one but they do not grow on different trees; they are all fruits of the same Spirit. Holiness is wholeness. The perfection of God is not found in any one attribute, but rather in the perfection of all, and in their harmonious balance in His character. When we are most like Him in holiness there is a beautiful balance of every worthy impulse and habit.

In our scripture Paul prays that we may have "long-suffering with joyfulness." God's man can patiently endure; but if endurance makes him grim and joyless, there is some fruit of the Spirit missing. A sanctified Christian is a joyful person, but that does not make him so happy-go-lucky that he cannot be relied upon.

This wholeness of holiness is God's plan to save us from warped personalities and sometimes from wrecked lives. Every man is in danger from his own strong points. "One never falls but on the side toward which he leans." And so I join in the spirit of today's text:

**Prayer for today**

*Thank You, Lord, for all the nurture of Thy Holy Spirit. Help me this day to walk worthy of Thee. Make my sanctified life fruitful in* EVERY *good work, in the measure that is pleasing to Thee. This I ask in Jesus' name. Amen.*

186

Read: Ephesians 3:14-21

*Now unto him that is able to do exceeding abundantly above all that we ask or think, according to the power that worketh in us, unto him be glory . . . Amen* (Ephesians 3:20-21).

## Power for My Special Problem

Am I tempted to think that my case is different from and more difficult than the spiritual problems of others? Am I thinking about some wrong spirit of which I am ashamed? Am I disturbed by my failure to more fully achieve some spiritual goal? I may ask grace for this also. I may be different from others and my special problem may seem impossible. But, thank God, there is power adequate for me. Paul commends us "unto him that is able to do exceedingly abundantly above all that we ask or think, according to the power that worketh in us."

Am I willing for God to control my life at this point also? Am I now continuing to yield my life wholly to God? If so, there is power for me. If I ask in faith, I may expect that wrong spirit to be corrected. I am promised the help of God to accomplish the task toward which His Spirit points me. Not in my own strength but by "the power that worketh in us." God will give me the victory if I really want it—if I want it more than anything else in the world.

Paul strengthens our faith when he writes, "How overwhelmingly great is His power for us believers. It is like the working of His mighty strength, which He exerted when He raised Christ from the dead" (Ephesians 1:19-20, Berkeley).

*Oh, we never can know what the Lord will bestow*
*Of the blessings for which we have prayed,*
*Till our body and soul He doth fully control,*
*And our all on the altar is laid.*
—Elisha A. Hoffman

# 10

**June 25**

READ: Galatians 5:16-18, 24-25

*If we live by the Spirit, let us also be directed by the Spirit* (Galatians 5:25, *Berkeley Version*).

## Walk in the Spirit

For the past three weeks we have been exploring the glorious possibilities of the clean and empowered life which are opened to us through the experience of entire sanctification. We turn our attention today to suggestions for maintaining a life of personal victory. In Berkeley's translation of our text a great Bible truth comes into clearer focus. The meaning is, If we have been made alive by the Spirit, let us also walk in the Spirit. Glorious and wonderful as our experience of God may have been during the first hours after receiving the Holy Spirit, the real test and the practical outcomes of Christian perfection show up in the days that follow. It is wonderful to receive the blessing of entire sanctification, but it is still more glorious to maintain the blessing and to live the sanctified life.

It is well to be able to look back to an experience when we knew that God forgave our sins. It is well to know the day that He sanctified us wholly. But spiritual life is not nourished by memories alone. The assurance of six years ago—or six weeks ago—is not enough. Have I had contact with God's Holy Spirit today? Have I thought about Him? Been checked by Him? Felt His prompting to say a kind word or to do a right deed that took a little courage? Have I asked counsel of Him? Renewed a promise to Him? Had my spirit gladdened by an inner assurance of His presence and approval of my life? This is to walk in the Spirit. It is this Spirit-directed life to which God calls me. It is this walk in the Spirit for which I pray.

> *Lord, I am pleading; hear Thou my prayer.*
> *Let me Thy blessed fellowship share.*
> *From day to day Thy servant I'd be.*
> *Grant me a closer walk with Thee.**
>
> —HALDOR LILLENAS

*© 1924 and 1952 by Lillenas Publishing Co.

188

READ: I Kings 8: 57-61

*And I will cause you to walk in my statutes* (Ezekiel 36: 27).

## Walk in My Statutes

God's full work of grace in the soul is a practical work. His Spirit leads me not only to approve His laws, but also to walk in them. The Holy Spirit will save me from a careless and merely verbal religion.

The sanctified life is one of progressive obedience. Walking in God's statutes is more than taking a single step. It is faithfully putting my feet down one after the other—always within the known will of God. Often I must take a step forward into a new area of His will that *has just been made known to me.* Today's promise means, I will cause you to move forward, seeing more of My will and doing more today than you saw and did yesterday.

Walking in the will of God is important, but the promise here is, I will *cause* you to walk. God not only shows us the way; He also supplies the power.

Does the Holy Spirit urge me to do something that seems hard? Do I have a natural tendency to shrink from it? How can I go forward? In prayer I tell God that I love Him. I tell Him that He knows what is best for me. I tell Him that I want to do His will. From some unseen reservoir of strength I feel courage flow into my spirit and I am able to do what before seemed impossible to me.

### Affirmation for today

*I do now commit my fears to God. I now remind Him that I have promised to do His will. I now accept the courage that comes from the Holy Spirit— courage to do what He is showing me today.*

**June 27**

READ: Acts 1:6-8

*Ye shall receive power, after that the Holy Ghost is come upon you* (Acts 1:8).

## Our Continuing Source of Power

If the life of holiness is to be a continuing experience, it must be a growing experience. There is no way to get permanent grace at an altar in a moment of time. Wesley writes, "The holiest of men still need Christ . . . for God does not give them a stock of holiness. But unless they receive a supply every moment, nothing but unholiness would remain" (*Christian Perfection*).

An accurate figure of God's sanctifying power is not a storage battery but a trolley. The trolley car has no ability to move itself but it is connected to a source of power adequate for every load that it must carry and for every hill along its route. In the use of this power the motorman has an element of freedom. He can drive in the center of the street or pull to the curb. However, his freedom extends only to the limit that the trolley car can move and still keep its connection with the power line.

Have you ever observed the motorman whose trolley has jumped the wire? His car goes nowhere and pulls no load. The motorman must again establish contact with his overhead source of power. So it is in the sanctified life. By an honest effort to know and do the will of God, we can keep the trolley on the wire. But we know that it is God who gives us our power—and He gives it moment by moment as we daily cultivate His presence.

> Ev'ry day, ev'ry hour
> Let me feel Thy cleansing pow'r;
> May Thy tender love to me
> Bind me closer, closer, Lord, to Thee.
> —FANNY J. CROSBY

READ: I John 2: 3-6

*Whoso keepeth his word, in him verily is the love of God perfected* (I John 2: 5).

## Continuing Obedience

The sanctified life does not change God's requirement for obedience. A true and satisfying life of Christian holiness always involves a careful and continuous endeavor to do the will of God. This is what we promised Him when we made our consecration and asked for the gift of the Holy Spirit.

Since our consecration vows to God were made once for all, they do not need to be made again and again, but we do need to remember them and honestly to live by them. Rev. C. W. Ruth used to say, "Instead of consecration being merely an act, it must become an attitude, to be worked out in daily life: not an occasional matter but a daily practice." It was in an hour of pledging our full obedience that God's Holy Spirit came to dwell in us. It is in continuing full obedience that the glory of His presence is made real to us again and again.

It was by this continued obedience to the known will of God that Jesus asked His disciples to prove their love for Him. He said, "If ye love me, keep my commandments" (John 14:15). To maintain a satisfying sanctified life, the counsel of Dr. Dougan Clark cannot be improved upon. "If at any time or in any thing you feel your will rising in opposition to God's will or providence, check such a rising at once. 'Thy will be done' must be the continual attitude of your heart and the frequent utterance of your lips."

### Prayer for today

*Not my will, but Thine; not my will, but Thine;*
*Not my will, but Thy will be done, Lord, in me.*
*May Thy Spirit divine fill this being of mine.*
*Not my will, but Thy will, be done, Lord, in me.**
—HUGH C. BENNER

*© 1951 by Lillenas Publishing Co. International copyright.

READ: Philippians 3: 7-11

*I delight to do thy will, O my God: yea, thy law is within my heart* (Psalms 40: 8).

## Continuing Consecration

Our continuing consecration is an impulse of the heart as well as a policy of the will. The Psalmist knew the joy of a life that is truly consecrated to God when he testified, "I delight to do thy will, O my God: yea, thy law is within my heart." It is this attitude of abounding love that is the secret of radiant Christian living in the high country of God. The people who are getting the most out of their religion are those who keep themselves fully consecrated to the will of God.

Dr. Philip Doddridge wrote out his own consecration thus: "This day do I, with utmost solemnity, surrender myself to Thee . . . I consecrate to Thee all that I am, and all that I have . . . to be all used entirely for thy glory . . . *as long as Thou continuest me in life* . . . ever holding myself in an attentive posture to observe the first intimations of Thy will, and ready to spring forward with zeal and joy to the immediate execution of it."

At the altar of prayer God does graciously accept our consecration which we deliberately make—sometimes with great struggle. But in response to our desire and struggle God gives to us deeper desire and less of struggle for the days ahead.

Some effort is still required but the joy of the Lord becomes our strength in the Christian life. And God wants to give us that joy.

### Prayer for today

*O God, I too have surrendered my whole self to Thee. By Thy grace I am today "holding myself in an attentive posture to observe the first intimations of Thy will, and ready to spring forward with zeal and joy to the immediate execution of it." Amen.*

READ: I John 3:18-19

*Let us ... love ... in deed and in truth. And hereby we ... shall assure our hearts before him* (I John 3:18-19).

## Keep Active in Service

If we keep our Lord's commandments and are faithful to our consecration vows, we shall be active Christians. Jesus says to us, "As my Father hath sent me, even so send I you"; "Go ye into all the world, and preach the gospel to every creature." If we would have the continuing presence of the Spirit, we must stay around where the Spirit is at work—we must busy ourselves with the tasks of the Spirit.

It is a wise provision of a holiness church which charges us with "seeking to do good to the bodies and souls of men; feeding the hungry, clothing the naked, visiting the sick and imprisoned, and ministering to the sick and needy, as opportunity and ability are given. Pressing upon the attention of the unsaved the claims of the gospel, inviting them to the house of the Lord, and trying to compass their salvation" (*Manual, Church of the Nazarene*).

If we are to maintain the joy and blessing of a close fellowship with the Holy Spirit, we must keep engaged in active expression of our Christian love. The Bible promises us, "And hereby we ... shall assure our hearts before him" (I John 3:18-19).

Does God seem far away? Am I worried as I feel for my spiritual pulse beat? I need to get out and do something for God. The exercise of Christian service will often bring deep spiritual breathing and a firm heartbeat that gives assurance of the indwelling Holy Spirit. Active Christians have little trouble with spiritual loss and uncertainty.

> *But if by a still, small voice He calls*
> *To paths that I do not know,*
> *I'll answer, dear Lord, with my hand in Thine,*
> *I'll go where You want me to go.*
> —MARY BROWN

**July 1**

READ: Colossians 2: 6-7

*Just as you once accepted Christ Jesus as your Lord, you must continue living in vital union with Him, with your roots deeply planted in Him, being consciously built up in Him, and growing stronger in faith* (Colossians 2: 6-7, Williams).

## We Live by Faith

A young Christian just recently sanctified once asked, "How do I keep the blessing?" The wise answer was, "Don't try to keep the blessing; let the Blesser keep you!"

Every spiritual gift which we receive from God is given in response to our faith. We receive entire sanctification by faith, and we are kept in this relationship to God by continuing faith. We cannot *by our own efforts* preserve any blessing that God has given to us in response to faith.

In our text Paul declares: "You must continue living in vital union with Him, with your roots deeply planted in Him . . . growing stronger in faith." In the sanctified life we are to be "rooted . . . in him" and thus grow as a tree grows; drawing life and strength from the soil in which it is embedded.

Dr. P. F. Bresee writes: "We stand by faith; God provides that into such a heart the divine Presence comes filling it with himself. He keeps it. The Bible insists upon, and we must have holiness of heart; but we cannot trust in a holy heart; we can trust only in Him who dwells within it."

Day by day the sanctified Christian turns to God in simple faith. Sometimes, in hours of severe test, we must turn to Him moment by moment. As the Holy Spirit once cleansed sin from my heart in response to my faith, so by faith He cleanses and fills me today.

**Affirmation for today**

*When my inner assurance begins to grow faint I resolve to pray, to obey, and to trust God until the assurance is strong again.*

194

READ: Hebrews 2:1-3

*We must pay the closer attention to what we have heard, lest we drift away from it* (Hebrews 2:1, R.S.V.).

## When Assurance Grows Faint

The consecrated, obedient, active, believing Christian is not likely to have serious difficulties at the point of continuing assurance regarding his entire sanctification. But these conditions are not always well fulfilled. John Wesley said: "Indeed, the witness of sanctification is not always clear at first; neither is it afterward always the same, but . . . sometimes stronger and sometimes fainter. Yea, and sometimes it is withdrawn" (*Christian Perfection*).

What shall we do in these hours of spiritual emptiness? The recurring witness of the Spirit is God's way of assuring us that He is pleased with our lives. When we miss that witness for days or weeks we need to ask ourselves why. Normally we shall find the explanation in ourselves. Uncertainty in our relationship to God comes most often when we grow content or careless. We become less sure of God's presence when our striving for improvement in Christian life and service slackens.

This uncertainty is God's way of protecting us from carelessly drifting away from the presence of His Holy Spirit. Spiritual uncertainty is like the silent red light on the instrument panel of an automobile. It flashes its warning to tell us that the oil is low and there is imminent danger to the motor. Under these conditions the very lack of assurance for which our hearts hunger is one more of God's gifts of grace to us. The Bible tells us that we must pay close attention to God's silent warning lest we drift away from all that He has given to us in this "so great salvation."

**Prayer for today**

*Thank You, Lord, for the inner checks of the Holy Spirit. Thank You for the warning silence when I am careless in the responsibilities of my love for You.*

**July 3**

READ: Romans 8: 14-17

*You have received no slavish spirit that would make you relapse into fear; you have received the Spirit of sonship* (Romans 8: 15, Moffatt).

## Continuing Assurance

We saw yesterday that lack of assurance is normally God's warning that we are close to spiritual trouble. But this is not always so. Sometimes we have extended periods when there is no assuring witness of God's presence even when we are being as faithful to Him as we know how to be. What shall we do in these hours of emotional uncertainty? Move closer to Jesus, and determine to trust Him more.

The most important part of Christian growth is establishing an unshakable confidence that, as long as we propose to walk with God, He will always be there to walk with us. We do not need always to be checking up to find out if He is there. Paul reminds us, "You have received no slavish spirit that would make you relapse into fear."

In our highest personal relationships we have assurance without constantly seeking it. A faithful husband has no slavish spirit of fear regarding the love of his wife. Having received the promise of that love, he lives confidently in it and for it. He often tries to express his love for her; he is thrilled when out of her heart she assures him, "I am yours, always yours." But something destructive happens when he presses for this assurance. The very confidence that he seeks is destroyed when he asks, "Do you love me? How can I be sure that you love me?"

When we are uncertain, let us first look to our relationships to God. If they are right, let us tell God that we love Him, that we intend to walk with Him to the end of our days, no matter how we feel. When we do this, His response and reassurance are never far away.

**Affirmation for today**

> *My Jesus, I love Thee;*
> *I know Thou art mine.*
> —WM. R. FEATHERSTONE

READ: I John 4: 16-19

*If the Son therefore shall make you free, ye shall be free indeed* (John 8: 36).

## Glorious Freedom

Today is July 4. In the United States we take a holiday to celebrate our political freedom. It is a worthy freedom, but are there not others to which we should also give attention? In our time, President Franklin D. Roosevelt reminded us of the four freedoms—freedom from want, freedom from fear, freedom for religious belief, and freedom of the press. The Christian has yet another for which he is grateful—freedom from fear in the presence of God. "There is no fear in love; but perfect love casteth out fear" (I John 4: 18).

The average man seeks to cast out his dread of God by forgetting Him but we Christians gain confidence by knowing God better. There was a day, as unawakened sinners, when we had no fear of God and no love for Him. Conviction for sins brought fear, but there was no love to relieve it. Forgiveness raised the glad cry, "We love him, because he first loved us." But even forgiven men are left at times with nagging fears due to carnality. God's Word assures us that there is something better than this.

When the Holy Spirit comes in His fullness, He brings a love that casts out this dread. With the love of God shed abroad in our hearts we have an inner security. When that love is made perfect we experience a confidence approaching boldness. It is this freedom from fear of which the Bible speaks, "Having therefore, brethren, boldness to enter into the holiest by the blood of Jesus . . . let us draw near with a true heart in full assurance of faith" (Hebrews 10:19, 22).

*Glorious freedom! Wonderful freedom!*
*No more in chains of sin I repine!*
*Jesus, the glorious Emancipator!*
*Now and forever He shall be mine.*
—HALDOR LILLENAS

197

READ: I John 3: 19-24

*Hereby we know that he abideth in us, by the Spirit which he hath given us* (I John 3: 24).

## The Daily Witness

A willing and progressive obedience is a continuing sign that we are sanctified wholly. The witness to the presence of God's Holy Spirit is not a dove perched upon the heads of God's people, but the dove nestled within their hearts. By the fruits of a holy life, by daily fellowship and communion with the Holy Spirit, God bears witness with our spirits that we are His children. This witness is daily renewed and it is satisfying to the heart.

In the long run there is no other witness that can be continuously satisfying. We thank God for that inner assurance which came to us at an altar of prayer. But today that assurance is in the past. At best, we had the witness that we *were* at that time sanctified wholly. What we need is the assurance that we are *now* well pleasing to God, that His Holy Spirit is living in us and working through us today.

Is your witness too far in the past? Is it faint? Uncertain? Seemingly gone? This does not necessarily mean that the Holy Spirit has gone. It means that you have paid too little attention to Him and your awareness of His presence has grown dim.

Do you want that assuring witness again? Then turn to Him now. Tell Him that you belong to Him. Remind Him that you love Him supremely. Ask Him to show you any place where you have been careless. Fix it up and begin to do His will at that point. Undertake today some service of love for Him. Your witness will soon return with satisfying assurance.

### Affirmation for today

*I shall today seek to make some conscious contact with God's Holy Spirit.*

READ: I John 3:18-20

*Let us ... love ... in deed and in truth. And hereby we ... shall assure our hearts before him* (I John 3:18-19).

## Do We Love?

In hours of uncertainty we dare not judge our state of grace in the light of tempting thoughts or impulsive emotions. We need some sound tests by which we may "assure our hearts before him."

Sincere love is the reassuring test proposed in this passage from I John. This was also Wesley's position. "What is Christian perfection?" Wesley answers his own question thus: "Loving God with all our heart, mind, soul, and strength. This implies that no wrong temper, none contrary to love, remains in the soul; and that all the thoughts, words and actions are governed by pure love."

When I harbor no spirit contrary to love, my spirit resembles the Holy Spirit, and I am a sanctified Christian. Who would quarrel with such an experience or who would question such a test? If I find an unloving and unlovely spirit, I surely want God to do something more for me. If God has given me a real spirit of love, I may be humbly grateful for such a blessing.

This evidence is something that is clearly given to us in consciousness. If we are honest with ourselves, we need have no uncertainty concerning the purity of our motives and the sincerity of our love. If as we examine our hearts we find sincere and full love to God, and if we find there only Christian love for all men, "Let us draw near with a true heart in full assurance of faith ... Let us hold fast the profession of our faith without wavering" (Hebrews 10:22-23).

**Affirmation for today**

*The love of God is shed abroad in our hearts by the Holy Ghost which is given unto us* (Romans 5:5).

**July 7**

READ: Matthew 6: 9-13

*Thy will be done in earth [in me], as it is in heaven* (Matthew 6: 10).

## Is My Consecration Still Complete?

The spiritual condition of the soul may be further checked by the depth of our consecration. Dr. Ralph Earle has written, "One valid test of a person's sanctification is the measure of his submission to the will of God." Here also we may examine ourselves without danger of confusion. This is the queston to ask, Is there any known reservation in my consecration to God? Such a test is valid and practical. It is not easy to be confused at this point.

John Wesley wrote, "A will steadily and uniformly devoted to God is essential to a state of sanctification, but not uniformity of joy or peace, or happy communion with God. These may rise and fall in various degrees, and may be affected either by the body or by diabolical agency in a manner which all our wisdom can neither understand nor prevent."

If our witness is weak, let us then test ourselves at the point of a will that is steadily and uniformly devoted to God. Can I today honestly pray, "Thy will be done in me, as it is done in heaven"?

If we discover in the hour of heart-searching that there is no conscious reservation, we have the right to assume that our consecration is complete and our acceptance with God is equally perfect. We have only to maintain this attitude of complete consecration, and go on about our business of loving and serving God. As we do, it will not be long until the Holy Spirit again makes His presence known to us wth completely satisfying assurance.

## My personal commitment

*Our Father which art in heaven, my love, my plans, my life are Yours. Work in and through me Your perfect will, now and forever.*

READ: Galatians 5:1, 22-23

*Stand fast therefore in the liberty wherewith Christ hath made us free, and be not entangled again with the yoke of bondage* (Galatians 3:1).

## Is There Some Fruit in My Life?

God's Word assures us that "the fruit of the Spirit is love, joy, peace, longsuffering, gentleness, goodness, faith, meekness, temperance." If these fruits are present in our lives we may assure ourselves that the Holy Spirit dwells in our hearts.

I do not depend upon any good works of mine to assure my standing with God. But I do depend upon God's declaration that the presence of His Holy Spirit makes a difference in my life. I know that love is better than hate, joy is better than unhappiness, peace is better than conflict. I had rather be long-suffering and gentle than to be impatient and rough. I would rather be good than bad. It is better to have faith than to doubt, and better to be meek than to be fierce. My prayer is to be temperate rather than to be extravagant.

I claim no credit for these attitudes. In whatever measure they possess me, they are the fruit of the Holy Spirit. Their presence is proof of God's Spirit at work in me.

My Christian life does not reflect all of these fruits in equal amounts. None of them is full-grown or perfect. But I thank God for every one that His Spirit is nurturing within me. I can see that some of these fruits are larger than when I turned my life wholly over to God and allowed His Spirit to fill me. This knowledge brings renewed confidence and assurance. I testify with another growing child of God:

> *Dear Lord:*
> *Ah ain't all Ah wants to be;*
> *Ah ain't all Ah ought to be;*
> *Ah ain't all Ah's gonna be;*
> *But still, thanks to de good God,*
> *Ah ain't what Ah used to be.*
> —AUTHOR UNKNOWN

201

**July 9**

READ: Acts 4:18-20

*We cannot but speak the things which we have seen and heard* (Acts 4:20).

## Testify to the Blessing of God

If we are to maintain our inner assurance, we must testify to what God has done in sanctifying our souls.

John Fletcher once testified: "Last Wednesday evening [the Holy Spirit] spoke to me by these words: 'Reckon ye also yourself to be dead indeed unto sin, but alive unto God through Jesus Christ our Lord' (Romans 6:11). I obeyed the voice of God; I now obey it and tell you all to the praise of His love, I am freed from sin, dead unto sin and alive unto God. I received this blessing four or five times before, but I lost it by not obeying the order of God, who has told us, 'with the heart man believeth unto righteousness, and with the mouth confession is made unto salvation.'

"Now, my brethren . . . I am resolved before you all to confess my Master. I will confess Him to all the world. And I declare unto you in the presence of God . . . I am now dead indeed unto sin and alive unto God, through Jesus Christ, who is my indwelling holiness."

And why should we hesitate to testify to God's sanctifying grace? In doing so, we do not boast of any merit of our own; we only magnify the power of God. David sang, "My soul shall make her boast in the Lord: the humble shall hear thereof, and be glad" (Psalms 34:2). May we not say from thankful hearts, "Unto me, who am less than the least of all saints, is this grace given" (Ephesians 3:8)?

> *Thee we would be always blessing,*
> *Serve Thee as Thy hosts above,*
> *Pray and praise Thee without ceasing,*
> *Glory in Thy perfect love.*
> —CHARLES WESLEY

READ: II Corinthians 4: 6-8

*We have this treasure in earthen vessels* (II Corinthians 4: 7).

## Human Saints

For several weeks we have been exploring the glorious possibilities of the clean and empowered life which are opened to us through entire sanctification. We turn now to another phase of the truth. Holiness makes possible a life of victory but not a life without battles.

The clearest possible understanding is needed as to what the experience of holiness has *not* done for us as well as what it has accomplished. If our expectations are false, we face disappointment and we are tempted to doubt: either to doubt that we were sanctified, or, more serious still, to doubt that there is any genuine reality in this second work of grace. Wesley said, "If I set the standards too high I drive people into needless fears." On the other hand, he continued, "If I set them too low I drive their souls into hell fire." We must try to find God's standard for ourselves somewhere between these two extremes.

It is always dangerous to ask, "How little of religion is enough?" We explore these minimum levels of sanctifying grace, not because we should be content to live here, but because we sometimes find ourselves in such circumstances. It is wise to move into the Canaan land of holiness as far and as fast as possible. But if one is unfortunately wandering near Jordan's banks, it is well to know on which bank he stands.

**Prayer for today**

> *Guide me, O Thou great Jehovah,*
> *Pilgrim thro' this barren land.*
> *I am weak, but Thou art mighty.*
> *Hold me with Thy pow'rful hand.*
> —W. WILLIAMS

READ: Acts 1:4-8

*It is not for you to know the times or the seasons, which the Father hath put in his own power* (Acts 1:7).

## I Accept What Thou Dost Give

"Ye shall receive power, after that the Holy Ghost is come upon you." The promise is crystal-clear. But what is the nature of that power? In our walk with God we shall avoid some dark days if we understand the limits as well as the wonder of His promised blessings.

In the light of this promised power these early Christians raised unchristian hopes. They wanted to know more than it is given man to know. Jesus told them plainly that the promise of the Father did not include that kind of power for men. There are some things that God "hath put in his own power."

God does not give us power to do or to get just anything that we want. The power of the Holy Spirit is not power to make money; it is not power to conquer our enemies or to bend others to our will; it is not intellectual power that enables us to see into the future or that makes us men of genius. If we have a measure of these abilities the Holy Spirit gives us power to keep them dedicated to holy purposes. If we do not have such abilities He gives us power to live useful and happy lives without them.

In this sense the power of the Holy Spirit is the power to accept our human limitations; the power to let God be God and gladly to acknowledge our dependence upon Him while at the same time we pledge Him our supreme allegiance.

**Prayer for today**

> *Our Father, I accept the kind of power Thou dost choose to give. "I bow my knees unto the Father of our Lord Jesus Christ . . . unto him that is able to do exceeding abundantly above all that we ask or think, according to the power that worketh in us . . . Amen* (Ephesians 3:14, 20-21).

READ: Romans 8:24-28

*Likewise the Spirit also helpeth our infirmities* (Romans 8:26).

## Human Infirmities

Because of his human limitations the sanctified Christian often falls short of a perfect manifestation of the spirit of love that God has put into his heart. But these human infirmities are not sins. The Bible teaches a difference between manifestations of carnality and expressions of our sin-weakened human nature. Paul reminds us that "we have this treasure in earthen vessels." Every sanctified Christian soon becomes aware that his vessel is pretty earthy.

We may fail because of ignorance; not understanding all of the facts in a situation, we do the wrong thing. We sometimes fail through weakness; not relying fully upon God, we fall short of high performance. Neither can rightly be called sin. Neither is intentional and therefore it does not bring guilt. But always this kind of failure brings to the sanctified Christian humiliation and regret. We are never to be satisfied with anything less than doing the will of God as fully as we know how.

When overtaken in such faults, we do not give up our faith in Christian holiness. Rather, having learned what God can do for us in the instantaneous experience of entire sanctification, we now press on to discover how the Holy Spirit can help us in our infirmities. The life of holiness is a life of spiritual victory through wholehearted love for Christ and complete loyalty to His will for us. We are pained by human frailties, but not paralyzed by them. We press on to a more perfect life and service tomorrow.

> *I want to live above the world,*
> *Tho' Satan's darts at me are hurled;*
> *For faith has caught the joyful sound,*
> *The song of saints on higher ground.*
> —JOHNSON OATMAN, JR.

**July 13**

READ: Hebrews 10: 35-39

*Cast not away . . . your confidence, which hath great recompence of reward* (Hebrews 10:35).

## You're Human, Too!

"Near the beginning of *Pilgrim's Progress* there is an interesting bit of conversation. Overburdened Christian had met Evangelist and had asked for help and direction. Evangelist pointed into the distance and asked, 'Do you see yon wicket gate?' Christian looked and honestly answered, 'No.' Then Evangelist, trying again, said, 'Do you see yonder shining light?' Christian strained his eyes and saw one spot that seemed less dark than the rest, and answered, 'I think I do.' 'Then keep that light in your eye,' said Evangelist, 'and go directly thereto, so shalt thou see the gate.'

"There are personality problems that are confusing, and oftentimes we almost lose sight of the 'wicket gate.' But there is a way out; and thus we have hope for tomorrow. We must confess that we have not found all the answers. We do not understand the full meaning of our complex personalities; we do not know the geography of all our moods and temperaments.

"Even with a definite transformation and being a real sanctified Christian, you will likely discover you're human too! In these moments, discouragement is a weapon used by the enemy to drag the child of God down to defeat. But that is the time to trust. We walk by faith a great deal of the way toward the city of God.

"The way of deliverance is continued unreserved surrender of your total personality to God. That means victory over sin and the power to live with courage, humility, and love. Remember He giveth more grace. No wonder Stevenson cried, 'The grace of God! We breathe it. We live it. It is the roof, the rafters, the floor and the nails of the universe'" (J. E. WILLIAMS).

**Prayer for today**

*"Heavenly Father, when the way is dark and my mind confused, help me to hold on. Help me to remember that You have never failed me yet, and I can still draw on Your fathomless grace. Amen."*

READ: Acts 23: 1-5

*Those who stood by said, "Would you revile God's high priest?" And Paul said, "I did not know, brethren, that he was the high priest; for it is written, 'You shall not speak evil of a ruler of your people'"* (R.S.V.).

## A Holy Disposition

Of the Apostle's behavior on this occasion Everett Lewis Cattell writes: "Now what about Paul? Was he Spirit-filled? Was he fully surrendered? Was he hid with Christ in God?

"We must make clear that all these questions concern disposition rather than outward or absolute perfection. There is proof that Paul was surrendered, that he was Spirit-filled. But the proof lies not in any experience which would make his answers, his words, the use of his tongue as perfect as those of Jesus.

"Rather the proof lies in the *disposition* which he manifested as soon as his error was revealed. Instantly, upon the rebuke of the bystanders, Paul came through with an apology. That indicated more truly the real heart of the man. And so it will with us. Caught off guard, a word is spoken, an attitude taken or a spirit shown for which we receive the Spirit's rebuke. If, in that situation, we allow self to re-affirm its independent stand, if we slip out of our hidden place in God, if a bit of enmity against God creeps back in, that will be manifest by an unwillingness to heed the check of the Spirit and a stubborn decision to go right on.

"But if there is love for Christ above all else and a desire to be altogether His, that disposition will show itself, even in so stern and tempestuous a nature as Paul's, with complete readiness to apologize and make right the incident. Note also Paul's action was instant—he did not wait for three or four days to cool off and then come around and merely try to act pleasant as though nothing had ever happened! The Spirit-filled heart does not hold grudges" (*The Spirit of Holiness*).

### Thought for today

"The steps of a good man are ordered by the Lord," said the Psalmist. George Muller added, "And the stops also."

**July 15**

READ: Ephesians 1: 15-20

*That ye may know . . . what is the exceeding great-ness of his power to us-ward who believe* (Ephesians 1: 18-19).

## Humanity in Ourselves

We do not see very clearly the line which divides carnality from human infirmity. Our inability to make this distinction often causes trouble. In *Terminology of Holiness*, Dr. J. B. Chapman writes: "There are many sincere people who very much need their own mercy to save them from unnecessary torment because of their weaknesses and tendencies that are involuntary and which are of the physical rather than the moral nature."

Mr. Wesley asks, How may we distinguish the temptations of the enemy and frailties of human nature from the carnal mind or corruption of the heart? He answers that sometimes "it is impossible to distinguish, without the direct witness of the Spirit." God may dwell with sanctifying power in the lives of men and women woefully weak and ignorant, if only their hearts are fully His.

After we have been sanctified wholly we should never doubt the grace that God has given to us. We must never use any substandard mood or act as an occasion to question the reality of the coming of the Holy Spirit. Instead, we should use these experiences as occasions to draw more freely upon God's help. Paul reminds us of "the surpassing greatness of his power over us believers—a power which operates with the strength of the might which he exerted in raising Christ from the dead" (Ephesians 1: 19-20, Moffatt). If the correction of my infirmity is no more difficult than raising Christ from the dead, God has power available through the Holy Spirit, whom He has given to me!

> *He cannot fail, for He is God;*
> *He cannot fail, He pledged His word;*
> *He cannot fail, He'll see you through;*
> *He cannot fail, He'll answer you.**
> —C. E. MASON, JR.

*© Singspiration, Inc. Used by permission.

READ: Romans 14: 10-13

*Let us no more pass judgment on one another, but rather decide never to put a stumbling-block or hindrance in the way of a brother* (Romans 14:13, R.S.V.).

## Humanity in Others

The man who tries to serve God and to live according to a standard of holiness is always in danger from the temptation to criticize others. He is keenly aware of God's will, and is eager for men everywhere to live by it.

God has standards for His people, and He too is eager for men to know and to live by those standards—but He has not set us up as judges. Our job is to be examples of the holy life and to be witnesses to the grace of God which He has given to us.

It is really one of our own human limitations—one of our infirmities—that makes it necessary for God to excuse us from being judges. We simply cannot know the motives of a fellow Christian. There are failures in the spiritual life which originate in carnality, but there are other shortcomings which arise from human infirmity even after a man has been sanctified wholly. To distinguish between these requires knowledge higher than ours.

In a fine passage in *Christian Perfection*, where he draws a bit of irony from the Book of Job, Mr. Wesley writes: "Can we pronounce, in all cases, how far infirmity reaches? what may, and what may not, be resolved into it? what may in all circumstances, and what may not, consist with perfect love? Can we precisely determine how it will influence the look, the gesture, the tone of voice? If we can, doubtless we are the men, and wisdom shall die with us."

### Prayer for the sanctified

*Lord Jesus, help me always to remember that Paul was preaching holiness also when he wrote, "Let us no more pass judgment on one another, but rather decide never to put a stumbling-block or hindrance in the way of a brother."*

**July 17**

READ: Psalms 25: 8-10

*Thine ears shall hear a word behind thee, saying,*
*This is the way, walk ye in it, when ye turn to the*
*right hand, and when ye turn to the left* (Isaiah
30: 21).

## Guidance of the Holy Spirit

"How can we know when we have crossed the line from
legitimate satisfaction of hunger to gluttony, from sensitive-
ness to self-pity, from zeal to envy, and from holy to unholy
speech?

"I have spoken of 'crossing the line.' Actually there is
an area between that which is clearly and wholly for the
glory of God and that which is clearly and wholly for the
glory of the isolated self—a sort of twilight zone. As one
enters it, the Spirit begins to whisper words of caution. These
grow more intense as we approach the line. Crossing, there is
a feeling of condemnation and guilt which intensifies the
further we go. It is not simple, partly because of our dullness
of hearing and perception, and partly because of the complex
nature of the situation—the intertwining of the legitimate
with the sinful in that shaded area. . . . It is impossible to
reduce the matter to simple rules or to define exactly the
line in all cases. *We are shut up to the voice of the Spirit as*
*our only guide.*

"No man can tell me when I cross the line, nor can I tell
another when he crosses his line. Nor is there any set of
rules which will help either of us. . . . It is a living way and
nothing short of the Living Spirit of God dwelling within us
can solve our problem. *But He does guide us!* There is never
a time when we are in danger of crossing one of these lines
but that He faithfully speaks! Yet never thunderously—only
with a still small voice. We can always hear—*if we listen!*"
(*The Spirit of Holiness,* by Everett Lewis Cattell.)

*He leadeth me! Oh, blessed tho't!*
*Oh, words with heav'nly comfort fraught!*
*Whate'er I do, where'er I be,*
*Still 'tis God's hand that leadeth me.*
—JOSEPH H. GILMORE

READ: Philippians 3:12-15

*Forgetting those things which are behind . . . I press toward the mark for the prize of the high calling of God in Christ Jesus* (Philippians 3:13-14).

## Strengthened to Strive

By growth in grace we may be strengthened at the points of our human infirmities. We should therefore expect to grow stronger where we have been weak. Even so, we shall never wholly escape the consequences of human infirmities while we live on this earth. John Wesley wrote: "We believe that there is no such perfection in this life as implies an entire deliverance . . . from manifold temptation, or from numberless infirmities, wherewith the corruptible body more or less presses down the soul" (*Christian Perfection*).

These are the facts. Are they discouraging? Not really. Rather they reflect the glory of human life. God has not made us perfect but He has made us improvable. He has set a goal before us and put within us the urge to attain it. He has removed the carnal nature which refuses to approve the goal or to love the God who planned it. He has given us His own Holy Spirit to inspire us when we are discouraged, to strengthen us when we feel weak, to bless us when, with Paul, "we press toward the mark."

We are made for growth—to face obstacles and to overcome them. A static perfection could not be a good perfection for a growing personality. The sanctified man has problems but he has also the freest possible access to the power of God to help him solve those problems rightly. Thanks be to God for His grace that leaves me dissatisfied enough to keep striving.

*Build thee more stately mansions, O my soul,*
*As the swift seasons roll!*
*Leave thy low-vaulted past!*
*Let each new temple, nobler than the last,*
*Shut thee from heaven with a dome more vast,*
*Till thou at length art free,*
*Leaving thine outgrown shell by life's unresting sea!*

—OLIVER WENDELL HOLMES

READ: Ephesians 6: 10-18

*Put on the whole armour of God, that ye may be able to stand against the wiles of the devil* (Ephesians 6: 11).

## Better Armor for More Pressure

God's whole armor of entire sanctification is provided to enable a man to stand. But to put on that armor is also to challenge the devil to use his whole arsenal of weapons against us.

Until a man tries by God's grace to live above sin, he is not aware of how deeply involved he has been. Until a man trusts the Holy Spirit to keep him from all sin, Satan never tries his utmost to test that man. He doesn't have to. The man commits sin and admits that he does. He is not seriously concerned about it, and expects to keep on sinning more or less. The devil knows that such a man is safely in his power. One sin leads to another. One sin anesthetizes the spirit so that the next sin hurts less. At last, God-given conscience is deathly quiet. The man does not suffer because he no longer resists. He does not feel defeat because he no longer tries to be victorious.

When we depend on the Holy Spirit for continuing sanctification, we must expect something different. Paul knew that the man who went all out for God was in for a fight— "We wrestle . . . against spiritual wickedness." Instead of God taking us out of the skirmishes at the fringe of the battle, He sends us with His combat teams to penetrate the enemy lines.

Our human nature inclines us to choose a small fight with our bare fists. God's plan is for an all-out battle—but equipped with His whole armor.

**Prayer for today**

*O God, I do not ask for fights less fierce, but help me to put on and to keep on the whole armor that You have provided.*

READ: I Corinthians 11:27-28

*Examine . . . your own selves, to see whether you are holding to your faith and showing the proper fruits of it* (II Corinthians 13:5, *The Amplified New Testament*).

## Examine Yourselves

The grace of entire sanctification and the life of Christian holiness must always be kept open to self-examination. Of course the abnormal mind can imagine spiritual illness that does not exist. And if a man always keeps the finger of his right hand on the pulse in his left wrist, he does no work with his hands. But dangers of self-examination should not deter us, for there are also dangers in carelessness.

Let us never close our eyes through fear that we shall discover some lack in our Christian experience. To do this is to shut ourselves off from the grace of God. Let us honestly examine our love for the Lord. Let us test our lives to see if our consecration is still complete. Let us ask the Holy Spirit to probe our motives to see if we are wholly sincere. Let us continue to trust God fully no matter what our self-examination reveals. Let us commit ourselves to the guidance of the Holy Spirit for the remedial steps which should follow every spiritual diagnosis. Let us never become discouraged and give up. Heart holiness always means going further and never going back.

Self-examination is always disastrous if I allow discouragement to conquer me. It is always wholesome when I respond positively and courageously. In our scripture Paul presses the need for holy introspection as we come to Communion. But he counsels no man to leave the Lord's table. Rather he says: "Let a man examine himself, and so [having made right anything that he found wrong] let him eat of that bread, and drink of that cup."

### Prayer for today

*Search me, O God, and know my heart: try me, and know my thoughts: and see if there be any wicked way in me, and lead me in the way everlasting* (Psalms 139:23-24).

**July 21**

READ: Mark 14: 32-36

*Abba, Father, all things are possible unto thee; take away this cup from me: nevertheless not what I will, but what thou wilt* (Mark 14: 36).

## Nevertheless What Thou Wilt

"We cannot understand fully all the struggle within the soul of our Lord when He prayed in Gethsemane to be spared the agony He saw before Him. But Jesus' petition did not end with, 'Take away this cup from me.' He prayed also: 'Nevertheless not what I will, but what thou wilt.' This *nevertheless* we can understand. We have been there.

"Sometimes we assume that all the responses of a completely consecrated life are automatic. *No!* Discipline and direction are still involved. Have we not, though the Spirit bore witness that our consecration was complete, experienced times when our immediate desires seemed to be in one direction and the Lord's will in another? Indeed! And here, precisely, is where many people take themselves off the altar.

"In God's plan of salvation there comes in every Christian life one great Gethsemane. What a man does there pretty well sets the course for the balance of his life. But the experience of entire sanctification does not mean spiritual automation. It is an experience of perfect love. When our wills seem to be at variance with His, or we cannot understand the *why* of His will, we say, in trust and love, *nevertheless.* At this point of discipline every man may have something of Gethsemane again.

"When our spirits are pressed to the breaking point, let us not forget to cry, 'Abba, Father.' We must never forget—though the sky is dark and the storm severe—that we have a Heavenly Father who loves us. When we are fighting a battle, even the battle of the will's struggle, we need not try to hide it from God, or to pretend that all is easy and automatic. Bring it out in the open to Him. Confess the struggle. Don't even hesitate to say, 'If it be possible.' Say whatever your soul must say, for it is a loving Father who listens to your cry."—PONDER W. GILLILAND.

214

READ: Isaiah 40: 27-31

*The eyes of the Lord run to and fro throughout the whole earth to shew himself strong in behalf of them whose heart is perfect toward him* (II Chronicles 16: 9).

## Strength When I Don't Feel Holy

A careful holiness teacher writes: "Holiness . . . is the renewal of the whole man in the image of Jesus. It is the utter destruction of all hatred, envy, malice, impatience . . . love of ease . . . and the like."

Does this mean that the sanctified man never feels like acting impatiently and never feels an inclination to be easy on himself by dodging a hard job? *No.* To be without these feelings would place us beyond temptation. God has not promised to keep us from feeling tempted. He has promised us power to stand.

In the sanctified life there are days when we honestly *feel* as if every evil tendency has been destroyed. We feel no impulse of any kind to be impatient, lazy, or proud. But there are other times when the allure of a wrong choice comes with such power that we can scarcely distinguish the feeling of temptation from the manifestation of carnality. In a moment of weakness or at the height of an unusually fierce assault from Satan we simply do not feel as if all impatience and love of ease have been destroyed.

How shall we reconcile these experiences? Let us in no case depend on our feelings for assurance of full salvation. Let us seek only to be sure that our hearts are perfectly loyal to God. Let us thank Him for sanctifying power when we feel it, and still thank Him when, for a time, we do not feel it. This sanctifying power is of God; He is always there. He is always waiting to show himself strong in our behalf so long as our hearts remain perfect in love toward Him.

> *Sprinkled with atoning blood,*
> *Still to my soul thyself reveal;*
> *Thy mighty working may I feel,*
> *And know that I am one with God.*
> —*Wesley's Hymns*

**July 23**

READ: I Peter 4: 12-13

*Beloved, think it not strange concerning the fiery
trial which is to try you, as though some strange
thing happened unto you* (I Peter 4: 12).

## Temptations Will Come

There is no state of grace this side of heaven which
exempts me from temptation. This is true even after God
has given me the fullness of the Holy Spirit. That is why
Peter exhorts us, "Beloved, think it not strange concerning
the fiery trial which is to try you, as though some strange
thing happened unto you."

In our justifiable enthusiasm for what God has done for
us in the work of entire sanctification, some of our preaching
and testimony leaves the impression that all spiritual battle
is ended when the second blessing is received. But we need
to be on guard at this point. If we are taught either ex-
plicitly or by mistaken inference that carnality is the only
source of the moral conflict, we are headed for trouble.

After we are sanctified we shall still find struggles—
sometimes fierce ones; Peter describes them as fiery trials.
If we do not anticipate some hard fighting, we shall be
thrown into confusion and be tempted to believe that we did
not "get the blessing."

Our text points out that we should not be surprised
at these fiery trials because they are common to all the
children of God. *The Amplified New Testament* puts it:
"Beloved, do not be amazed and bewildered . . . as though
something strange—unusual and alien to you and your
position—were befalling you." Temptations will come to the
sanctified but we have a promise: "God is faithful, who will
not suffer you to be tempted above that ye are able; but will
with the temptation also make a way to escape" (I Corinthians 10: 13).

> *A wonderful Saviour is Jesus, my Lord.*
> *He taketh my burden away.*
> *He holdeth me up, and I shall not be moved.*
> *He giveth me strength as my day.*
> —FANNY J. CROSBY

READ: Matthew 3: 16—4: 11

*Then was Jesus led up of the spirit into the wilderness to be tempted of the devil* (Matthew 4: 1).

## Temptation and Desire

A sincere young woman, seeking to live the sanctified life, asked her pastor: "If I had been sanctified wholly, I certainly wouldn't have felt this way, would I?" Here is a point where the devil often tries to defeat us.

In all genuine temptation we are aware of powerful inner urges. The Bible tells us, "Every man is tempted, when he is drawn away of his own desire" (James 1: 14, Wesley's translation). The question of the distraught soul is, Are these desires of mine a sign that carnality still reigns within? Or are they such experiences of temptation as are consistent with the indwelling Holy Spirit?

It will help us if we remember that Jesus himself was tempted immediately after the Spirit of God descended upon Him. Our Lord was also tempted through the channels of His most insistent desires. He was hungry and was tempted to do the wrong thing to get satisfaction. He wanted men to know the power of God, and was tempted to resort to a selfish display for proof. Because He yearned for the loyalty of men from all kingdoms He was tempted to try a short cut to His goal.

The devil often tempts us through our strong human desires. But in the sanctified heart there is a desire that is greater than any of these. The sanctified man honestly desires to do the whole will of God. We are always safe when we test the reality of our sanctification against this desire, and we are always in danger if we test it against any other.

> *My desire, to be like Jesus;*
> *My desire, to be like Him.*
> *His Spirit fill me, His love o'erwhelm me—*
> *In deed and word, to be like Him.**
> —LILLIAN PLANKENHORN

*© Lillian Plankenhorn. Used by permission.

**July 25**

READ: James 1:12-15

*Blessed is the man that endureth temptation: for when he is tried, he shall receive the crown of life, which the Lord hath promised to them that love him (James 1:12).*

## Only Yielding Is Sin

"We cannot prevent Satan from ringing our doorbell, but we do not need to invite him in to dinner." In dealing with the problem of temptation in the sanctified life Dr. H. Orton Wiley points out in *Christian Theology* that "no temptation or evil suggestion becomes sin . . . until it is tolerated or cherished by the mind." In terms of conscious experience this means that no momentary desire for the wrong is to be considered an evidence of carnality. Furthermore the temptations of the sanctified may be prolonged. I may experience repeated suggestions of evil arising out of normal human nature or from direct satanic attack. James reminds us that God's blessings are for the man who *endures* temptation—not the man who never faces it.

God's Word tells us, "Then desire [any wrong desire] when it has conceived gives birth to sin" (v. 15, R.S.V.). When does a wrong desire conceive? When does it really come to life, and become an occasion of sin in me? Only when I yield in my heart of hearts; only when I reach the point that I would carry out the evil suggestion if opportunity made it possible.

"Blessed is the man that endureth temptation"—because as long as he is enduring he has not yielded. No inner sin is present unless I tolerate and encourage the thought of evil. As long as I am resisting I know that my heart is right toward God and that there is no spirit within me that is contrary to His will.

> *I'll yield not to temptation, for yielding is sin.*
> *Each vict'ry will help me some other to win.*
> *I'll fight faithfully onward, dark passions subdue.*
> *I'll look ever to Jesus; He'll carry me through.*
> —H. R. PALMER (slightly adapted)

READ: James 1: 16-18

*Of his own will he brought us forth by the word of truth that we should be a kind of first fruits of his creatures* (James 1: 18, R.S.V.).

## The Physical Hungers

We saw yesterday that, even though we have been sanctified wholly, our temptations may be fierce and long. We may continually seek to rid our minds of some evil suggestion and yet have that suggestion repeatedly thrust back into consciousness. To draw an illustration from an experience that baffles many sincere young Christians may be helpful.

It is as natural for sex desire and sex thought to thrust themselves into consciousness under normally recurring physical conditions as it is for one to feel hungry and to think about food when the stomach is empty. The one desire is no more evidence of carnality than the other. God made us this way and He did it on purpose "that we should be a kind of first fruits of his creatures."

Dr. Dougan Clark has said, "God does not design to *annihilate* our physical appetites and propensities, but to *sanctify* them. He does not wish to make us anything else than men and women, but He does wish us to be *holy* men and women."

The very nature of the sex instinct and the necessary inhibitions of its normal expression among unmarried young people make of it a recurrent source of temptation. To feel these desires and to have corresponding thoughts enter the mind is no necessary indication of carnality in the soul. However, the holy heart seeks to resist instantly every suggestion of satisfying bodily hungers in ways that are forbidden by the Heavenly Father, whom we love and serve.

### Affirmation for today

*I discipline my body and make it serve me* (I Corinthians 9: 27, *Berkeley Version*).

**July 27**

READ: James 1: 12-18

*Blessed is the man that endureth temptation: for when he is tried, he shall receive the crown of life, which the Lord hath promised to them that love him* (James 1: 12).

## God Has a Purpose

Our text may appropriately be read, "Blessed is the *sanctified man* that endureth temptation." It is not the will of God that any of His children should succumb to the tempter and fall into sin. But it is equally clear that God allows these temptations to come to us (yes, even after we have been sanctified wholly), and He will continue to allow them as long as we live. Jesus reminds us, "In the world ye shall have tribulation" (John 16: 33).

When we are tempted it is not because there is something wrong with us, or with our experience of entire sanctification. It is because something is right! God allows temptation to come, not because He can't prevent it, but because He plans to use it for our good and for His glory. Divine love has good purposes to bring to pass in our lives through testing.

If we look upon our temptations as evidences that God does not care, we fail to trust Him. If we fear that He cannot give us victory over our tests, we shall never become stalwart Christians. We fall into despair over temptations only when we do not see God's purpose in them. When we fret about our trials, and resent them, to that extent we reject God's plan for us to grow strong through testing. If on the contrary we can see God's hand at work in the pressures of the sanctified life, and if we can trust Him to give us victory, we shall be "perfecting holiness in the fear of God." It is for this victory that God has given us the power of the Holy Spirit.

### Prayer for today

*Father in heaven, teach me that temptations are to be faced and not feared. Help me always to remember that You filled me with your Holy Spirit, not to save me from pressure, but to make me strong in the midst of it. Amen.*

READ: I Peter 5: 8-11

*But the God of all grace . . . after that ye have suf-
fered a while, make you perfect, stablish, strengthen,
settle you* (I Peter 5: 10).

## God Wants Me to Be Strong

God's work of entire sanctification is not to exempt us
from the lifelong process of building character but rather to
better equip us for it. The Father did not spare His only
Son from temptation. The Bible tells us, "In all things it
behoved him to be made like unto his brethren . . . he himself
hath suffered being tempted" (Hebrews 2:17-18). If God did
not spare His Son, I dare not ask to be excused. God wants
me to be strong, and I want His will to be done in me.

God's purpose is to allow enough trial to test me to the
limit. But He promises enough grace to prevent me from
breaking at that limit. Does your temptation seem severe?
It always does, or it would not be a temptation. But God has
a purpose in that testing. "After that ye have suffered a
while," He intends to "make you perfect, stablish, strengthen,
settle you."

Our scripture portrays clearly the three persons present
in the temptations of a child of God. There is our "adversary
*the devil,*" who is always seeking to destroy us. There is the
*child of God,* who is to do two things: (1) recognize that his
temptations are the same kind that other Christians have and
(2) resist the devil, standing firm in his faith. Finally, there
is always present with us in every temptation "the *God of
all grace,* who hath called us unto his eternal glory by Christ
Jesus."

**Prayer for today**

*Father in heaven, quickly show me Your face in
every hour of temptation. At an altar of consecration I once said, "Not my will, but thine, be done."
That is still my consecration today. Give me courage
to do the right. Let me know that You are near.
Make me a stronger Christian when You have
brought me past my hour of anguish.*

**July 29**

READ: Philippians 3: 7-12

*I count all things but loss . . . that I may know him, and the power of his resurrection, and the fellowship of his sufferings* (Philippians 3: 8, 10).

## I Want to Be Like Jesus

I do not enjoy temptation or trials but, oh, how I yearn to be like Jesus! I cannot be like Him if I am seeking only "the power of his resurrection." I am most like Him when I am ready also to accept "the fellowship of his sufferings."

We often think of God's grace as enabling us to endure temptations, but can we go further than this? The Bible teaches us that committed Christians can find a source of deep joy even in testings. "Beloved, think it not strange concerning the fiery trial which is to try you, as though some strange thing happened unto you. *But rejoice, inasmuch as ye are partakers of Christ's sufferings*" (I Peter 4: 12-13). When my goal is to be like Jesus, I can rejoice in any experience where I seem to be a little bit like my Lord.

When I am tempted, I can be like Him. He too knew the struggle with evil, but He did not yield to it. He too shrank from the fierce encounter but was ready to accept whatever the Father sent.

Can I really find some joy in the midst of my tests? I can if, more than all else, I want to know Christ's fellowship. I can if, in my tests, I place my hand in His, and walk side by side with Him. I can if with Him I say to the Father, "Not what I will, but what thou wilt" (Mark 14: 36). This is to know what Our Lord knew in the hour of His deepest test. This is to know "the fellowship of his sufferings."

*Be like Jesus, this my song,*
*In the home, and in the throng.*
*Be like Jesus all day long,*
*I would be like Jesus.**

—JAMES ROWE

*© 1940, renewal, The Rodeheaver Co. Used by permission.

READ: II Corinthians 12: 7-10

*He said unto me, My grace is sufficient for thee: for my strength is made perfect in weakness* (II Corinthians 12: 9).

## I Need to Depend on God

Paul was a sanctified Christian. In spite of this fact—or probably *because* of it—he was beset by a strong and recurring temptation. He says this temptation came, not because he was failing God, because God had already done so much for him. Paul called this troublesome thing a thorn in his flesh, and declared it was a messenger of Satan sent to give him a bad time. He prayed earnestly three times for God to deliver him from the attack of Satan. God could have done so, but He did not. Why?

God's answer to Paul's prayer gives us another reason why a Heavenly Father allows the sanctified Christian to be tempted. We need to learn to depend on God. The spiritual life is a personal partnership—a mutual and glad partnership of God's Holy Spirit and my spirit. If God had given to me at the altar enough grace to carry me to the end, I would miss the wonder of the renewed fellowship that I have when I come to Him and am helped and reassured by Him.

God did not remove the thorn, but when it hurt the worst, Paul heard God's voice most clearly. And that voice transformed his day! Is it really good to go our own painless way, seldom feeling our need of God, and hence seldom hearing Him? Paul says *No*—a thousand times no. And in our own dark hours when God's presence becomes most real to us we join in the Apostle's testimony: "Most gladly therefore will I rather glory in my infirmities, that the power of Christ may rest upon me."

### Praise for today

*O my Father, I gladly acknowledge this wonder. It is better to be buffeted and to feel Thy help than never to be battered at all. Thanks for every sanctifying process of Thy Spirit that impels me to lean hard on Thee. Amen.*

**July 31**

READ: I John 3:19-20

*If our heart condemn us, God is greater than our heart, and knoweth all things* (I John 3:20).

## A Defeat Need Not Destroy Us

It is possible for the sanctified person to yield to temptation and thus fall into condemnation. One may be overcome at a weak point in a moment of sudden attack from Satan. This kind of defeat is not a sin of ignorance because, had the Christian thought about it, he would have known his conduct to be wrong. Yet such defeats must be distinguished from willful sin.

A failure of this kind brings condemnation immediately, but such condemnation does not mean that one is immediately a backslider and a practicing sinner. God is not so ready to leave us. The feeling of condemnation is God's reminder to save us, not His notice that He has left us. John tells us, "If our heart condemn us, God is greater than our heart, and knoweth all things." If we are truly repentant, God knows it and deals with us in mercy. If we have been thus defeated we should at once acknowledge our defeat, confess it to God, and ask forgiveness, but never give up our faith.

Probably every sanctified Christian has had need of God's mercy in such situations. Dr. J. A. Huffman writes: "Throughout my Christian life, I have made it a practice to right anything which was wrong, promptly upon discovering it. There have been many blunders on my part; but the blessed Holy Spirit has been faithful in all His dealings with me. In the language of the late Joseph H. Smith, 'I have not slept outside of Canaan since the day that I entered that experience many years ago.'"

### Help for today

*The steps of a good man are ordered by the Lord: and he delighteth in his way. Though he fall, he shall not be utterly cast down: for the Lord upholdeth him with his hand* (Psalms 37:23-24).

READ: I John 3:1-6

*Whosoever abideth in him sinneth not* (I John 3:6).

## In Him Is No Sin

In *Magnificent Obsession*, Lloyd Douglas has Robert Merrick testifying to his grandfather, "I'm tied up to the Major Personality! . . . like a beam of sunshine to the sun! . . . I'll not lose my power unless He loses His!"

The goal of Christian holiness is a life above sin. But our source of power is continual contact with God. "Whosoever abideth in him sinneth not." If we have fallen short of our goal, it is because we have not yet found the full secret of abiding in Him. As I look back, can I locate the point where I ceased to abide in Him and moved across the line into the area of self-dependence?

Perhaps it was only minutes before my sin. I felt a check of the Holy Spirit but I failed to pay attention to Him. At that instant my abiding in Him ended and His promise to keep me from sin ceased to be effective. Perhaps the point of departure was further back and less conscious. I started the day late and in a hurry; I did not make time to let God speak to me from the Bible. I did not take time to tell Him of my love and to feel again the reassurance of His presence as I prayed.

There is no promise to keep me above sin except as I abide in Him. There is no way to abide in Him once and for all time. There is a way to come to Him in a decisive moment of commitment and cleansing. But the commitment of that hour is only the beginning of a life that commits every hour. The faith for cleansing is a faith to be cultivated daily and to be exercised in every hour of need. Full freedom from sin depends upon abiding in Him every conscious moment. "In him is no sin."

> *His will I have joy in fulfilling,*
> *As I'm walking in His sight;*
> *My all to the Blood I am bringing.*
> *It alone can keep me right.*
> —BALLINGTON BOOTH

**August 2**

READ: John 15: 4-6

*If a man abide not in me, he is cast forth as a branch, and is withered* (John 15: 6).

## Even the Sanctified Can Backslide

At times difficulty arises in our walk with God—not over some one wrong act. Rather there is a gradually increasing, almost unnoticed, lack of attention to the spiritual life. Through failure to abide in Christ, we have withered.

It is possible to backslide completely after having been sanctified wholly. Paul warns us to "grieve not the holy Spirit of God" (Ephesians 4: 30). Carelessness can cause the love of God to grow weak in our souls. When love is weakened, disregard is near. When we disregard God, we may next grieve Him away by blighting indifference or by willful rebellion. The Holy Spirit does not remain where He is not made welcome and where His will is rejected.

If perchance after we were sanctified we have become careless of our vows to God, if we have not been as aggressive in the spiritual life as we should have been, what shall we do? Shall we in hours of awakening throw away all of our experience from the past and assume that we are utterly backslidden and are to begin entirely anew?

*No.* Let us not suppose that God throws us over as if we were parties involved in an immature lovers' quarrel. God is not so ready to abandon us. But we must cease to be careless or we shall eventually lose our souls. Let us ask God to forgive our neglect. Let us tarry until we are conscious again of God's approval and the blessing of His presence. Let us draw close and walk hand in hand again.

> *Try again! Why don't you?*
> *Try again! Oh, won't you?*
> *Jesus at your side doth stand*
> *And offers you His aid.*
>
> —HARRY BRIGGS

READ: Luke 11: 11-13

*If ye then, being evil, know how to give good gifts unto your children: how much more shall your heavenly Father give the Holy Spirit to them that ask him?* (Luke 11: 13)

## God Is Loath to Leave Us

We saw yesterday that it is possible to backslide even after we have been sanctified wholly. With this solemn fact before us there is another word that must be said. God is more willing to give us His Holy Spirit than earthly parents are to give good gifts to their children. And God is more loath to take that Gift from us than the best earthly parent would be to take back a present given to a child. Jesus prayed that we might have a Comforter who would abide with us forever.

The Holy Spirit comes to us when we really want Him more than we want anything else in the world. He will remain with us as long as that desire is in our hearts. He will not leave us even though because of human frailty we sometimes act as if we did not love Him supremely. He gives us time to regain spiritual perspective, time to consider our attitudes and actions, time to evaluate them in terms of our consecration. If we deviate from perfect love toward Him, He yet has perfect love for us and will not leave us unless forced out by our willful refusal to respond to that love.

Very rarely then should we allow ourselves to believe that the Holy Spirit has left us after He has once come in His fullness. If we walk in the light as it comes to us, very rarely should it be necessary for us to return to the altar, having given up our faith and abandoned what God has done for us. We are far more prone to abandon God than He is to abandon us.

*Ever present, truest Friend,*
*Ever near, Thine aid to lend,*
*Leave us not to doubt and fear,*
*Groping on in darkness drear.*
—MARCUS M. WELLS

**August 4**

READ: Psalms 25: 1-6

*Unto thee, O Lord, do I lift up my soul. O my God, I trust in thee: let me not be ashamed* (Psalms 25: 1-2).

## It Is Better to Try Again

In my hours of sincere self-examination I ask God to look into my heart to see if there is any wicked way in me. What shall I do when God shows me that sin has again stained my soul? It is better to try to do right, to fail, to repent, and to try again than never to try at all. It is better to believe that God can give me victory over temptation than to believe that sin must always win the victory over me.

My goal and my prayer are for a life above sin. If I have failed, the failure has been in me. At some point I walked away from Christ instead of drawing closer to Him. As I look back, can I recognize the place where I began to draw away? The place where I should have moved closer to Him?

Did I forget that high moment of consecration when I turned my whole life over to God? Did I fail in my full dependence upon divine power? What then shall I do? Give up my goal? Forget my prayer? Deny my faith? *No.* Rather I start again toward my goal. I revive my hope. I reassert my faith. I begin again this moment walking in the sanctifying power of the Holy Spirit.

### Prayer for today

*Do not forsake me, gracious Lord, for trees of deepest root are torn up by the violence of the storm, and lofty, firm mountains are rent asunder by the force of the earthquake. Suffer me not, therefore, gracious Lord, to be tempted above that I am able to bear, for Thou art faithful and good, lest my soul be shamed. I pray not for my flesh, being well aware that it must suffer and die in time, but this alone I ask: Strengthen me in warfare; assist and keep me, make a way for me to escape in temptation; deliver me, and let me not be put to shame, for I put my trust in Thee.*

—MENNO SIMONS, founder of the Mennonites

READ: I John 2:1-3

*If any man sin, we have an advocate with the Father, Jesus Christ the righteous* (I John 2:1).

## Keeping the Experience

In *Free Indeed,* Dean Bertha Munro has given superb counsel to the sanctified Christian who has stumbled.

"It is possible to grieve the Holy Spirit away by disobedience and persistent neglect, and without His presence to lose the seal of our final salvation. But He was not eager to go, and He will gladly return unless we deliberately spurn Him. The enemy's deadliest weapon is the black cloud of discouragement he causes to settle between us and God when we realize our loss.

"If we could pierce the cloud, we should see the Father looking our way. God is concerned when a good man fails. We should see His hand stretched out to lift us up. The image is that of a little boy who has stumbled and fallen but, because he still clutches his father's hand, can be pulled to his feet again. It is possible for the sanctified child of God to slip, but very improbable that he will be satisfied to strain away from the Father's hand and lie in the mud. He has a taste for white raiment and the Father's smile.

"The rule is, Sin not. The safety proviso is, If you sin, remember that your Advocate, Jesus, is praying for you.

"The steps back are simple and direct: Go back to your consecration and build it up; make fresh connections with the Holy Spirit; set your love to work. For in one of these areas your relationship broke down. These are your safety zones."

*He gave His own Son to redeem me,*
*And He'll never forget to keep me.*
—F. A. GRAVES

**August 6**

READ: Romans 8: 35-39

*In all these things we are more than conquerors through him that loved us* (Romans 8:37).

## More than Conquerors Through Him

In *More than Conquerors*. Milton S. Agnew tells the story of Handley Page, well-known British aviator. Page said that his most thrilling experience happened in Arabia. He was in the middle of a long flight over the desert. His plane was an early model with an unpressurized cabin. To his horror he heard a rat gnawing behind him. Unable to leave the wheel, he grew tense speculating on the damage the rat could do by gnawing the insulation off the electric wires and destroying the controls of the plane. What could he do?

"Suddenly," he says, "it occurred to me that a rat is made for low altitudes. I pushed the plane skyward to a height at which the rarefied atmosphere made it difficult to breathe. The gnawing of the rat grew fainter and fainter, and finally stopped altogether. When I reached my destination I examined the plane and found the rat, dead."

The evils which gnaw at the vital lifelines of our spirits cannot survive at the high levels of holy living. It is not God's plan that we should in our own strength frantically try to kill off the evil tendencies which beset us. Rather we are to turn our lives skyward, to rise toward God on wings of prayer, and faith. As we thus bring ourselves into His presence, we discover with glad amazement that the dangers which threatened us have no further power to do us harm.

**Prayer for today**

*Heavenly Father, I turn my face toward Thee. I feel the cleansing power of Thy presence. Center my thoughts on thyself until every temptation that would draw me from Thee is broken and my unfettered spirit is attracted by none but Thee.*

August 7 *12*

READ: I John 3: 2-3

*Beloved, now are we the sons of God, and it doth not yet appear what we shall be* (I John 3: 2).

## Possibilities of Grace

In his stimulating book, *The Meaning of Sanctification*, Charles Ewing Brown has a chapter with the intriguing title "Entire Sanctification as a Bundle of Possibilities." This title points the way to the truth that we are to consider for the next several weeks.

The cleansing which occurs when the Holy Spirit comes in His fullness removes immediately the strain and defeat caused by carnality. But such cleansing and baptism hold promise of even more. Not all that God proposes to do for us through entire sanctification is done in a moment of time. When we are sanctified, the Holy Spirit comes to abide with us and to work His will through us for all the rest of our days of the sanctified life.

As we follow the Holy Spirit we may expect to discover measures of Christian grace in ourselves beyond what we can even now imagine. We are encouraged in God's Word to add to our faith many graces: virtue, knowledge, temperance, patience, godliness, brotherly kindness, and charity. Freed from carnality, indwelt by all the fullness of God himself, what possibilities for growth in grace must lie out before us!

Sheridan Baker, in the introduction to his *Hidden Manna*, relates that soon after he entered the sanctified life he began to turn his attention away from "what had been *done for him*" to what "he now saw *before him.*" We would join him in that vision, for entire sanctification is no closed door; it is rather the open road to God's tomorrow in our lives. Isaiah has called it "The way of holiness."

> *Let me then be always growing,*
> *Never, never standing still;*
> *Listening, learning, better knowing*
> *Thee and Thy most blessed will,*
> *Till I reach Thy holy place,*
> *Daily let me grow in grace.*
>
> —FRANCIS RIDLEY HAVERGAL

**August 8**

READ: Isaiah 35: 8-10

*An highway shall be there, and a way, and it shall be called The way of holiness* (Isaiah 35: 8).

## Holiness Is a Way

"One of the most challenging descriptions of the life of holiness is given by the Old Testament prophet Isaiah in his word picture of 'The way of holiness.' He says some remarkable things about this way. It is a way which runs through the reclaimed desert, part of God's great 'reclamation project' which began with the coming of Christ (vv. 3-7). It is a clean way, for 'the unclean shall not pass over it.' It is a plain way wherein wayfaring men need not err. It is a safe way, for lions and ravenous beasts are excluded. It is a way for the redeemed to walk. It is a joyous way. And it is a homeward way.

"But underlying all of this is the simple yet striking idea that many of us seem to have missed. It is a *way*. Instead of a place to be reached, holiness is a way to be traveled. Rather than our entrance being a termination or an end, it is a starting point. Holiness is not a milestone to be passed, but a growing life to be lived.

"It is appalling to find people who have professed the sanctifying grace of God for years who are less spiritual than they were a week after their initial victory. Prayer holds less victory for them. The Bible is still largely a closed Book. The fellowship of other Christians has little attraction. Public worship is more social than spiritual. Service is more drudgery than delight. They are clean but not keen, religious but not radiant, good but not godly" (W. T. PURKISER).

> *My soul, be on thy guard;*
> *Ten thousand foes arise;*
> *The hosts of sin are pressing hard*
> *To draw thee from the skies.*
> —GEORGE HEATH

READ: Isaiah 35: 8-10

*It shall be called The way of holiness* (Isaiah 35: 8).

## Holiness Is a Way (continued)

Yesterday in our exploration of the way of holiness we saw that some Christians lead dwarfed lives. Their spiritual development stops almost as soon as they are born. "That these things ought not to be, scarcely needs to be said. It is possible that the causes of spiritual atrophy are many. But surely one of the most deadly is the failure to keep in mind at all times that holiness is a way. It is a pilgrimage from here to eternity. There is no place to stop and camp—at least not permanently.

"All normal life is marked by growth. Whenever growth totally stops, death begins. The body and the mind that cease to develop commence to die. And this is true of the spiritual nature. To 'grow in grace, and in the knowledge of our Lord and Saviour Jesus Christ' is not a matter of choice but of necessity.

"But traveling the way of holiness does not just happen. It isn't the aimless wandering of a tramp. It takes effort and purpose to make a journey and to arrive at a desired destination. We must resist the idea that where we are is where we should stay for the rest of our lives. True, it is easier to drift than to travel. It is comforting to camp among familiar scenes, to linger over victories already won. But the call of God's far horizons is upon us, and we must not stay" (W. T. PURKISER).

*O for a heart that is whiter than snow!*
*Then in His grace and His knowledge to grow;*
*Growing like Him who my pattern shall be,*
*Till in His beauty my King I shall see.*

—*Hymns of the Living Faith*

**August 10**

READ: Philippians 3: 7-11

*I count all things but loss for the excellency of the knowledge of Christ Jesus my Lord* (Philippians 3: 8).

## I Press Toward the Mark

The title of Lloyd Douglas' book *Magnificent Obsession* has stirred a restless yearning in thousands who are lured by the God-given pull of an ideal. What was Paul's magnificent obsession? What was the excellency toward which he was pressing? Was it not to be more and more Christlike? Every time the Apostle's thought turned to his Master, the vision of that glorious ideal caught him up in its motivating power.

The clearer our own vision of God's ideal for us, the more earnestly we shall press toward that goal. Here is God's plan for growth in the Christian life. The experience of heart holiness wonderfully undergirds this divine plan for progress.

The sanctified Christian grows in grace more rapidly because he sees more clearly what the will of God is. We are promised, "When he, the Spirit of truth, is come, he will guide you into all truth" (John 16: 13).

The sanctified man strives more earnestly to realize the full will of God in his life because his heart has already been fully devoted to God's will.

Moreover, when we are filled with the Holy Spirit we overcome spiritual weaknesses more readily because we have more of the power of God within. The Bible tells us, "The Spirit also helpeth our infirmities" (Romans 8: 26).

We are sanctified wholly in order that we may more rapidly "grow in grace, and in the knowledge of our Lord and Saviour Jesus Christ" (II Peter 3: 18).

**Testimony for today**

> *When I think of thy ways*
> *I turn my feet to thy testimonies;*
> *I hasten and do not delay*
> *to keep thy commandments.*

> PSALMS 119: 59-60, R.S.V.

234

READ: Philippians 3:12-15

*Reaching forth unto those things which are before ...
Let us therefore, as many as be perfect, be thus
minded* (Philippians 3:13, 15).

## Let Us Be Thus Minded

Is there any place in the Christian life where I can honestly say, I have it made? Perhaps in heaven we may reach some such high plane, but even that is doubtful. How can a static heaven be satisfying to us in whom God has implanted the urge to grow? It is certain that to satisfy our deepest human needs here on earth we must keep always pressing toward goals that are yet beyond us. When yesterday's goals become today's achievements, the Holy Spirit lifts our vision to new heights to be scaled tomorrow.

Those who are entirely sanctified and filled with the Holy Spirit are often most conscious of the distance between their own present exemplification of God's love and the vision of the ultimate possibilities of that love. Within six months of his death our beloved and saintly Dr. J. B. Chapman said publicly, "I sometimes find it hard to be as good a man as I know I ought to be."

To be as good a person as I know I ought to be; to be more sensitive to the leading of the Holy Spirit; to be more generous with the limitations of my fellowmen—here there is reflected a great incompleteness. Here there is wide room for improvement. But this, too, is a part of Christian perfection—if there be within me an urgent desire to move as far and as fast as possible toward God's ideal for me. Paul prays that this sense of incompleteness might be the attitude of all who are deeply spiritual: "Let us therefore, as many as be perfect, be thus minded."

**Thought for today**

*Paul denied perfection as a winner, but he professed perfection as a runner.*—J. PAUL TAYLOR.

August 12

READ: I John 3: 1-3

*We are children of God now, beloved; what we are to be is not apparent yet, but we do know that when he appears we are to be like him* (I John 3: 2, Moffatt).

## We Must Not Surrender to Discouragement

What attitude shall I take when, after I have been sanctified, I discover in myself conduct that is less than Christlike? The normal reaction is discouragement. When I see some glorious manifestation of grace in the life of another sanctified Christian, I am tempted to say, "I guess I must be mistaken about my own experience. If I really had the Holy Spirit in my heart, I too would manifest perfect love that way." But to yield to this temptation is to cripple the faith upon which our continuing sanctification depends. If persisted in, such doubts blight our faith and will destroy our souls.

We are hard pressed at times to know what minimum Christian behavior is consistent with entire sanctificaton. In these hours we must never forget that God's plan is for us to grow in the perfection of Christian conduct. Jesus spoke of the Holy Spirit as the Comforter, or Strengthener. One purpose for His coming is to make us stronger Christians tomorrow than we have been today.

God overlooks much weakness in a spiritual babe—even a sanctified babe! But there is one unchanging principle governing our relationship to God in the life of Christian holiness: He overlooks more shortcomings *in the early sanctified life* than later on. God expects us to grow in grace. We may not be very good representatives now, but if we belong wholly to God today, there is bright prospect for tomorrow.

### Hope for today

*Beloved, now are we the sons of God, and it doth not yet appear what we shall be; but we know that when he shall appear, we shall be like him* (I John 3: 2).

READ: II Corinthians 6:17—7:1

*Having therefore these promises, dearly beloved, let us cleanse ourselves from all filthiness of the flesh and spirit, perfecting holiness in the fear of God* (II Corinthians 7:1).

## We Must Never Be Indifferent

The devil will not allow us to become strong Christians if he can prevent it. If he cannot discourage us over our shortcomings in the sanctified life, he will encourage an attitude of indifference. We are sometimes tempted to shrug our shoulders and say: "Oh, well, everyone is different. That measure of victory is fine for others, but it is not possible for me." With a comic strip character we are tempted to say: "I yam what I yam, and I can't be any yammer!"

Such false resignation in the face of recognized weakness is but poorly masked spiritual indifference. This unconcern is as disastrous as discouragement—and less Christlike. If I am discouraged by my failure it is clear proof that I recognize my conduct as unworthy of a Christian. It is also proof that I am not content to live a life inconsistent with my Christian profession. On the other hand, indifference to any unloving attitude has in it the seeds of carnality. Such indifference quickly cuts the nerve of all growth in holiness. If I do not care about my bad behavior, my spirit is not like the spirit of Jesus. He cared when any man did wrong.

The attitude of the sanctified heart must always be a strong desire for a greater measure of the spirit of Jesus. God's Word exhorts us, "Since we have these promises, beloved, let us cleanse ourselves from every defilement of body and spirit, and make holiness perfect in the fear of God" (R.S.V.).

> *A charge to keep I have,*
> *A God to glorify;*
> *A never-dying soul to save,*
> *And fit it for the sky.*
> —CHARLES WESLEY

**August 14**

READ: Ephesians 5: 22-27

*Wives, submit yourselves unto your own husbands . . .*
*Husbands, love your wives* (Ephesians 5: 22, 25).

## Holiness, Habits, and Health

"It is possible for a habit to be physically amd mentally unhealthful without being morally unholy. But holiness can help us even here. Holiness is fundamental to abundant living.

"There are some men who love their wives; they are Christians and are unquestionably morally sound, yet they have a habit of speaking roughly or discourteously. Such men know that 'their bark is worse than their bite.' But the habit keeps the family in constant hidden fear and insecurity. Such a habit should by all means be broken. Children can be lastingly injured emotionally by it.

"There are wives who love their husbands and would not kill them even if they had a gun and knew how to shoot it. Yet they nag, pick, find fault, and keep their husbands in a state of constant suffering. A cutting tongue hurts! A whining voice hurts; and a picking, critical attitude hurts. The wife is so accustomed to speaking sharply that she does not know she does it. But any habit which makes it impossible for our mates to relax and enjoy us will cost a high price even if it can be accepted in our concept of Christian living.

"Bad habits make us misfits among others, tense in our own systems, and insecure in our living. They are hard to break but they are too costly to live with. Fundamentally, a habit is morally wrong if it injures my health, lessens my usefulness, hurts another, or diminishes my influence for Christ. If I persistently tolerate such a habit, it becomes incompatible with my profession of holiness. I should not give up my profession, but should I not immediately bring up my standard of living?" (MILO ARNOLD.)

**Prayer for today**

*Dear Lord, help me to hear myself as others hear me, and to become the kind of person that You want me to be.*

READ: Romans 8: 12-14

*If ye through the Spirit do mortify the deeds of the body, ye shall live* (Romans 8: 13).

## Through the Spirit

Growth in the life of holiness is not accomplished by sheer determination and human effort. We make progress in the things of God when we yield ourselves to Him. In all spiritual achievement God provides the power; we simply appropriate what He offers.

Paul writes: "If ye *through the Spirit* do mortify the deeds of the body, ye shall live." It is the Holy Spirit who brings the power for spiritual mastery and growth. After we have sought to be sanctified wholly and have received the witness of the Spirit, we may discover weaknesses which we thought would never trouble us again. When we find these character faults, they are to be regarded as areas for spiritual growth. This is as much a part of the Holy Spirit's ministry as is heart cleansing.

What God did not do for us immediately at an altar of prayer may yet be done for us by the indwelling Holy Spirit in answer to specific prayer on a thousand occasions. God expects us to do all within our power to conquer and control these forces of old habits and the pull of temptations which yet remain after we have been sanctified wholly. He expects us to do all within our power—and it is within our power to depend upon Him. The mastery of such weaknesses and the consequent strengthening of the soul is one of the continuing possibilities of grace to be demonstrated in the sanctified life. This, too is achieved through the Spirit—the sanctifying Spirit of God.

*He is able to make me stand.*
*He will hold me by His hand.*
  *He will keep my feet on the King's highway*
  *'Til I reach that land of perfect day.*
*He is able! Hallelujah!*
*He is able to make me stand.*

—AUTHOR UNKNOWN

**August 16**

READ: II Peter 1: 5-11

*And beside this, giving all diligence, add to your faith* (II Peter 1: 5).

## Add to Your Faith

Our text begins, "And beside *this*." Beside what? Beside the precious promises which assure us of our salvation through faith. God has a richness and depth of life in fellowship with himself that is far beyond what we know today. There are as-yet-unrealized possibilities of a godly life open to every sanctified Christian. There are glorious possibilities of going deeper and further with Christ. It is the work of the Holy Spirit to go before us and to lead us into these riches of God's grace. It is a part of the romance of the sanctified life that it is a growing experience. We cannot now know all that God plans to do for us if we will keep fully yielded to the leadership of His Holy Spirit.

God's plan for my growth in grace is by means of the spiritual ideals which He sets before me. When the awareness of some as-yet-unrealized possibility of grace makes me uncomfortable, the Holy Spirit is by this very awareness urging me to take definite steps in that direction.

If in these hours of new light we yield either to indifference or to despair, we shall fail to realize God's purpose for us. These are the times when we add to our faith, if we respond obediently to such enlarged vision. Thus we move toward the fuller realization of one more of the bundle of possibilities that a complete dedication to God opens up to our lives.

**Prayer for today**

*Dear Lord, You have shown me new light today. I shall move forward into the circle of that light. Let me add to my faith. Show me the steps that lead closer to Your perfect will for me. Amen.*

READ: Ephesians 3: 14-21

*For this cause I bow my knees unto the Father of our Lord Jesus Christ . . . that Christ may dwell in your hearts by faith . . . that ye may be filled with all the fulness of God* (Ephesians 3: 14-19).

## Filled with All the Fulness of God

"All the fulness of God"! What a wonder! The sanctified life begins in a moment of glorious crisis, the moment when we give ourselves utterly to God and He gives himself fully to us. But the sanctified life is more than a glorious beginning —it can be a yet more glorious fellowship across the years of our days.

Begun in consecration and faith, it continues in obedience and trust. Started by coming to God with a fundamental soul need, it is deepened and enriched by our continued coming to Him always with all the needs of our lives. Beginning with a heart-warming certainty of the presence of the Holy Spirit, we may continue with this glad assurance of His unseen presence until that day when we shall see God face to face.

May the writer and the reader join the Apostle Paul in this prayer, for each other, and for every true child of God? "For this cause I bow my knees unto the Father of our Lord Jesus Christ, of whom the whole family in heaven and earth is named, that he would grant you, according to the riches of his glory, to be strengthened with might by his Spirit in the inner man; that Christ may dwell in your hearts by faith; that ye, being rooted and grounded in love, may be able to comprehend with all saints what is the breadth, and length, and depth, and height; and to know the love of Christ, which passeth knowledge, that ye might be filled with all the fulness of God" (Ephesians 3: 14-19). Amen.

*There is a place of full release,*
*Near to the heart of God;*
*A place where all is joy and peace,*
*Near to the heart of God.*
—C. B. McAfee

**August 18**

READ: Romans 6: 17-22

*Now being made free from sin, and become servants to God, ye have your fruit unto holiness, and the end everlasting life* (Romans 6: 22).

## Fruit unto Holiness

As a sanctified Christian what do I most want God to do for my own spirit? Now? At this point in my spiritual pilgrimage? What today is my own greatest spiritual need? What fruit of the Spirit seems least developed in my life?

It is the purpose of God that this specific victory shall be the next of the many unfolding possibilities of grace which He would yet make known to me. Sometimes such victories can be immediate and dramatic. In answer to earnest prayer and faith, God can alter an attitude or break the chains of habit. But if this victory does not come suddenly it may nevertheless be a real victory in the sanctified life. Partial success in spiritual effort is not failure. If I am stronger today than I was a year ago—that is progress. If I am stronger next year than I am now—that is victory.

Is not God, by these experiences, trying to show us that the work of the Holy Spirit is twofold in our lives? He does for us some things in a moment of time: He eradicates the carnal mind and fills the soul with himself. But He has another ministry to perform for us across the years: He teaches us how to make our conduct ever more consistent with the perfect love which He has placed within the soul. God can in time, and through grace and discipline, correct many human frailties and add many spiritual graces which He does not impart at a public altar.

### Praise for today

*Now unto him that is able to do exceeding abundantly above all that we ask or think, according to the power that worketh in us, unto him be glory in the church by Christ Jesus throughout all ages, world without end. Amen* (Ephesians 3: 20-21).

READ: Galatians 2:11-14

*Despise not the chastening of the Lord . . . for whom the Lord loveth he correcteth* (Proverbs 3:11-12).

## When I Have Been Criticized

In our scripture for today "Peter had failed to be true to his vision, and Paul administered rebuke. That Peter received his reproof in the right spirit may be inferred from his second epistle. Here Peter refers to Paul's epistles 'in which are some things hard to be understood.' Peter's loyalty to the brother who talks over his head is clearly evident when he says of these same difficult writings that the 'unlearned and unstable wrest [them], as they do also the other Scriptures, unto their own destruction.' There is not a trace here of bitterness for a past rebuke.

"Brothers in the faith ought to hold one another up to their best. For this the word of reproof given in love and meekness is necessary. With it goes the necessity of a deep identification with Christ that will enable us to take a rebuke with patience, meekness, and without bitterness.

"But what if the rebuke is unjust or given with censoriousness? First of all, remember that we never have anything to lose by making such a thrust the occasion of deep heart-searching. If it is false we have lost nothing. If there is any truth in it and we mend the matter, we have gained. If we either vocally or in our minds fly instantly to defense and marshal arguments against a rebuke, we lose great benefit. Let the searching take place first. And mark you, let it be a searching of heart for things needing to be made right rather than a searching for bits of goodness with which to offset the rebuke or to prove it unjust, and certainly rather than a searching for evil in the person who administered the rebuke so that we can justify ourselves 'tit for tat.' Rebuke is the occasion for one of the deepest testings of the reality of our surrender. To learn to take it is to grow in grace" (*The Spirit of Holiness*, Everett Lewis Cattell).

**August 20**

READ: Romans 14:11-13

*Let us not therefore judge one another any more: but judge this rather, that no man put a stumblingblock or an occasion to fall in his brother's way* (Romans 14: 13).

## Conquering Criticism

"A missionary, who had precipitated an ugly situation by a certain speech, told me, when I asked whether he really felt led to make that speech: 'No. I felt I must say it quickly for fear I would be checked before I got it said.' That was more honest than most of us care to be, but how often has that been our experience?

"An infinite amount of trouble and misunderstanding among Christians arises out of this persistent temptation to judge others, imputing motives which we have no right to impute. It is true that we are to exercise righteous judgment. The critical faculty is a part of the equipment God has given us. But here is where a legitimate God-given quality can become the agent of self.

"It has not yet dawned in the minds of many Christians that pride of opinion is just as damning and must be dealt with just as decisively as any other sin. Of course the answer always is, 'But I'm right!' That is the way we always feel about our judgments. But suppose two sanctified people hold opposite views. Each feels the other is wrong. Actually both are wrong if there is not a disposition to yield! So I must grow in grace. I must stop passing judgment on whether my brother is sanctified when he wears things I cannot wear without pride, or speaks more explosively than I would let myself under provocation, or seems too sensitive about the criticisms I have given for his good. I just do not know whether he has crossed his line in these matters or not, and he is not judged before God by my line" (*The Spirit of Holiness,* by Everett Lewis Cattell).

### Questions for today

*Is my point of criticism necessary? Is it kind? Have I prayed about it?*

READ: Luke 10: 25-28

*Thou shalt love the Lord thy God . . . with all thy mind* (Luke 10: 27).

## What Are My Habitual Thoughts?

I was typing the sentence, "Holy life is to worship God by pouring out the heart in prayer, praise, and giving thanks." In the last word I made a mistake and typed an *i* for an *a*. Instead of "giving thanks" the phrase came out "giving thinks." It was not a bad mistake! We do worship God by giving thought to our Christian lives.

What does it mean to love God with all my mind? Is it not to cultivate the right thoughts? Thoughts dedicated to God? Aimed at goodness? Motivated by Christian love? Thinking about how to do my daily task in God's way? Concerned with the work of God's kingdom?

It is a sobering test, but a fair one to apply: Does this thought glorify Jesus? In His life here on earth would He have entertained it? When my answer is *No*, the thought must go.

Loving God with all my mind is to shut out the unworthy. But it is more. Does this kind of devotion to God say something also about mere time-killing thoughts? Too much television trivia and too little attention to God? But even this is still negative.

Do I love God with the constructive power of my intellect? Does an appreciable amount of my thought center on what God wants to do in me? Am I trying to understand and make plans for my spiritual growth toward His likeness? How much time do I spend wrestling in thought with the concerns of the Kingdom? The Bible tells us, "Those who live according to the Spirit set their minds on the things of the Spirit" (Romans 8: 5, R.S.V.).

### Prayer for today

*Probe me today, O God, and help me to increase the spiritual content of my thought life. In Jesus' name I ask it. Amen.*

**August 22**

READ: I Corinthians 6: 12, 19-20

*Everything [morally right] is permissible to me—
allowable and lawful; but not all things are helpful
—good for me to do, expedient and profitable when
considered with other things* (I Corinthians 6: 12,
A.N.T.).

## Sanctified Leisure Time

Time is a sacred trust. The wise use of it is a sincere
concern of those who seek to consecrate all of life to God.
Especially is this true of leisure, for leisure is time peculiarly
our own. Time spent in earning a living is determined largely
by the demands of our occupation. Time given to eating and
sleeping is controlled by the requirements of the body. But
how we use our leisure is strictly our responsibility. In this
sense it is the most ethically important kind of time that we
have.

What kind of free time schedule is God's kind of schedule
for me? We are helped with our answer to this question
when we recall that holiness means *wholeness*. God is concerned with every part of life and so He wants me to be concerned with all of it—physical, mental, social, and spiritual.
The body needs rest and a change of activity; does my leisure
provide it? The effective mind must be fed with a variety of
interests; does my free time provide mental re-creation or
wreck-creation? Wholesome human life requires enriching
social contacts; do I schedule some hours of sharing myself
with others? The human spirit needs ever-recurring periods
spent in the presence of God; is there in my schedule some
unhurried time for talking to Him? for listening to God?
for seeking to know His will for me as revealed in the Bible?

When I consecrated my all to God I gave Him both
vocation and vacation. My free time was set apart to be
managed under the guidance of the Holy Spirit.

### Affirmation for today

*I will this day prayerfully examine my leisure-
time schedule to see how well it reflects my consecration to the whole will of God.*

READ: Philippians 4:10-13

*I can do all things through Christ which strengthen-
eth me* (Philippians 4:13).

## I Can Do All Things Through Christ

Does God offer a man power to keep on going when he
feels like quitting? That is a high claim, but holiness enables
us to walk in high country! Paul shows us the power available.
He was in jail when he would have preferred to be free; he had
to write a letter when he would rather have gone to visit the
church at Philippi.

But Paul had found the power he needed. "I have learned,
in whatsoever state I am, therewith to be content. I know
both how to be abased, and I know how to abound: every
where and in all things I am instructed both to be full and to
be hungry, both to abound and to suffer need. I can do all
things through Christ which strengtheneth me."

Where did Paul learn these lessons of living above the
disappointments and frustrations of life? He learned them
where we may learn them—from the Holy Spirit, who reminds us of the example of our Lord. It was Jesus who faced
life's darkest hour and prayed, "O my Father, if it be possible,
let this cup pass from me: nevertheless not as I will, but as
thou wilt" (Matthew 26:39). It was Jesus who said, "But the
Comforter, which is the Holy Ghost, whom the Father will
send in my name, he shall teach you all things, and bring all
things to your remembrance, whatsoever I have said unto
you" (John 14:26).

This strength that comes from God is not sheer endurance.
To endure is better than to collapse. But one can endure
while at the same time being discouraged, resigned to circumstances, surrendering life's high goals, and living inef-
fectively. The power of God is better than that.

### Prayer for today

*My Father, today I accept Thy power not only
to carry my burden but also to know the joy that
Thou dost give in spite of burdens. Help me to grow
in this grace also.*

**August 24**

READ: Acts 1: 7-9

*But ye shall receive power, after that the Holy Ghost
is come upon you: and ye shall be witnesses unto me*
(Acts 1: 8).

## Pentecost as a Preparation for Service

We have seen that entire sanctification makes us better
persons and prepares us for heaven. But that is not all.
"Believers are not sanctified wholly simply for security in
the next world, but also for service in this world. Full salvation is not a dead-end street, stopping at the door of the
sanctified man's home. It is not a house where he lives,
but a highway where he travels" (J. Paul Taylor). Jesus
promises us the gift of the Holy Spirit to prepare us for our
share in His work; "But ye shall receive power, after that
the Holy Ghost is come upon you: and ye shall be witnesses
unto me." Entire sanctification brings a bundle of possibilities for Christian service as well as an exhaustless grace
for holy living.

This ministry of entire sanctification as a preparation for
Christian service was indicated by Paul when he wrote to
Timothy, "If a man therefore purge himself from these, he
shall be a vessel unto honour, sanctified, and meet for the
master's use, and prepared unto every good work" (II Timothy 2: 21).

From all of us who are true Christians, God expects a
portion of our income, a part of our time, and a measure of
our thought and planning to be given for the furtherance
of His work in the world. Christian life begins at Calvary,
but effective service begins at Pentecost.

Is my consecration such that God can call on me for
some service today? Does the Holy Spirit so fill my spirit
that His concerns are also my concerns? Is the song writer's
prayer my sincere prayer also?

> *Bless me, Lord, and make me a blessing;*
> *I'll gladly Thy message convey.*
> *Use me to help some poor needy soul,*
> *And make me a blessing today.*
>
> —J. H. ZELLEY

READ: Acts 2:46-47

*Go ye into all the world, and preach the gospel to
every creature* (Mark 16:15).

## Service for a Sanctified Layman

Because God has not called me to be a preacher, do I
count myself out of His active service? Do I think that only
these especially called persons are included in the Great
Commission? This was never the purpose of our Lord. Our
scripture reading for today tells of the activity of the whole
Church—preachers and lay people—upon whom the Holy
Spirit had been outpoured. "And all that believed were together . . . And they, continuing daily with one accord [were]
in the temple, and breaking bread from house to house . . .
praising God, and having favour with all the people."

The preachers were busy preaching; lay members attended services and testified to their neighbors. These Spirit-
filled Christians were all busy doing the things that the Lord
had told them to do. They stirred the community for righteousness until "the Lord added to the church daily such as
should be saved."

If my sanctified life is to bring me increasing satisfaction
I must find some place of regular service for my Lord. Do I
have a place within the church where I can do something for
Christ? I cannot do everything, but by God's help I can do
something.

The Sunday school needs teachers; young people need
guides in their weekly services. Children and teen-agers need
concerned Christian leaders in weekday activities. There are
cars to be driven to bring folk to the house of God. There are
carpenters' jobs and decorating tasks to improve the building
and equipment of the church. There are shut-ins to be visited
and neighbors to be invited to God's house.

God has given me the power to do something for Him.
Am I doing what I could be doing for the Lord, whom I
love?

### Affirmation for today

*I will, by God's help, spend some time this week
or offer to give some time for the work of my church.*

**August 26**

READ: Acts 6:1-8

*Then Philip went down to the city of Samaria, and preached Christ unto them* (Acts 8:5).

## More Service for Sanctified Laymen

Is God's provision for effective Christian witness limited to preachers? Our scripture reading for today answers a resounding *No*.

Stephen, who was so effective in testimony, and Philip, who was used of God to bring a revival to Samaria, were both laymen. They had not been called to preach; in fact the apostles had assigned them to lay activities because they were not preachers. But these men were sanctified laymen. They felt they must have some part in Christian service. They did their share, along with the other five men, in caring for the Grecian widows of the Church, but all the while they gave clear testimony to the work of God in their souls.

We are given a share in spreading the good news, not because we have been called to preach, but because we have been called out of sin; not because we have been given a place in the pulpit, but because we have been given the power of the Holy Spirit. The radiance of the sanctified life is maintained as we share it with others.

I may not be a Stephen or a Philip but God has need of me in the task of reaching my acquaintances with the gospel message. The Bible tells us, "In a great house there are articles not only of gold and silver, but also of wood and of earthenware; and some are for honourable, and others for common use" (II Timothy 2:20, Weymouth). As a Christian, I do not try to tell God how He must use me. I only ask that He fill me with himself, and use me where I can help.

*If Thou hast any errand, Lord,*
*Send me and I'll obey.*
*Use me in any way Thou wilt,*
*And make me a blessing today.*
—J. H. ZELLEY

READ: Matthew 16: 21-23

*The God of our Lord Jesus Christ . . . give unto you the spirit of wisdom . . . the eyes of your understanding being enlightened* (Ephesians 1: 17-18).

## Clarified Vision

How does entire sanctification fit us for more effective Christian service? One answer is that the man who is filled with the Holy Spirit sees more clearly the nature of God's work. The closer we draw to Him, the more nearly our vision and our concerns become like God's own.

One of the saddest chapters in the earthly life of Jesus was the failure of His followers to share His vision. When He began to tell them how He must suffer to accomplish God's will, Peter challenged the Master: "Be it far from thee, Lord: this shall not be unto thee." In response Jesus said: "Out of my way, Satan! . . . you stand right in my path, Peter, when you look at things from man's point of view and not from God's" (Matthew 16: 23, Phillips).

How different was Peter's vision after Pentecost! He could now see that God might use even suffering to accomplish His purposes: "Therefore let those who suffer according to God's will do right and entrust their souls to a faithful creator" (I Peter 4: 19, R.S.V.).

Only when the Christian has been sanctified wholly does he have God's full preparation for service. Only then do we begin to see clearly the purposes and methods of God. When we have had the eyes of our understanding enlightened by the power of the Holy Spirit, we no longer challenge our Lord's guidance. We accept His way in full confidence that it is right. With a Spirit-filled Peter, our Spirit-filled hearts gladly sing, "To him be glory and dominion for ever and ever. Amen" (I Peter 5: 11).

> *Silently now I wait for Thee,*
> *Ready, my God, Thy will to see.*
> *Open my eyes, illumine me,*
> *Spirit divine!*
> —CHARLES H. SCOTT

**August 28**

READ: Acts 8: 26-40

*The Spirit said unto Philip, Go near, and join thyself to this chariot. And Philip ran thither to him* (Acts 8: 29-30).

## Ready Obedience

A saintly little lady nearly eighty years of age testified in prayer meeting: "I've learned that when God tells me to do something, I have to go and do it right away." Here is the kind of response that God wants from every one of His children.

The sanctified man renders better Christian service because all of his powers are fully dedicated to God. When we make our consecration vows we say:

> *"I'll go where You want me to go, dear Lord,*
> *Over mountain, or plain, or sea;*
> *I'll say what You want me to say, dear Lord;*
> *I'll be what You want me to be."*

With such a consecration, when God has some bit of work to be done, He can call on us, knowing that we will obey. There will be no debating of the issues after we have said, "Thy will shall be my will." There is no shirking of duty when we have given our talents to God to be used as He might need them. In the sanctified heart there is a readiness to put aside our own plans when the Holy Spirit whispers that He has need of an hour or two of our time.

God's work is always in trouble when He must try to get it done with half-committed Christians. The risk is too great that such persons will neglect or say *No* to some prompting of the Spirit. Does God have in me a good service risk? I want to be that kind of Christian.

> *Open my mind, that I may read*
> *More of Thy love in word and deed.*
> *What shall I fear while yet Thou dost lead?*
> *Only for light from Thee I plead.*
> —CHARLES H. SCOTT

READ: Acts 4: 29-31

*And when they had prayed . . . they were all filled with the Holy Ghost, and they spake the word of God with boldness* (Acts 4: 31).

## Courage for Service

Every Christian needs to know something of the experience of these early Spirit-filled men and women. Every Christian needs to discover courage for witnessing—the courage that comes through the work of the Holy Spirit in us.

Uncle Bud Robinson used to tell of holding a meeting in a large church of 788 members. Of these only 8 could be counted on to lead in prayer. One of the 8 was a timid little lady who had to be notified a day in advance if she was to be called on. In the meeting she was sanctified wholly and the next night testified on the street, attracting such a crowd that traffic was blocked!

Sometimes the crisis experience of entire sanctification brings this immediate release from old fears. The Christian at once launches into a life of radiant activity. Because this happens we may think holiness of heart ought automatically to make every Christian a courageous and effective witness immediately. But this is not true.

Courageous Christian service, like maturity in Christian graces, is most often a result of growth after entire sanctification. T. M. Anderson writes: "Sanctification does not rid all persons of a timid and shy spirit. They may be persons who are naturally timid and retiring in disposition. It is constitutional with them, and not moral lack. No seeking at an altar will overcome it. *Yet this robber of the saints must be overcome.*"

Do I want this thief of my spiritual effectiveness conquered? He can be, when I join earnestly in the prayer of these early Christians.

### Prayer for today

*And now, Lord . . . grant unto thy servants, that with all boldness they may speak thy word* (Acts 4: 29).

**August 30**

READ: Acts 4: 31, 33

*They were all filled with the Holy Ghost, and they spake the word of God with boldness* (Acts 4: 31).

## Courage to Witness

What may I expect the Holy Spirit to do for me when I am afraid to witness for Jesus? What is God's will for me at this point? The Bible replies: "God hath not given us the spirit of fear; but of power, and of love, and of a sound mind. Be not thou therefore ashamed of the testimony of our Lord" (II Timothy 1: 7-8).

On the eve of the Crucifixion, Peter was so fearful that he denied his Lord. In Gethsemane, John was among those who "forsook him, and fled." But only a few weeks later, those who heard the preaching of these men marveled "when they saw the boldness of Peter and John" (Acts 4: 13). What had happened to them? Luke answers the question: "Then Peter, filled with the Holy Ghost, said unto them . . ." (4: 8). It was after this sermon that Peter and John were threatened by the rulers and specifically warned to testify no more. But they, with others, went to prayer. "And when they had prayed, the place was shaken where they were assembled together; and they were all filled with the Holy Ghost, and they spake the word of God with boldness."

If we are not sanctified and lack courage to speak for Christ, we may expect the baptism with the Holy Ghost to give us greater boldness. If we have been sanctified wholly and still feel timid about witnessing, the Holy Spirit will give us courage in answer to our specific prayer.

> Oh, use me, Lord, use even me
> Just as Thou wilt, and when, and where,
> Until Thy blessed face I see,
> Thy rest, Thy joy, Thy glory share!
>
> —*The Salvation Army Tune Book*

READ: Ephesians 6: 18-20

*Grant unto thy servants, that with all boldness they may speak thy word* (Acts 4: 29).

## Power Through Courage

Miss —— was a sanctified young woman. She knew that Christ wanted her to be a witness for Him, but she was timid. As she left on her assignment, tears of fright were in her eyes. She said to her pastor: "I'm scared to death, but this is what I was saved to do, and I'm going to do it!" God gave her power as she exercised her courage.

When we have been saved from our sins and sanctified wholly, there is a natural impulse to share our good news with others. But that first impulse alone is not enough to keep us witnessing for Christ. After the Day of Pentecost there were circumstances that threatened to silence even the 120 who had been filled with the Holy Spirit. But they knew what their Lord had asked them to do. With determination they resolved to witness for Christ. They prayed, "Grant unto thy servants, that with all boldness they may speak thy word." God answered that prayer. They felt anew the power of the Holy Spirit "and they spake the word of God with boldness" (Acts 4: 31).

Dr. Harold Reed tells of a personal covenant that opened channels for added power to witness. He says: "After receiving the Holy Spirit in my late teens, I made a promise to God that I would give my personal testimony to anyone who spent as much as one half-day with me in work, in travel, or any other association. This promise has been kept with few exceptions across several decades. As a result I have had opportunity to lead a number into the experience of salvation."

### Affirmation for today

*I will, by God's help, be courageous and give my witness for Christ.*

**September 1**

READ: Matthew 9:35-38

*He was moved with compassion on them* (Matthew 9:36).

## Love for Souls

Jesus said when the Holy Spirit came to a Christian's life the Spirit would not speak of himself but would show us the things of Christ. Our scripture for today shows us our Lord's deepest concern. It was for the souls of men. "When he saw the multitudes, he was moved with compassion on them, because they fainted, and were scattered abroad, as sheep having no shepherd" (Matthew 9:36). When we have been filled with the Holy Spirit, we become more like Jesus in this respect also.

The Holy Spirit gave this concern for the souls of men to Catherine Booth. Speaking of a meeting which she had addressed at Southsea, she said: "O! how I yearned over them! I felt as if it would be a small thing to die there and then if that would have brought them to Jesus."

Does the baptism with the Holy Spirit always give me immediately this all-consuming passion for souls? No, but I cannot draw close to Christ without beginning to feel it. In *The Way of Holiness*, Samuel Logan Brengle writes: "Holiness increases this desire and makes it burn with a quenchless flame. The zeal of other people blazes up, burns low, and often dies out, but the zeal of a man with a clean heart, full of the Holy Ghost, increases year by year. . . . Others do not grieve if souls are not saved, but he feels that he must see souls saved or die. . . . And this zeal for the salvation and sanctification of men leads him to do something to reach them. . . . He finds that, as he follows the Spirit, the Lord fills his mouth with truth and gives him something to say."

**Truth for today**

*"It is certain that God can use us more in the salvation of men the higher and holier our lives are. Those who will not give themselves* UTTERLY *will never be able to set others free."*

READ: Acts 8: 5-8, 26-40

*And the angel of the Lord spake unto Philip, saying, Arise, and go toward the south . . . And he arose and went (Acts 8: 26-27).*

## Power for Increasing Service

The power of the Holy Spirit is not all given to me at an altar of prayer. God has planned that my usefulness in the sanctified life should be an ever-enlarging experience.

Philip went down to Samaria without any special revelation from God (Acts 8: 5). While he was busy in this part of God's work an angel came to open a new door (8: 26). As Philip obeyed this guidance, the Spirit himself led him on to yet new opportunities (8: 29), and finally "the Spirit of the Lord caught away Philip" for some new Christian service (8: 39-40).

As a sanctified Christian, am I willing to do the humblest bit of service, if only I can see that it will help God's work along? As we busy ourselves with such service, God will open new and larger opportunities to us. As I reflect upon my consecration I am moved to say again:

*"If Thou hast any errand, Lord,*
*Send me, and I'll obey.*
*Use me in any way Thou wilt,*
*And make me a blessing today."*
—J. H. ZELLEY

No act of worship draws us so close to God as the endeavor to share in His work.

### Prayer for today

*Lord Jesus, I would know the fellowship of Thy work. Show me some small task today and I shall do it. Lead me to another service tomorrow, and I shall follow Thee. "Thy kingdom come. Thy will be done in earth, as it is in heaven." Amen.*

**September 3**

READ: Romans 12:1-2, 6-8

*Who then is willing to consecrate his service this day unto the Lord?* (I Chronicles 29:5)

## Sanctified to Win Another

Can God use me to lead a friend to Jesus? This is the question we are to ask ourselves each day this week. The answer is *Yes* but it is always a conditional Yes—Yes, if I am a sanctified Christian. Yes, if my life is still consecrated, still set apart to serve Christ.

Have I somewhere at an altar of prayer made a full consecration to God? Is my life now fully surrendered to Christ? Is my deepest desire to serve Him and to be used by Him? Do I know the Saviour so well and love Him so much that I want to tell someone else about Him? Am I completely dedicated to see happen in the lives of my friends what Christ most wants to happen there?

Our scripture reminds us that God has given us different gifts and opportunities for reaching others, but dedication to the task is required of us all. Our practical service must be given from warm hearts; the teacher is to teach devotedly; the exhorter must mean it; our offerings are to be given freely and gladly; and our kindnesses are to spring from hearts of love. If these be true of us, then Christ is using us and will use us to make someone else hungry to know Him.

"Who then is willing to consecrate his service *this day* unto the Lord?"

But the question of our text is specific: Am I dedicated to doing something about it today? Will there be some time for intercessory prayer? Some deed of helpfulness? Some word of witness for my Lord? I resolve that it shall be so.

> *Open my mouth and let me bear*
> *Gladly the warm truth ev'rywhere;*
> *Open my heart and let me prepare*
> *Love with Thy children thus to share.*
> —CHARLES H. SCOTT

READ: John 17: 15-21

*As thou hast sent me into the world, even so have I also sent them into the world* (John 17: 18).

## Give Me the Spirit of Jesus

Can God use me to lead a friend to Jesus? Yes, if I have in me the spirit of Jesus—if I see things as He saw them and if I am stirred by the facts that stirred Him. Our Lord was persuaded that it was worth giving His life to save a lost man—and He gave it. That was Jesus' sense of mission. Is it not a similar sense of urgency that He looks for in us after we have given ourselves fully to Him?

In the Garden of Gethsemane, on the eve of the Crucifixion, Jesus prayed for us. What was the burden of His prayer? He prayed that we might remain here to help Him accomplish the work for which He was giving His life. Will we sincerely open our hearts to the implications of His intercession for us? "I pray not that thou shouldest take them out of the world. . . . As thou hast sent me into the world, even so have I also sent them into the world . . . that the world may believe that thou hast sent me."

That is the mind of Christ. It was for this that Paul prayed when he wrote, "Let this mind be in you, which was also in Christ Jesus" (Philippians 2: 5). It is for this deeper identification with Christ that we offer our prayer today.

### Self-dedication

*We bind unto ourselves today, Thee our God; Thy power to hold us, Thy hand to guide us, Thine eye to watch us, Thine ear to hear us, Thy wisdom to teach us, Thy Word to give us speech, Thy presence to defend us; this day and every day; in the Name of the Blessed Trinity Father, Son, and Holy Ghost; unto whom be the Kingdom and the Power, and the Glory, for ever and ever.*—ST. PATRICK.

**September 5**

READ: John 4: 31-38

*Say not ye, There are yet four months, and then cometh harvest? behold, I say unto you, Lift up your eyes, and look on the fields; for they are white already to harvest* (John 4: 35).

## The Time Is Now

Can God use me to lead a friend to Jesus? Yes, if I will try, and if through the encouragement and help of the Holy Spirit I keep on trying even when I have not succeeded.

The Holy Spirit dwelling in us will show us how to do God's work if we will listen to His counsel. Is not our most frequent source of failure simply that we have put it off? Jesus' first disciples said, It is four months until harvest-time. Do we not too often listen to the enemy when he says, Later will be better? But hear the Master: "The fields . . . are . . . already to harvest." Jesus declares, The time is *now*— always now. If we try to win a soul, our spirits will rejoice, and men will be brought to Christ, for "he that reapeth . . . gathereth fruit unto eternal life."

But soul winning often takes time. If it takes God a year to produce a harvest of winter wheat, shall we not be patient with the laws of spiritual sowing and reaping? Sometimes we joyfully reap where another has sowed; shall we not, therefore, gladly sow that another may reap? The man who runs the drill expects a harvest as truly as he who takes the combine to the field.

Be it sowing or reaping, I shall try to influence someone toward Jesus this week. I take this word from God as my promise: "He that goeth forth and weepeth, bearing precious seed, shall doubtless come again with rejoicing, bringing his sheaves with him" (Psalms 126: 6).

**Truth for today**

*When we try to work with God we always succeed better than we know.*

READ: Luke 15: 4-7

*What man of you having an hundred sheep, if he lose one of them, doth not leave the ninety and nine in the wilderness, and go after that which is lost, until he find it?* (Luke 15: 4)

## Go After That Which Is Lost

At the visitation center in our church I sometimes see a little printed reminder. The Holy Spirit puts me under conviction each time it confronts me. It is this: "Most men who are lost, are lost because no one planned to win them." Can God use me to lead a friend to Jesus? Yes, if I care enough and will dare enough. Jesus gave the parable of the lost sheep to show us the essential qualifications of the soul winner. They are two—knowledge and action.

Unsaved men and women are lost. I say it—but do I believe it? Yes, I believe it—but do I *really* believe it? I think that I really believe it, but am I making any plans to win the unsaved?

The shepherd knew that a lost sheep was in desperate danger. That knowledge galvanized him into action. He laid aside 99 per cent of his usual duties to concentrate upon the most important need of the hour. When a soul is lost, is anything more important than showing him the way to Christ?

The first problem of soul winning is the soul winner. How much of Christ do I have to share? How deeply am I concerned? How responsive will I be to the prompting of the Holy Spirit today? When the shepherd knew that his sheep was missing, he went "after that which was lost," until he found it. Do I know of a lost friend? Have I been concerned enough to lay aside some other less important things to go after him?

> *Teacher Divine, use me, I ask!*
> *Grant to me strength for my sacred task.*
> *Thy Spirit move me, Lord, I pray;*
> *Help me to win some soul today.**

—KATHRYN B. PECK

*© 1960 by Lillenas Publishing Company. All rights reserved.

**September 7**

READ: Ephesians 3: 14-21

*For this cause I bow my knees unto the Father . . .*
*that ye might be filled with all the fulness of God*
(Ephesians 3: 14, 19).

## God Is Able

Can God use me to win a friend to Jesus and to lead him on into entire sanctification? Yes, if I sincerely believe that Christ can do as much for my friend as He has done for me.

I shall be best prepared to go to my friend when I have meditated long enough upon the wonder of what God has done for my own life. How deep is the peace that comes from knowing my sins are forgiven? What sorrows have I been spared by inviting Christ to guide my choices? What heartaches, caused by old sins, have been healed by forgiveness and restoration? What tension and turmoil have been removed by God's sanctifying power? What inner strength for difficult days has come to me through the presence of the Holy Spirit?

It was the wonder of God's blessing upon a human life that lifted Paul's spirit. In the glow of that realization he could pray for others: "That Christ may dwell in your hearts by faith; that ye, being rooted and grounded in love, may be able to comprehend with all saints what is the breadth, and length, and depth, and height; and to know the love of Christ, which passeth knowledge, that ye might be filled with all the fulness of God."

Do I, today, sense again something of this ministry of God to my own spirit? And do I believe that Christ can do for my friend what He has done for me? If I do, I shall scarcely be able to wait to tell him:

> *I have a peace; it is calm as a river—*
> *A peace that the friends of this world never knew.*
> *My Saviour alone is its Author and Giver,*
> *And, oh, could I know it was given to you!*
> —S. O'MALEY CLUFF

READ: Acts 4:20, 29, 31

*It is God which worketh in you both to will and to do of his good pleasure* (Philippians 2:13).

## The Spirit-filled Life

Can God use me to win a friend to Jesus? Yes, if I will let Him prepare me for the task. Before our Lord sent His first followers out to win others He commanded them, "Tarry ye in the city of Jerusalem, until ye be endued with power from on high" (Luke 24:49). But even a second trip to the altar and being sanctified wholly is not all the preparation that I need to win another to Christ. Before these early sanctified Christians "spake the word of God with boldness," they offered a special prayer for courage. As a result of their prayer they were filled to overflowing with a new outpouring of the Holy Spirit. The preparation for doing God's work has not been changed. Have I waited in the presence of God, earnestly desiring and confidently expecting to be filled afresh with the Holy Spirit?

Soul winning is God's work, and God's work can best be done by us when we are most like Him. When I am filled with God's Spirit, He helps me to see my friend's need, He gives me courage to speak, and guides me in what to say. When He prompts me to witness to a friend, He goes before me to prepare the way. After I have gone, He lingers to repeat the message.

Can God use me to win a friend to Jesus? The other way to ask the question is, Do I have enough of God in my life to share with my friend? Is my life filled to overflowing with His Spirit?

> *O fill me, with thy fullness, Lord,*
> *Until my very heart o'erflow*
> *In kindling thought and glowing word,*
> *Thy love to tell, thy praise to show.*
>
> —*Wesleyan Methodist Hymnal*

**September 9**

READ: Ephesians 6: 10-20

*Praying always . . . for me, that . . . I may speak boldly, as I ought to speak* (Ephesians 6:18-20).

## Be Strong in the Lord

Can God use me to win a friend to Jesus? Yes, if I speak boldly as I ought to speak. Recently a young man gave his Christian witness to an attendant in a service station and found a warm response. Afterward he asked me, "Why does it scare you so to speak about Jesus?" The answer is that the devil does everything in his power to stop even the most Spirit-filled Christian from speaking a word for Christ. We wrestle "against principalities, against powers, against the rulers of the darkness of this world, against spiritual wickedness in high places." Dr. Henry Clay Trumbull witnessed personally to more than ten thousand people in forty years of personal soul winning. But said he, "In every instance I was tempted not to have the interview."

Even after forty years of a Spirit-filled life of service, Trumbull had to resist the devil in order to witness for Christ. The strongest Christian needs again and again to hear this encouraging word from God: "Be strong and of a good courage, fear not . . . for the Lord thy God, he it is that doth go with thee" (Deuteronomy 31:6). Even the Apostle Paul knew the opposition of the devil and requested special prayer that "I may open my mouth boldly, to make known the mystery of the gospel."

As a sanctified Christian, I join in that prayer. O God, give me courage that "I may speak boldly as I ought to speak." Use me to win a friend to Christ.

**Truth for today**

*Courage is fear that has said its prayers.*

READ: John 16:12-13

*Do not be worrying beforehand about what you should say, but say whatever is given you at that time, for it is not you that will be speaking, but the Holy Spirit* (Mark 13:11, Williams).

## He Will Guide You

In the Spirit-filled life may I expect God to tell me what I ought to say and to guide me in what I ought to do? The answer from God's Word is *Yes*, but that answer must be thoughtfully examined. Divine guidance is a privilege of the Christian life—indeed a mark of the child of God. The Bible tells us, "As many as are led by the Spirit of God, they are the sons of God" (Romans 8:14). But this high privilege is surrounded by some safeguards.

Who were the men to whom Jesus spoke in our text? Under what circumstances were they encouraged not to worry about saying the right thing? What was the area of truth in which they might depend implicitly upon the immediate inspiration of the Holy Spirit?

These men were God's men; they had made following Jesus the business of their lives. They were soon to tarry for the promised outpouring of the Holy Spirit. They were men who would arouse opposition in giving their Christian witness. It was this kind of men, doing this kind of work, and encountering this kind of opposition, to whom Jesus gave the promise of on-the-spot, unpremeditated, Spirit-inspired answers.

Is this promise for me? Under comparable conditions, yes. Am I a child of God? Have I tarried for the baptism with the Holy Spirit? Am I making it my business to be a follower of Jesus? Am I trying to witness for Him? Then I need not be afraid. His Holy Spirit is with me and will guide me. I may rest in Him to prompt the right thoughts and words without worry and without nerve-destroying strain.

**Promise for today**

*Thus saith the Lord God, the Holy One of Israel . . . in quietness and in confidence shall be your strength* (Isaiah 30:15).

September 11

READ: Acts 8: 26-39

*The Spirit said unto Philip, Go near, and join thyself to this chariot* (Acts 8: 29).

## The Holy Spirit Guides Us

Our Lord wants us always to be alert to witness for Him, but sometimes the Holy Spirit gives us special assignments.

For ten days I had done what I could by prayer and in the public services to win Mr. ——— for Christ, but had failed. The last Sunday of the revival the Holy Spirit impressed me that I must make an effort to deal personally with him before the meeting closed. The pastor agreed to take me to the home, but emergency calls upset our plans. I decided that without transportation I could not make the call. But the Holy Spirit would not let me give up that easily. He reminded me that I could at least call by telephone or take a taxi to the house.

Under this urging of the Holy Spirit, I called Mr. ——— and found the pastor already there. He came for me. In the living room of the home I greeted the man and his wife, and talked briefly about my special feeling of concern for him throughout the revival. When I asked if we could pray he said hesitantly, "Well, I guess a prayer never hurt anybody." I prayed that he would yield his life to God and that God would save him now.

When I finished, the pastor urged Mr. ——— to pray for himself. He prayed a faltering but sincere prayer of confession and testified that God had forgiven his sins.

Four weeks later the pastor wrote: "The man we prayed with on May 28 had a heart attack and died on June 23. He left a clear testimony that he was ready to go."

I'm glad the Holy Spirit wouldn't let me omit that call.

### Prayer for today

*Spirit of God, keep me sensitive to Thy leading. Show me what to do and I will obey.*

READ: Psalms 119: 129-135

*The entrance of thy words giveth light* (Psalms 119: 130).

## Thy Word Is a Light

Today we come to a turn of the road in our exploration of God's high country of holiness. Thus far we have followed a logically organized study of this great Christian truth. Always we have looked at the Biblical foundation for our faith, but from this point forward we shall do so more intently.

We turn now to an examination of both Old and New Testament passages that have significant relevance for holiness teaching. We shall begin in Genesis and finish in Revelation. Some of these scriptures have already been used in our earlier explorations, but we shall seek to probe their meanings more deeply. Some of them have been little used in holiness teaching but they deserve attention.

As we begin this special approach let us recall Bishop Foster's testimony to the place of Christian holiness in the Bible: "It breathes in the prophecy, thunders in the law, murmurs in the narrative, whispers in the promises, supplicates in the prayers, sparkles in the poetry, resounds in the songs, speaks in the types, glows in the imagery, voices in the language, and burns in the spirit of the whole scheme. . . . Holiness! holiness needed! holiness required! holiness offered! holiness attainable! holiness a present duty, a present privilege, a present enjoyment . . . It is the truth glowing all over . . . the glorious truth which sparkles and whispers, and sings and shouts in all its history, and biography, and poetry, and prophecy, and precept, and promise, and prayer. . . . The wonder is that all do not see, that any rise up to question a truth so conspicuous, so glorious, so full of comfort" (*Christian Purity*).

The answer to the Bishop's wonder is found in the profound truth of our text: "The *entrance* of thy words giveth light." God's Word becomes light only as we sincerely open our hearts to its truth.

**Prayer for these days**
*Spirit of God, make Thy words light for my way.*
*In Jesus' name I ask it.*

**September 13**

READ: Luke 24: 25-27

*Beginning at Moses and the prophets, he expounded unto them in all the scriptures the things concerning himself* (Luke 24: 27).

## Holiness in the Old Testament

In our search for the truths of Christian holiness can the Old Testament help us? Or must we confine our study to the clear light of New Testament revelation?

The light is certainly clearer in the New Testament. If the Old Testament had been adequate there would have been no need for the better revelation of the New. At the same time there is no truth clearly revealed in the New Testament that is not foreshadowed in the Old. In our scripture for today Jesus pointed out New Testament truth from Old Testament sources. God is the same, yesterday, today, and forever.

Where God has revealed a partial truth He has thrown some light on the whole truth. The basis for man's holiness is to be found in the character of the God revealed in this Old Testament commandment: "Ye shall be holy: for I the Lord your God am holy" (Leviticus 19: 2).

The holiness teaching in the Old Testament was not as clear to the men who first received it as it is to us today. Without the full revelation in Christ we would see it no more clearly than did they. But God has given us a clearer understanding. In the light of our Lord's promise to send the Holy Spirit upon His people, these half-visible truths of earlier revelation shine clearly like phosphorescent signs at night. Holiness is taught in the Old Testament.

**Prayer for today**

*O Holy Spirit, Thou Guide to all truth, give me eyes to see and a deep desire to accept the truth from Thy Word, wherever that truth may appear.*

READ: Isaiah 6:1-7

*Thine iniquity is taken away, and thy sin purged* (Isaiah 6:7).

## Types and Symbols of Holiness

Not every Old Testament dual phrase teaches holiness as a second blessing, but holiness is taught in the Old Testament. We may test our use of a passage by asking, Does this truth ring true in view of the whole teaching of the Bible? Is this Old Testament foreshadowing of holiness doctrine consistent with New Testament truth?

Some Old Testament passages suggest parallels to the experience of Christian holiness. We may rightfully use them as types or illustrations though we do not present them as Biblical proofs for our belief. One such parallel is the experience of the Israelites crossing the Red Sea and later crossing the Jordan River. These were first and second crises through which Israel reached God's promised land.

There are, however, other Old Testament passages that teach clearly the essence of New Testament doctrine. David saw that his acts of sin came from an unholy disposition. With true New Testament insight he prayed, "Create in me a clean heart, O God; and renew a right spirit within me" (Psalms 51:10).

Isaiah saw the true character of God when he heard the seraphim singing, "Holy, holy, holy, is the Lord of hosts." He then cried out, "Woe is me! for I am undone; because I am a man of unclean lips." God heard this cry for holiness and sent a heavenly messenger to cleanse the seeker. Here there is more than type and symbol. Here the holiness of God confronts the sinful nature of man, and the human spirit cries for cleansing.

### Prayer for today

*Almighty God, unto whom all hearts are opened, all desires known, and from whom no secrets are hid; cleanse the thoughts of our hearts, by the inspiration of the Holy Spirit, that we may perfectly love thee, and worthily magnify thy holy name, through Christ our Lord* (Communion service prayer of the Anglican church).

269

**September 15**

READ: Genesis 5: 21-24

*And all the days of Enoch were three hundred sixty and five years: and Enoch walked with God: and he was not; for God took him* (Genesis 5: 23-24).

## Holiness Before the Flood

"A remarkable biography! Nowadays men write hundreds of pages about their heroes, and do not say as much as that. But there is a good reason. There is not so much as that to say.

"Enoch's age was most ungodly, and men had very little religious light. They had no Bible. They had no law. They had only the promise of the Seed that some time would come to bruise the Serpent's head. But Enoch held on to that promise, and in its light and hope he walked with God for three hundred years.

"I imagine Enoch made up his mind that it was *possible* to walk with God; to be of the same mind and heart and purpose as God. I think he not only believed in the possibility but he made up his mind that he would. He put his will into this matter and determined that as for him he would walk with God. *He took such steps as were necessary to do so.* He separated himself in spirit from the ungodly people about him, and he raised his voice against their evil ways. He became not only a negatively righteous man, but a positively holy man.

"For three hundred years God was his Friend, his Counsellor, his Comforter, his Constant Companion. Oh, what fellowship that was! What an opportunity to gain wisdom! How easy to be good and do good! How life must have almost burst with fulness of gladness! Walking with God! Talking with God! Communing with God! Having mutual sympathy with God—entering into union with God. And all this by faith, by simple trust, by childlike confidence. This was Enoch's reward, and it may be yours, my brother, my sister, if you will meet the conditions as Enoch did" (SAMUEL LOGAN BRENGLE).

**Question for today**

*Do I walk with God?*

READ: Genesis 32: 3-12, 22-30

*Thou saidst, I will surely do thee good* (Genesis 32: 12).

## God Confronts a Man Again

Shall we say that Jacob's blessing at Jabbok was an experience of entire sanctification? Certainly the Holy Spirit was not then available to men in the New Testament sense. But are there not in this account striking parallels to the lives of men whom we have known as they have come into the experience of Christian holiness?

Was Jacob's experience a "second blessing properly so called"? Let us not be dogmatic, but all can agree on this much: here was a crisis in Jacob's spiritual life—and it was not the first one. When we agree on the reality behind our words, we become more generous with each other in our efforts to describe the workings of God. Here was God's encounter with a man who had already met Him at Bethel (Genesis 28: 10-22). Jacob considered himself to be a servant of God. He already had a measure of trust in the Lord and knew something of the divine power available to a man who prays. He who already knew God in a measure, came to Him for further help—and he found God in a deeper experience.

Many a man has been pushed to prayer and to further confrontation by God when he has thus found his problems to be greater than his resources. In this Jacob is typical. He had previously found ways of his own to outwit his opponents and to outmaneuver his problems. Now he had a situation that was beyond him.

In verse 24 we read: "And Jacob was left alone." These words are not in the record by accident. Here is a significant fact of the spiritual life. We do not do business with God until we give Him our full attention. When we are alone with God, things begin to happen in our lives.

### Affirmation for today

*When I need help, I shall get alone and let God speak to me.*

**September 17**

READ: Genesis 32: 24-26

*I will not let thee go, except thou bless me* (Genesis 32: 26).

## I Will Not Let Thee Go

It is God who takes the initiative in the struggle for the soul. It was the heavenly visitor who at first grappled with Jacob. Who was he—an angel of God? Or God himself in human form? We cannot be sure, but we know that God here made His power real to Jacob—and Jacob recognized the divine character of the struggle.

It was God who took the initiative but it was Jacob who resisted. The contest was long because God never gives up the struggle for a soul until He has done His best to bring us under His sovereign rule. The angel put Jacob's thigh out of joint in order that the man might know the power of God and be persuaded to yield himself to God's love. Here is the divine blow that both wounds and heals. A man may thereafter walk with a limp, but he never regrets it while he walks in divine fellowship.

God takes the initiative and presses the struggle, but He leaves the final decision to us. At this point the initiative passes from Seeker to the sought. At daybreak God said, "I will press myself upon you no longer. I am ready to go my way." But Jacob now knew who it was with whom he wrestled. He sensed the high significance of this encounter and desperately declared: "I will not let thee go, except thou bless me." Here is the one human command that God delights to obey. When I truly want His blessing, I may have it.

> *Yield to me now, for I am weak*
> *But confident in self-despair;*
> *Speak to my heart, in blessings speak,*
> *Be conquered by my instant prayer.*
> —*Hymns of the Living Faith*

READ: Genesis 32: 26-30

*Thy name shall be . . . Israel [a prince of God]: for . . . thou hast power with God and with men* (Genesis 32: 28).

## And He Blessed Him There

"I will not let thee go, except thou bless me, is music to the ear of God; for when we are in that mood He can ask us the right questions. And so the query came: "What is thy name?" What kind of man are you? It is never easy for the carnal heart to answer that question—to confess its carnality. It is never easy—but it is that confession which brings the blessing. With the final surrender came a man's acknowledgment of his need: My name is Jacob; I am rightly named. I am at heart selfish, crooked, a cheater.

"He needed to have self beaten out of him; he needed to recognize God as lovingly striving with him; he needed to yield himself up to Him; he needed to have his heart thus cleansed and softened, and then opened wide by panting desire for the presence and benediction of God; he needed to be made conscious of his new standing, and of the higher life budding within him; he needed to experience the yearning for a closer vision of the face, a deeper knowledge of the name,—and then it was possible to pour into his heart a tenderness and fulness of blessing which before there had been no room to receive" (A. Maclaren).

Jacob's confession was made—and God's blessing was given. "Your name shall no more be called Jacob, but Israel, for you have striven with God . . . and have prevailed" (R.S.V.). Every man who makes this confession may have this blessing. And he who receives it knows that there has been a crisis in his spiritual life. Jacob called the place Peniel, which means "The Face of God." A man may call it what he will, if he has had the experience.

### Question for today

*Can I also bear Jacob's testimony, "I have seen God face to face, and my life is preserved"?*

**September 19**

READ: Exodus 13:11-13

*Sanctify unto me all the firstborn . . . both of man and of beast: it is mine* (Exodus 13:2).

## Recognizing God's Priorities

Do the exhortations of our scripture for today seem like strange voices from a strange land? They were given first to men of another day and a different culture but they clothe universal truths. In them we find Old Testament foundations for New Testament holiness. Every man who is rightly related to God finds that his life is different because he has consecrated himself and his possessions to his Creator.

Why did God require the dedication of the first-born to himself? Perhaps because among the Israelites this first-born son was more highly honored than any other child—and God would have our best. The parents were not to look upon this child as their own until they had first given the five-shekel redemption offering and solemnly presented him to God. After thus recognizing the divine title to their child, they received him back again.

The firstborn of the animals represented the material possessions of a pastoral people. Thus was their wealth consecrated to the service of God. The calves, lambs, and kids were used for the sacrifices of the Tabernacle. Under these requirements God's people gave of their wealth for their worship. They gave their best, and they gave as God had prospered them.

The colt of the ass was ceremonially unclean and thus not suitable for sacrifice. But the man who raised donkeys must also meet God's priorities. The colt must be redeemed with a lamb suitable for sacrifice, or the colt must be destroyed. Does this seem unnecessarily strict? Perhaps so, but we never go wrong when we try to do God's will in even the smallest detail. Holy living then and now bids us:

> *Give of your best to the Master;*
> *Give Him first place in your heart;*
> *Give Him first place in your service;*
> *Consecrate every part.*

—H. B. G.

READ: Exodus 13: 11-14

*And when in time to come your son asks you, "What does this mean?" you shall say to him, "By strength of hand the Lord brought us out . . ."* (Exodus 13: 14, R.S.V.).

## The Testimony of Holy Living

We saw yesterday that there were genuine spiritual values in God's Old Testament laws for the sanctification of His people. We have reserved perhaps the most important of those values for our thought today.

A man may sacrifice an animal to the glory of God but he does not thus consecrate a son. A godly parent does not sacrifice his first-born, but he does recognize God's claim upon the child. And not only upon the first-born, but upon every child of the home. God declares, "Behold, all souls are mine; as the soul of the Father, so also the soul of the son is mine" (Ezekiel 18: 4).

Holy living is the only finally effective way that we have of consecrating our children to God. The Hebrew parent was required to be careful in his religious observances in order that his son might one day ask him, "What does this mean?" The question was to give God's man opportunity to declare his faith to his child: It is because of what the Lord did for me when I came out of Egypt (Exodus 13: 8).

Is any service for God too difficult, is any consecration of self too demanding, if in that devotion my child sees God in my life, and grows hungry to know Him?

A "preacher's kid" saw his sanctified father mistreated. Later the boy watched his dad get blessed under the ministry of the man who had done the wrong. Here in his own language is the boy's reaction: "I said then, Holiness is real—and I want it."

> *Let the beauty of Jesus be seen in me,*
> *All His wonderful passion and purity.*
> *O Thou Spirit divine, all my nature refine,*
> *Till the beauty of Jesus be seen in me.*
>
> —T. M. JONES

**September 21**

READ: Exodus 20: 1-17

*I am the Lord your God: ye shall therefore sanctify yourselves, and ye shall be holy; for I am holy* (Leviticus 11: 44).

## Holiness and the Ten Commandments

"To live godly is to live in the fear and love of God. To be obedient to all His known will. To worship God *only,* according to the first commandment; to worship Him *spiritually,* according to the second; to worship Him *reverently,* according to the third commandment; to worship Him *statedly,* according to the fourth" (J. B. CHAPMAN).

Christian holiness does not stop with the first four commandments. Holiness of heart also provides the right inward basis for living with our fellowman. Holiness is a spirit of love that accords honor to the parents who have given me life and a home. Holiness makes me similar to God in His high regard for human life. Sanctification is a safeguard from adultery; I hold my own body as a temple of God, and I would not encourage another to sin against Him. How can a holy man, who loves his neighbor as himself, steal from that neighbor, or bear false witness against him, or covet what he has?

To live the life of holiness "is to worship with the hand by tithing the income and making gifts according to the ability which God giveth. It is to worship with the mind by reading God's Word and meditating upon His power, wisdom and love. It is to worship Him with the heart by pouring out the spirit in prayer, praise and giving thanks. . . . To live godly is to live in gracious communion, fellowship and agreement with God" (J. B. CHAPMAN).

**Praise for today**

*Oh, how love I thy law!*
*It is my meditation all the day.*
(Psalms 119: 97)

READ: Leviticus 18: 1-5

*Ye shall do my judgments, and keep mine ordinances, to walk therein* (Leviticus 18: 4).

## I Am the Lord Your God

"I am the Lord your God." This is the beginning and the end of the holy life. Could any message be clearer than our Old Testament Bible reading for today? "You shall not do as they do in the land of Egypt, where you dwelt, and you shall not do as they do in the land of Canaan, to which I am bringing you. You shall not walk in their statutes. You shall do my ordinances and keep my statutes and walk in them. I am the Lord your God" (R.S.V.).

The life of holiness sets us apart as different men because we serve a different Deity. The Egyptians and the Canaanites were unholy people because they served unholy gods. The holiness of Israel was rooted in her covenant relationship to God. He had chosen them to be His people; they had accepted Him as their God. When we accept God, we agree to obey Him.

Walking according to the divine law means a life of separation from former sinful practices. Paul reminds us: "Among them we all once walked, as we indulged our fleshly desires and carried out the inclinations of the lower nature and the lower thoughts" (Ephesians 2: 3, Berkeley). But serving a holy God separates us also from the unholy practices of our current society. As a Christian I do not thoughtlessly pattern my life after my neighbors—even when they are upper-income, cultured neighbors. I serve the Lord God. Always my test in the life of holiness must be, Is this the will of God for my life?

### Affirmation for today

*I delight to do thy will, O my God: yea, thy law is within my heart* (Psalms 40: 8).

**September 23**

READ: Leviticus 18: 4-5; 19: 1-2

*Ye shall be holy: for I the Lord your God am holy*
*(Leviticus 19: 2).*

## God Is Holy

We saw yesterday that the choice of a man's God deter-
mines the kind of life that he lives. Today we see what kind
of God chose Israel, and what kind of God is "the God and
Father of our Lord Jesus Christ."

When God reveals His own nature in one sentence, it is
this: "I the Lord your God am holy." A holy God is a God
concerned with fairness, honesty, and justice. The perfect
revelation of God's holiness is to be seen in his Son. Of our
Lord, the Bible declares: "You have loved right and hated
wrong! That is why God, your God, has anointed you . . .
beyond all your comrades" (Hebrews 1: 9, Goodspeed). My
heart responds to a God who is like Jesus.

But goodness is more than justice, and God is more than
fair. Holiness is not only righteousness; it is also love. "The
God and Father of our Lord Jesus Christ" is interested in
men, interested in helping them. Our welfare is His deepest
concern because God loves every person whom He has created.

It is God's love for us that makes Him yearn for men to
be holy. He knows that we can never be truly happy until
we are good. Until we are like Him, we never really live.
"I, the Lord, am your God. So you must keep my statutes
and ordinances, by the observance of which man shall live"
(Leviticus 18: 4-5, Smith).

Who can quarrel with goodness? Who can reject sincere
love? This is God's nature, and it is this life to which He calls
us.

### Truth for today

*He hath shewed thee, O man, what is good; and*
*what doth the Lord require of thee, but to do justly,*
*and to love mercy, and to walk humbly with thy God?*
*(Micah 6: 8)*

278

READ: Numbers 13: 1-3, 25-33; 14: 6-9

*My servant Caleb . . . has a different spirit and has followed me fully* (Numbers 14: 24, R.S.V.).

## The Different Spirit

In this familiar story we have no doctrine of second-blessing holiness. But there is here a clear picture of what God can do for men who follow Him fully.

What was this different spirit that Joshua and Caleb had? Men with the natural spirit were fearful because their problems loomed larger than their resources: "We be not able to go up against the people" (13:31). The different spirit declared, "Let us go up at once, and possess it; for we are well able to overcome it" (13:30). The natural man sees the strength of his enemies: "They are stronger than we." But he who fully follows God sees more clearly the enemy's weakness: "Their defense is departed from them" (14:9).

All twelve of the spies were chosen people, and all of them were leaders in their tribes (13:3), but ten of them needed to follow God more fully. It is a sad day when a professed man of God can look at a good country and bring "an evil report of the land" (13:32). It is the Holy Spirit who enables a man to look at the same territory and declare, "It is an exceeding good land" (4:7).

Self-centered men saw only the threat to themselves: "It is a land that eateth up the inhabitants" (13:32). He who follows the Lord sees how God makes nourishment out of opposition: "They are bread for us" (14:9). The carnal mind has a craven spirit: "We were in our own sight as grasshoppers" (13:33). Spirit-filled man knows his true stature because he knows who is on his side: "The Lord is with us" (14:9).

### Prayer for today

*Spirit of God, so fill my life with thyself that I too may have that different spirit. Amen.*

**September 25**

READ: Numbers 14: 6-9

*If the Lord delight in us, then he will bring us into this land* (Numbers 14: 7).

## An Exceeding Good Land

The land of Canaan always represented to the Hebrews the supreme blessing of God. When Abram was called to leave Ur of the Chaldees, God promised him a homeland in Canaan. When Moses led Israel out of Egyptian bondage, the people of God were on the march to Canaan.

Among holiness people the land of Canaan has been a favorite figure of God's highest spiritual blessings. Egypt with its poor diet of leeks and its bitter slave bondage has symbolized the miserable life of the sinner. Escape from Egypt by crossing the Red Sea has been a figure of conversion. Wilderness wanderings have been used to picture the unhappy life of the Christian who has escaped sin's enslavement but who has not yet crossed the Jordan river into the Promised Land. God's best for Israel was Canaan, so the sanctified life has often been described in those terms. Here is the glad testimony of a satisfied, sanctified Christian:

> *I'm over the Jordan tide;*
> *The waters did there divide.*
> *I'm in the land of Canaan,*
> *Abundantly satisfied.*
>
> *I am in the land of Canaan,*
> *This land of corn and wine.*
> *The atmosphere is pleasant;*
> *The fruit is large and fine.*
>
> —I. G. MARTIN

God has promised, "If ye be willing and obedient, ye shall eat the good of the land" (Isaiah 1: 19).

## Prayer for today

*O God, I want Thy best for my life. I do now yield myself entirely to Thee. Lead me into the land of Thy promise.*

READ: Deuteronomy 10:11-13

*What doth the Lord thy God require of thee, but to fear the Lord thy God, to walk in all his ways, and to love him, and to serve the Lord thy God with all thy heart and with all thy soul?* (Deuteronomy 10:12)

## An Early Vision of High Religion

Our scripture foreshadows Christian holiness both symbolically and really. The symbol is the land of Canaan into which God told Moses to lead His people. But the real holiness teaching is found in the kind of relationship to God that Moses here describes.

To fear the Lord is the basis of all worthy religion. This Biblical word does not mean to be afraid of God. It means rather to recognize God and to acknowledge my relationship to Him. God made me; He preserves me and sets up the laws by which my life is governed. To fear the Lord means to respect God's authority and to fashion my life accordingly.

To truly walk in the way of God is "to walk in *all his ways.*" Israel was to live after God's ordinances rather than according to their new neighbors' customs, or even according to their own inclinations. To walk in all of God's ways means that I shall never choose one of my own ways in preference to one of God's ways.

But this careful duty of holy living is not an unwilling slavery. We serve God because we love Him. We often think about Him and we delight to talk with Him.

To love God thus is to serve Him with all the heart. The young man who is in love wants above all else to please the girl he loves. The young woman in love puts herself out to discover and to do what her beloved enjoys. It is our best human picture of the soul's true love for God. The song writer knew the secret of this high religion when he wrote:

> *I serve Him because I love Him;*
> *I love Him because He first loved me;*
> *I give Him my heart's devotion*
> *For time and eternity.**

—HALDOR LILLENAS

*© 1920 and 1948 by Lillenas Publishing Co.

**September 27**

READ: I Chronicles 28: 9-10

*Know thou the God of thy father, and serve him with a perfect heart and with a willing mind* (I Chronicles 28: 9).

## Serve God with a Perfect Heart

No man is ever confronted by God with higher demands than these—but no Christian is permitted to live on a lower level. This charge was given by David to his son Solomon as he ascended the throne of Israel and prepared to build the Temple. But in its widest application it is the divine charge to every human being who ascends the throne of life and is thus responsible to make himself "the temple of the living God."

If we have been blessed with godly parents, we are to seek to know God at least as well as they knew Him. If we had no help from a Christian home, we are responsible to know the God of a spiritual father or mother. We who know the Lord stand on the shoulders of some man or woman of God who went before us.

Our text is Old Testament teaching but it is a clear insight into the nature of all true religion. Every man who knows God is charged to "serve him with a perfect heart." Others translate it "an undivided heart," and "a whole heart." All are accurate and all describe the kind of life that is envisioned and made possible today by the experience of entire sanctification.

This service to God is to be the service of a willing mind. In verse 8, David charged the leaders of Israel: "*Seek out all the commandments of Jehovah*" (A.R.V.). It is not enough to do God's will only as far as we now know it; we must ever be seeking for deeper insight into it.

> *Open my eyes, that I may see*
> *Glimpses of truth Thou hast for me;*
> *Place in my hands the wonderful key*
> *That shall unclasp, and set me free.*
>
> *—Wesleyan Methodist Hymnal*

READ: Psalms 24: 3-6

*Such are the men who . . . seek the presence of the God of Jacob* (Psalms 24: 6, Moffatt).

## Holy Men for a Holy God

In the Psalms we sometimes find our clearest and most moving theology. It is such a passage through which God speaks to us today. This psalm was written for the specific occasion when David brought the ark of the covenant to Jerusalem, but it speaks universal spiritual truth. Here is how sinful men may prepare themselves to live with a holy God.

"Here is inquiry after better things. What shall I do to rise to that high place where the Lord dwells, that I may be acquainted with him? What shall I do that I may be of those whom God owns for his peculiar people?

"God's people shall have communion with him. They are such as keep themselves from all gross acts of sin. They are such as make conscience of being inwardly as good as they seem outwardly. It is not enough that our hands be clean before men, but we must also wash our hearts from wickedness. This is a pure heart, which is sincere and without guile in covenanting with God, which is purified by faith, and conformed to the image and will of God.

"They join themselves to God, to seek him; not only in earnest prayer, but in serious endeavours to obtain his favour, and keep themselves in his love.

"They shall be blessed: they shall receive the blessing from the Lord and those whom God blesses are blessed indeed. They shall be justified, and sanctified. These are the spiritual blessings which they shall receive, even righteousness, the very thing they hunger and thirst after" (Matthew Henry, 1662-1714).

### Promise for today

*Blessed are they which do hunger and thirst after righteousness: for they shall be filled* (Matthew 5: 6).

**September 29**

READ: Psalms 101: 1-3

*The Lord appeared to Abram, and said unto him, I am the Almighty God; walk before me, and be thou perfect* (Genesis 17:1).

## Perfect Before God

The experience of entire sanctification is sometimes called *Christian perfection.* The term is used because the Bible speaks in this language of a man's relationship to God. It would be incorrect to speak of Christian perfection in the Old Testament because Christ had not yet come. But the New Testament experience has a clear Old Testament parallel.

The Bible says: "Noah was a just man and perfect in his generations" (Genesis 6:9). In our text for today God commanded Abram: "Walk before me, and be thou perfect" (Genesis 17:1). The Levites were instructed: "Thou shalt be perfect with the Lord thy God" (Deuteronomy 18:13). We are assured that "Asa's heart was perfect with the Lord all his days" (I Kings 15:14). David prayed, "Give unto Solomon my son a perfect heart, to keep thy commandments" (I Chronicles 29:19). The Bible says of Job: "That man was perfect and upright, and one that feared God and turned away from evil" (Job 1:1, A.R.V.). David promised God: "I will walk within my house with a perfect heart" (Psalms 101:2). In life's most serious moment, when called to account before God, Hezekiah could testify: "I have walked before thee in truth and with a perfect heart" (Isaiah 38:3).

In the light of Christian standards there were moral flaws in the lives of all of these men, but the Bible repeatedly calls them perfect. There must be something significant to which God's Word testifies in these passages. Is this not the perfect heart? The perfect desire and full intention to do the whole will of God? Is not God here saying clearly, Your life can be entirely satisfying in My sight—you can, in this sense, be perfect before Me?

### Prayer for today

*O God, when evening comes today, and when the shades are drawn on my life, may I too be able to say, "I have walked before thee in truth and with a perfect heart." In Jesus' name I ask it. Amen.*

READ: Isaiah 6: 1-8

*I saw also the Lord sitting upon a throne high and lifted up* (Isaiah 6: 1).

## I Saw the Lord

Is it permissible to compare Isaiah's cleansing with the experience of Christians upon whom the Holy Spirit is poured out today? We must not read too much into the experiences of these early men of God, for we know that "the Holy Ghost was not yet given" in the New Testament sense. But God here did for a man's spirit something remarkably parallel to the baptism with the Holy Ghost and fire.

No place in the Old Testament do we come closer to the New Testament experience of entire sanctification than when Isaiah had this vision of God. If this was not indeed the same experience, it is a remarkably accurate preview of the glorious cleansing and empowering that came to Christ's followers on the Day of Pentecost.

Isaiah was already a devout man of God. He was a counselor to Judah's king and a prophet to her people. He knew how to find divine resources in the crises of life. At this critical hour in the nation's history the young statesman came to the Temple to pray.

When we earnestly seek Him, God reveals himself in a new and fuller measure to those who already know Him. To the man who cares enough about God to seek Him in His sanctuary, God gives an added vision of himself "high and lifted up." Those who have received the Holy Spirit in sanctifying power testify that the experience is just that kind of further and more satisfying contact with God.

> *Teach me to love Thee as Thine angels love,*
> *One holy passion filling all my frame;*
> *The baptism of the heaven-descended Dove,*
> *My heart an altar, and Thy love the flame.*
> —*Hymns of the Living Faith*

**October 1**

READ: Isaiah 6:1-4

*In the year that king Uzziah died I saw also the Lord sitting upon a throne* (Isaiah 6:1).

## Doors to a New Experience with God

What are the circumstances that have power to lift a Christian's vision until he sees his Lord in a new perspective? How are the doors opened to a new experience with God?

Our text does more than merely to date Isaiah's vision; it tells us *why* as well as *when.* Uzziah had been a strong monarch but now he was dead. Threatening clouds of war were gathering to the north of Judah. The new king was barely twenty-five years of age. Were those young hands strong enough to hold the reins and to guide the nation? Isaiah was disturbed to the depths; but he was wise enough to take his concern to God in prayer.

Is the new vision of God to be found as simply as that? Yes. It is like the worried shopper, her arms filled with packages. She comes to a closed door and has no free hand to open it. But as she simply moves forward an electric eye releases unseen power that opens the closed door and she moves through it into God's world on the other side.

It was disturbance over the dead king that made possible Isaiah's vision of the living God. Had there been no empty earthly throne, he would never have seen the throne of God. In our walk with the Lord, have we come to some dead-end street? Some closed door? This can be the occasion for release to a wider experience. If we but keep moving toward God in prayer, there is a power that opens the door.

### Prayer for today

*Who, dear Lord, ever came to Thee with a pious heart and was rejected? Who ever sought Thee and found Thee not? Who ever sought help with Thee and did not obtain it? Who ever prayed for Thy grace and did not receive it? Who ever called upon Thee without being heard?*—MENNO SIMONS, about 1538.

READ: Isaiah 6:1-5

*Woe is me! for I am undone; because I am a man of unclean lips* (Isaiah 6:5).

## Conviction for Cleansing

"He who had uttered this cry was one who had kept himself from his iniquity, holding the mystery of the faith in a pure conscience; and yet in that terrible light he saw and avowed himself as a man undone, saw stains in himself which he had not imagined before, discovered impurities which he had not dreamt of before, saw his own sin and his people's sin, till that mighty cry of anguish was wrung from him. Yet that moment, with all its dreadfulness, was a passage into a true life" (R. C. TRENCH).

Was it the song of the seraphim that convicted Isaiah of his deep need? Was it not the message of the holiness of God that rang from the lips of this heavenly choir? In a flash of convicting personal insight the young prophet knew that he could not join in that song. The need for forgiveness is here, but there is more. Isaiah was conscious that his deeper need was cleansing from unholiness. Until that happened, his lips were unworthy to join the seraphim as they sang,

*Holy, Holy, Holy, Lord God Almighty!*

Until he was cleansed and joined that choir, he could not truthfully sing:

*All Thy works shall praise Thy name*
*In earth, and sky, and sea.*

To understand God's will for a holy life is to see our duty to be clean. In the hour of conviction we know our own need and we know that we must have all the help that God can give us.

*I hate the sin which grieves Thy loving heart;*
*Speak, precious Lord, and bid it all depart.*
*Thy temple cleanse, and make my heart Thy home;*
*Come, King of Kings, and reign thyself alone.**
                                    —GEORGE BENNARD

*© 1940, renewal, The Rodeheaver Co. Used by permission.

**October 3**

READ: Isaiah 6: 1-7

*Thine iniquity is taken away, and thy sin is purged* (Isaiah 6: 7).

## Like a Refiner's Fire

How shall we picture God's power to cleanse the human spirit? The Bible often uses the figure of fire, and that was the form in which God made the experience real to the prophet.

Isaiah knew the fires that burned continually in the Valley of Hinnom, cleansing Jerusalem by consuming the city's refuse. He knew also how the refiner applied fire to the crucible to cleanse his gold of impurities. As the melting metal grew hotter and hotter, the lighter-weight dross came to the surface and was skimmed off. When the hottest fire released no further impurity, the work was done. When the refiner could see his own image clearly reflected in the pure molten metal, he was satisfied. God thus proposes to purge the dross from our lives, and when He has cleansed us, to see in us a clear reflection of His own image.

Isaiah saw that the cleansing fire which brought him moral purity came from the altar of God. In Old Testament times this altar was the altar of burnt offering, where atonement was made for sin. But our Offering for sin is Christ. It is through His atonement that we have forgiveness and sanctification. "Wherefore Jesus also, that he might sanctify the people with his own blood, suffered without the gate" (Hebrews 13:12). Oh, blessed provision for our cleansing! Millions have borne witness to the power of Christ to deal with sin—a power that takes away a man's guilt and cleanses the deeper stain. Today I join in their glad praise:

> *Blessed be the name of Jesus!*
> *I'm so glad He took me in.*
> *He's forgiven my transgressions;*
> *He has cleansed my heart from sin.*
> —M. J. HARRIS

READ: Isaiah 6:1-8

*Also I heard the voice of the Lord, saying, Whom shall I send, and who will go for us? Then said I, Here am I; send me* (Isaiah 6:8).

## Here Am I

When our hearts grow responsive to the touch of God, our ears are opened to better hear His voice. When our lives are most aglow with the love of God, our hearts spontaneously respond, "Here am I; send me." Cold religion is a contradiction in terms. Our relationship to God is deeply satisfying only when our lives are aglow with His touch upon us, and when we are fervent in our response to Him.

Our highest worship is not in the consciousness of our need, nor the recognition of God's glory, nor in our rapture at His touch. What is the highest form of worship? Is it not to be doing God's will in daily life?

A part of the defilement from which we are cleansed is indifference to the needs of God's kingdom, a lack of concern for the souls of men. When the Holy Spirit comes in His fullness, there is a new readiness for service; a new kind of power takes hold of our lives. God breathes into sanctified hearts a love for men that is akin to His own love for lost humanity. He imparts to us a readiness to keep speaking, even when men's ears are heavy. We keep trying because the Spirit of God has not quit. We try to show men God's way even when they close their eyes. We try again, because God bids them look again. Having been cleansed by His power and filled with His Spirit, we are made ready for service.

### Truth for today

*Blessed are they who with purged eyes see, and with yielded hearts obey the heavenly vision, and turn to the King and offer themselves for any service He may require, saying, "Here am I; send me"* (A. MACLAREN).

**October 5**

READ: Isaiah 35:1-10

*In the wilderness shall waters break out, and streams in the desert. And the parched ground shall become a pool, and the thirsty land springs of water* (Isaiah 35:6-7).

## God's Gift to the Thirsty

What was the glorious vision that God gave to the prophet causing him to sing the glad song of this thirty-fifth chapter of Isaiah? It was the vision of God's supreme revelation to us in His Son. He inspired Isaiah to look seven hundred years into the future and describe the coming of Christ. Note verses 5 and 6: "Then the eyes of the blind shall be opened, and the ears of the deaf shall be unstopped. Then shall the lame man leap as an hart, and the tongue of the dumb shall sing." Are not these gracious words an accurate picture of our Lord's miracles during His earthly ministry?

But Isaiah looks beyond the earthly ministry of Jesus. He sees Pentecost and speaks of the outpoured Holy Spirit. "In the wilderness shall waters break out, and streams in the desert. And the parched ground shall become a pool, and the thirsty land springs of water."

Jesus himself used this same figure and probably referred to Isaiah's prophecy when He cried, "If any man is thirsty he can come to Me and drink! The man who believes in Me, as the Scripture said, will have rivers of living water flowing from his inmost heart" (Phillips). The Bible tells us clearly that this experience is to be the work of the Holy Spirit. "This spake he of the Spirit which they that believe on him should receive; for the Holy Ghost was not yet given; because that Jesus was not yet glorified" (John 7:38-39).

**Prayer for today**

*O God, our Father, we thank Thee for Thy Holy Spirit, who is to be with us, and in us as a never-failing stream of refreshment and strength. We do now open our hearts to His full ministry. In the name of Jesus. Amen.*

290

READ: Isaiah 35:1-10

*An highway shall be there, and a way, and it shall be called The way of holiness* (Isaiah 35:8).

## Way of Guidance

God here pictures for us the truth of holiness as a highway across a dangerous desert. It is indeed God's highway to high country. In a barren wilderness where we should otherwise be lost and perish, He has planned the way of holiness for our safe conduct to the Celestial City. If we are to find our eternal home with God, we must have a clear knowledge of His will for us.

How does God guide us in the way that we should go? (1) He has given us the truths of His Word: "Holy men of God spake as they were moved by the Holy Ghost" (II Peter 1:21). The Holy Bible is God's way of guiding our feet into the highway of holiness; and it is His way of keeping us traveling along that highway until we reach the end of our earthly pilgrimage.

The guidance of Scripture is basic, but we often need answers to details of our personal problems where the Bible is not specific. For these decisions Jesus promised (2) that when the Holy Spirit came He would be our Guide. "I have yet many things to say unto you, but ye cannot bear them now. Howbeit when he, the Spirit of truth, is come, he will guide you into all truth" (John 16:12-13).

How often have we prayed to know God's will for our lives and the blessed Holy Spirit has given both a knowledge of what to do and a deep assurance that His guidance was right! It is an experience with God which we must have again and again.

> *Holy Spirit, faithful Guide,*
> *Ever near the Christian's side,*
> *Gently lead us by the hand,*
> *Pilgrims in a desert land.*
> —MARCUS M. WELLS

**October 7**

READ: Isaiah 35: 8-10

*And a highway will be there; its name will be, The Holy Way; the unclean and the sinner may not go over it"* (Isaiah 35: 8, *The Basic Bible*).

## Way of Cleanness

God's way is always different from the ways of the sinful world. The highway of holiness runs above the surrounding plains of evil. It leads by a straight course toward heaven instead of wandering in aimless circles. The way of holiness therefore separates those who travel on it from men who travel the ways of the world. The American Revised Version translates our text, "The unclean shall not pass over it; but it shall be for the redeemed."

The term unclean refers to people. Bishop Lowth translates, "No unclean person shall pass through it." God's way is the holy way, not only because holiness is the goal to which it leads, but still more because only holy feet may tread it. The Bible declares that the unclean and the sinner are excluded.

Holiness is Godlikeness. To be unclean is to be unlike God and therefore to be shut out from the way that leads to God. A holy life is a way of separation from this world and a way of nonconformity to its evils.

This highway of holiness is a toll road. There is a price to be paid if we are to travel on it, and that price is to be cleansed from sin. But the price is fair and the journey is rewarding. At the end we shall come to Zion with songs and everlasting joy upon our heads; we shall obtain joy and gladness, and sorrow and sighing shall flee away.

> *Since Thou would'st have us free from sin,*
> *And pure as those above,*
> *Make haste to bring Thy nature in,*
> *And perfect us in love.*
>
> —*Wesley's Hymns*

READ: Isaiah 35: 8-10

*It shall be called The way of holiness; the unclean shall not pass over it* (Isaiah 35: 8).

## Way of Purity

God's first concern for us is that we shall be free from sin, that we shall be pure in heart. That is why His way of holiness is a sinless way. Isaiah saw it seven hundred years before Christ was born: "It shall be called The way of holiness; the unclean shall not pass over it; . . . but the redeemed shall walk there." Moffatt puts the promise into poetry:

> *A stainless highroad shall appear,*
> *its name "The Sacred Way";*
> *no soul unclean shall tread it,*
> *no impious foot stray over it;*
> *no lions shall ever haunt it,*
> *no wild beasts leap on it;*
> *but on it the redeemed shall walk,*
> *those whom the Eternal has set free.*

Am I today on the way of holiness? If so, the Holy Spirit keeps me pure. The Holy Spirit is first and foremost the Spirit of holiness. So that if I am not clean, no matter what my gifts, no matter what my wisdom, no matter what my intellectual force, no matter what my supernatural and miraculous power, I do not have the Spirit of God in me. If the Holy Spirit is in me, He is making me clean.

This way of holiness is the highway to heaven. Only the pure in heart know God truly here; only the pure in heart may see Him hereafter.

> *Oh, make me clean! Oh, make me clean!*
> *Mine eyes Thy holiness have seen;*
> *Oh, send the burning, cleansing flame,*
> *And make me clean in Jesus' name!\**
> —GEORGE BENNARD

\*© 1940, renewal, The Rodeheaver Co. Used by permission.

**October 9**

READ: Isaiah 35: 8-10

*And a highway shall be there; and it shall be called*
*The way of holiness . . . he himself shall be with them,*
*walking in the way* (Isaiah 35: 8, Bishop Lowth).

## Way of Divine Companionship

Often our struggles with the difficulties in life bring rewards of unusual blessing. The clause in verse 8, "but it shall be for those," is a difficult spot for Bible translators. For this clause there are about as many translations as there are translators. But the difficulty has also brought its blessings.

One of the revised versions has a marginal reading, "He shall be with them." Bishop Lowth reinforces that truth when he translates our text, "He himself shall be with them, walking in the way."

Here Isaiah foreshadows the most glorious truth of this experience of Christian holiness. God sends His Holy Spirit to be the intimate Companion of our earthly journeys. Yea, He is more than a Companion. Jesus promised, "I will pray the Father, and he shall give you another Comforter, that he may abide with you for ever; even the Spirit of truth; whom the world cannot receive, because it seeth him not, neither knoweth him: but ye know him; for he dwelleth with you, and shall be in you" (John 14: 16-17).

The way of holiness is "the way of the Holy One." This way is a holy way because all who travel the road have intimate fellowship with God himself in the person of His Holy Spirit. Jesus walked with two disciples in intimate fellowship along the road to Emmaus. Dr. E. Stanley Jones has reminded us that our Lord could not remain here in His physical presence to walk your road and mine. So He sent the Holy Spirit to be "the Christ of every road."

> *What a fellowship, what a joy divine,*
> *Leaning on the everlasting arms!*
> *What a blessedness, what a peace is mine,*
> *Leaning on the everlasting arms!*
> —ELISHA A. HOFFMAN

294

READ: Isaiah 35: 8-10

*It shall be called The way of holiness . . . it shall be for . . . wayfaring men, though fools, shall not err therein* (Isaiah 35: 8).

## The Way for Wayfaring Men

A cultured young man, with a Ph.D. degree, brought an earnest gospel message in a youth rally. After the service a sharp teen-ager remarked to a friend, "If a guy like that believes in religion, it's O.K. for me."

Have you ever been tempted to believe that religion is only for sissies? Have you ever felt that holiness was only for the oddballs?

God has provided a salvation that is suitable for even the abnormal and the eccentric. The way is so clear that fools need not err therein. But the way of holiness was not designed for nitwits.

What a difference is made by a mere punctuation mark! Read our text one way and it sounds as if the road was made for fools: "It shall be for those: the wayfaring men, though fools, shall not err therein." But swap a colon and a comma and see what a difference. "It shall be for those, the wayfaring men: though fools shall not err therein."

The way of holiness is for wayfaring men. God has planned His best for those who are going somewhere—for men and women who are on the way. I must never hang my head for trying to be the kind of person God wants me to be. With Paul, I square my shoulders. "I am not ashamed of the gospel of Christ: for it is the power of God unto salvation to every one that believeth" (Romans 1: 16).

> *"Called unto holiness," children of light,*
> *Walking with Jesus in garments of white;*
>
> . . . . . . . . . . . . . . . . . . . . . . . . . . . . .
>
> *Lift up your heads, for the day draweth near*
> *When in His beauty the King shall appear.*
> —MRS. C. H. MORRIS

**October 11**

READ: Isaiah 65: 1-2 (R.S.V.).

*I was ready to be sought by those who did not ask for me; I was ready to be found by those who did not seek me. I said, "Here am I, here am I, to a nation that did not call on my name. I spread out my hands all the day to a rebellious people, who walk in a way that is not good, following their own devices* (Isaiah 65: 1-2, R.S.V.).

## The Seeking Spirit of God

In this scripture is laid bare the yearning heart of God as He seeks to lay hold upon the lives of men for their own highest welfare. In its historical setting this is God's call to the people of Israel—His own chosen people. In its universal application this call is the yearning of the eternally contemporary God who is always seeking men. Within this broader framework is there not a permissible application to God's call to the higher life of holiness?

The people of Israel stood in a special relationship to God. They were His people, though they did not walk close to Him. They were content in their limited contact and did not ask to know Him better. He was ready to reveal himself to them but they did not seek Him. He called to them repeatedly, "Here am I; here am I," but they did not turn to listen. There was not an hour in the day that God was not seeking to reach the unresponsive. They were rebellious because they did not want to listen to God's call. They walked in a way that was not good—not good because it was the way of their own devices.

### Prayer for today

*Search my heart, O God. Are You ready to give me what I have not asked? Are You eager to share a fullness of yourself that I have not sought? I confess that the way of my own devices is not good. I hear Your call. I pause to listen more intently. I turn from my own devices to Your design for my life. I ask for Your way. I ask for You. And wonder of wonders—You give yourself to me!*

READ: Jeremiah 7: 21-23

*Obey my voice, and I will be your God* (Jeremiah 7: 23).

## I Will Be Your God

Man is incurably religious. In every age and in all localities he seeks for God. In Japan we find him in the Shinto temple; in Burma he worships at a Confucian shrine; in India he bows at a Hindu altar; in Arabia he prays with his face toward Mecca; in Africa he follows the witch man's magic; in Europe and America he attends the church of his choice—but everywhere he is seeking God.

Deep in man's soul there is a longing to know God in a satisfying way. Augustine has written, "Thou hast made us for Thyself, and the heart never resteth till it findeth rest in Thee."

Men everywhere hunger to know God, but soul hunger does not assure satisfaction. The search is sometimes futile, or only partially rewarding, for God will not satisfy the soul of man with less than the full truth. Better it is that a man continue to hunger than to have his soul satisfied with husks which cannot nourish the spiritual life. God is a holy God. He gives himself to us only in the measure that we desire to be holy people. His counsel is, "Obey my voice, and I will be your God." Do our hearts cry out for more of God? Let us ask Him to make us holy. Do we hunger for His presence? Let us pray to be cleansed from all that is unlike Him.

### Prayer for today

*Create in me a clean heart, O God; and renew a right spirit within me. Thou desirest not sacrifice; else would I give it: thou delightest not in burnt offering. The sacrifices of God are a broken spirit: a broken and a contrite heart, O God, thou wilt not despise* (Psalms 51: 10, 16-17).

READ: Jeremiah 24: 6-7

*I will give them an heart to know me, that I am the Lord . . . they shall return unto me with their whole heart* (Jeremiah 24: 7).

## The Responsive Heart

Can the realities of the spirit be likened to the most sacred experiences that we know in the body? What is it like to have a heart that responds to God? Like the gladness that comes with the warm handclasp of a friend? Like the oneness we feel when an older brother puts an encouraging arm around our shoulders? Like earth's closest companionship in the embrace of the one whom we love? To know the love of God is all of these—and more.

The heart of stone is cold, dead, hard, and self-centered. God proposes to give in its place a heart that is warm, living, pliable, and responsive to Him.

Am I indifferent to things that are good? God can make me concerned. Am I unresponsive? God promises, "I will . . . give you a nature that can be touched" (Moffatt). Am I rebellious? God proposes to make me His loyal ally. Is my love for God all but dead? He will rekindle it until it burns with a steady flame.

And wonder of wonders! None of these transformations is made against my will, for He changes my deepest desires. I am powerless to bring these changes to pass. In my present carnal condition I cannot even truly desire them. But I can see that I ought to want them. I know that I ought to love God with my whole heart, soul, and mind. I know that I ought to, but I cannot. I can only acknowledge my needy condition and ask for the new heart.

**Prayer for today**

> Give me a love that knows no ill;
> Give me the grace to do Thy will.
> Pardon and cleanse this soul of mine;
> Give me a heart like Thine.*

—J. W. VAN DEVENTER

*© 1948, renewal, The Rodeheaver Co. Used by permission.

READ: Ezekiel 11: 19-20

*I will take the stony heart out of their flesh* (Ezekiel 11: 19).

## The Stony Heart

A stone is hard, it is cold, it is unresponsive, and it resists all efforts to move or to reshape it. This is the Bible picture of the human heart corrupted by sin and alien to God.

This is the condition of the willful sinner. He is unmoved by the call of God. He wants God to let him alone. When urged by the people of God or prodded by the Spirit of God, he becomes downright rebellious and antagonistic. One would think it was literal stones of which the Scripture speaks, but it was of men of whom it was written. "Having eyes, they see not; having ears, they hear not; neither do they understand."

But is this condition true only of a man who has never known God? No, there is in the heart of even the saved man a tendency to hardening of his spiritual arteries.

It was the stony heart that troubled Mrs. Hannah Whitall Smith even after she had been saved. She testified: "It was not my outward walk that caused me sorrow . . . it was the sins of my heart that troubled me—coldness, deadness, want of Christian love . . . roots of bitterness, want of a meek and quiet spirit . . . *Sin* still had more or less dominion over me, and I did not come up to the Bible standard."

God has a gracious promise for every child who is thus troubled, "I will take away the stony heart out of your flesh."

> *Spirit of the living God,*
> *Fall fresh on me.*
> *Melt me, mold me, fill me, use me.*
> *Spirit of the living God,*
> *Fall fresh on me.*
>
> —DANIEL IVERSON

**October 15**

READ: Ezekiel 36: 23-25

*Then will I sprinkle clean water upon you, and ye shall be clean* (Ezekiel 36: 25).

## Ye Shall Be Clean

To be holy means to be free from sin, to be entirely clean in the sight of God. Moffatt translates our text, "I will pour clean water over you, cleansing you from all your impieties." The impurities from which God proposes to cleanse us are our impieties, those things in our lives that are unlike himself.

God's purpose is that we shall be like Him, and that we shall help others to be so. This was His purpose in creation. It is still His plan for our lives.

We are not called to be the people of God on account of already being holy; God calls us in order that we may become holy. God showed Ezekiel that He was saving His people out of Babylonian captivity and was taking them back to their homeland in Canaan. But this external restoration was to be accompanied by an inner transformation. There must be a cleansing and a renewing of their hearts. Thus God leads every repentant sinner back to the promised land of forgiveness and fellowship. But He proposes to do more. He consecrates His redeemed people to "serve him without fear, in holiness and righteousness before him, all the days of our life" (Luke 1: 74-75).

As the careful housewife washes a dish clean of all that is distasteful and then rinses it to be sure it is as clean as it ought to be, so God proposes to cleanse His people and fit us for His own use. With glad hearts we sing:

> *The cleansing stream, I see, I see!*
> *I plunge, and, oh, it cleanseth me!*
> *Oh! praise the Lord, it cleanseth me,*
> *It cleanseth me, yes, cleanseth me!*
>
> —PHOEBE PALMER

READ: Matthew 10:37-39

*From all your idols, will I cleanse you* (Ezekiel 36: 25).

## From All Your Idols

Idol worship and the need for cleansing from it were both literal and real for the Hebrews. From the time they entered Canaan they were tempted to dilute their devotion to God by worshiping the idols of the heathen. The Canaanites worshiped the god of fertility and they had good crops. Would not the same worship produce the same results for the farmers of Israel? This was their temptation and to that temptation they yielded again and again. They did not forsake Jehovah entirely, but neither did they trust Him completely.

For us this promise is not literal but it is no less real. We are repulsed by the thought of praying before images of stone. But are there no idols from which our worship needs to be cleansed? Have I known what is God's will for my life, but have tried to forget it and do something else because God's will seemed hard? Have I tried to love God but my love has not been strong enough to keep me faithful to His will? These are the idols of today—wrong loyalties and unfaithful service. Can God help me at these points? He can. The promise is, "From all *your* idols, will I cleanse you."

After the return from Babylon, Israel was never again troubled by idol worship. Cleansed and filled by the Holy Spirit, it is possible for us to love God with all the soul, with all the mind, and with all our strength. It is to this holy life of undivided loyalty that He summons us.

*Jesus calls us from the worship*
*Of the vain world's golden store,*
*From each idol that would keep us,*
*Saying, "Christian, love Me more."*
—CECIL F. ALEXANDER

**October 17**

READ: II Corinthians 5:17

*A new heart also will I give you* (Ezekiel 36:26).

## A New Heart

When we see the holiness of God, and sense our own unholy character our spirits cry out for a change. What we need is not new surroundings but a new self. No change counts much for a man except one that changes him.

It is at this point that God proposes to meet our needs; He changes our lives by changing our hearts. Because we are changed persons we have different desires. We can testify with Paul, "Therefore if any man be in Christ, he is a new creature: old things are passed away; behold, all things are become new."

The new heart which God promises is nothing less than a new self. We are different persons. Moffatt translates our text, "I will give you a new nature." This substitution of a new heart for the old one implies a radical change in the character and direction of our desires. It is an internal revolution. From this changed heart there will come changed conduct, new habits, and a different destiny.

Does the life we are now living reflect a heart made new by the Holy Spirit? Or do we still desire the things of the world rather than the things of God? Does this world absorb our attention and conquer us when "we ought to rule it and use it for heaven"?

"A new heart will I give you." This is God's promise. Never have men needed it more than we do. Shall we not take God at His word and accept it?

### Prayer for today

*Lord, give me this new heart, this new nature, these new desires and attitudes. Give me a heart like Thine.*

READ: Ezekiel 36: 24-27

*A new spirit will I put within you* (Ezekiel 36:26).

## A New Spirit

My spirit is seen in my basic attitudes, and those attitudes faithfully reflect the kind of person that I am.

If I am selfish, can I become generous? If I am critical, can I become appreciative? If I was born in a negative mood and have all of my life lived in reverse gear, can my spirit be changed so that I have a helpful, positive attitude? Although it seems too good to be true, God's answer to all of these questions is a glad *Yes.*

The people to whom this promise was first made had a bad spirit. They defiled the land "by their own way and by their doings" (v. 17). They had oppressed their neighbors to the point of bloodshed. They were so indifferent to God that they had set up idol worship (v. 18)—and yet God gave them this promise.

If God can remake such lives as these, surely there is help for me also. This is the good news of the gospel. God not only forgives our past sins; He also changes our bad attitudes. But how?

It is through His indwelling Presence. God's Spirit has always been with His people in some measure. But since Pentecost that Presence has been unique. Jesus said of the Holy Spirit, "Ye know him; for he dwelleth with you, *and shall be in you*" (John 14:17). From the inside God can and does work to make us like himself. We may have new spirits when we accept His Spirit.

> *Thou canst fill me, gracious Spirit,*
> *Tho' I cannot tell Thee how.*
> *But I need Thee, greatly need Thee;*
> *Come, oh, come, and fill me now!*
> —E. H. STOKES

**October 19**

READ: Joel 2: 27-29

*I will put my spirit within you* (Ezekiel 36: 27).

## My Own Spirit Within You

Our closing prayer yesterday was the heart cry of the human spirit longing to be holy. God never fails to answer that prayer.

How can mortal man become like God? The divine answer is, "I will put my spirit within you." I can be like God if He gives me a spirit—an attitude—that is like His own. That is promise enough, but that is not all that God promises. Perhaps that is as far as men could see before Pentecost. But in the light of Jesus' promise we now see that the word *spirit* should have a capital *S. The Berkeley Version* translates it, "I will put My Spirit within you." And Moffatt emphasizes it thus: "I will put my own spirit within you."

God in me! That is the extravagant promise. And the New Testament verifies it: "I will ask the Father to give you another Helper to be with you for ever, even the Spirit . . . you know him, because he remains with you and will be within you" (John 14: 16-17, Moffatt).

How can a man become like his Creator? We most resemble God when we are most filled with God's own Holy Spirit. Holiness is to be God-possessed as well as to be God-like. We do not know how the human spirit can be invaded and transformed by the Holy Spirit. But neither do we know how a live current of electricity can invade and charge a dead wire with power. We do not understand how it can be, but we can open our hearts to the Spirit's coming and make glad use of His power.

> *Spirit of burning, come!*
> *O that it now from heaven might fall,*
> *And all my sins consume!*
> *Come, Holy Ghost, for thee I call.*
> —*Wesley's Hymns*

READ: Ezekiel 36: 26-28

*I will . . . cause you . . . to be careful to observe my ordinances* (Ezekiel 36: 27, R.S.V.).

## Keep My Judgments, and Do Them

It is God who sanctifies me. It is the Holy Spirit who enables me to meet the requirements of God. But there are requirements. God declares, "Ye shall keep my judgments and *do* them." It is His power but I must act. Jesus made this truth clear when He declared, "Not every one that saith unto me, Lord, Lord, shall enter into the kingdom of heaven; but he that doeth the will of my Father which is in heaven" (Matthew 7: 21).

God requires us to do His commandments but we do them *after* He has given us the *new heart* and *new spirit.* "I will . . . cause you to . . . be careful to observe my ordinances." This is God's promise and His standard. We are always to be careful to do His will—but He promises always to help us.

Is this standard of holiness too high? Is it unreasonable and impossible? This is spiritual life on a high level, but it is the high country to which God's Word points us; it is the country to which His Spirit calls us; it is the climb on which He promises to go with us.

By the help of the Holy Spirit, I can always try carefully to do God's will—never in my own strength alone, but never careless in my efforts. Always trying, but always relying on His help. Thus fully committed to God's will, and always turning to Him for the power to enable us, we may enjoy the consciousness of God's approval. This is Christian perfection.

### Prayer for today

*O God, by Thy grace I shall be careful to do Thy will today—and every day. Amen.*

**October 21**

READ: II Corinthians 6: 16-18

*You shall be my own people . . . I will keep you clear of all your impurities* (Ezekiel 36: 28-29, Moffatt).

## Ye Shall Be My People

A lad from a drunken home had been befriended by a passing stranger. In his effort to thank his new friend, the boy said wistfully, "Mister, I sure wish you were my dad." Here is echoed one of life's deepest heart cries. We need to belong, to be loved, to be important to somebody.

There are those who never know the security of belonging to a loving home, but no man needs to be an orphan from God. The divine promise is, "You shall be my own people."

But how shall we know this assurance that comes from belonging to the family of God? The answer is clear. "This thing commanded I them, saying, Obey my voice . . . and ye shall be my people: and walk ye in all the ways that I have commanded you" (Jeremiah 7: 23). The closer we walk to God, the deeper is our sense of belonging to Him. Holiness, on our part, is simply to give ourselves to God as completely as we know how. Sanctification means to separate ourselves from all that is unlike God and to accept His promise to keep us cleansed from sin.

To commit myself to do the whole will of God; to be able to invite God to look into my heart and to know that He will find there no opposition to His will, nothing but deep love and a real desire to serve Him—this is what it means to be a sanctified child of God. This is the new Garden of Eden on earth. That blessed fellowship makes the heart sing:

> *And He walks with me, and He talks with me,*
> *And He tells me I am His own,*
> *And the joy we share as we tarry there,*
> *None other has ever known.**
>
> —C. AUSTIN MILES

*© 1940, renewal, The Rodeheaver Co. Used by permission.

READ: Ezekiel 36: 27-31

*I will put my spirit within you . . . Then shall ye remember your own evil ways* (Ezekiel 36: 27, 31).

## Then Shall Ye Remember

In order to reclaim and cure the alcoholic, the doctor sometimes prescribes a daily dose of antibuse. This drug causes a violent reaction when mixed with alcohol. If the man takes a drink while the antibuse is in his system, the reaction makes him extremely nauseated. The memory of his last illness is motivation enough to cause him to leave liquor alone.

Does God have some kind of moral and spiritual antibuse to help save men from sinning? He promised it to Israel. Here were people who backslid again and again. Their besetting sin was idolatry. As we read the history of Israel it appears that nothing could cure them of slipping back into their old evil ways. But God gave them this blessed promise, "I will put my spirit within you, and cause you to walk in my statutes . . . Then shall ye remember your own evil ways, and your doings that were not good, and shall loathe yourselves in your own sight for your iniquities and for your abominations." God kept His promise. It is a fact of history that after the return from exile Israel never again lapsed into idolatry.

It is a good thing for a man to remember his past sins when that memory brings a loathing for evil. It is still better when the memory brings gratitude for cleansing, and a deeper dependence upon God for power to live a holy life. This ministry of memory is one of the blessed ways that the Holy Spirit works in us.

### Prayer for today

*Spirit of the living God, may the vision of Thy holiness create in me a revulsion for every sin that once enticed me. By the power of Thine indwelling presence keep me holy and happy and useful. In Jesus' name. Amen.*

**October 23**

READ: Ezekiel 36: 32-36

*The nations will know that I am the Lord . . . when through you I vindicate my holiness before their eyes* (Ezekiel 36: 23, R.S.V.).

## Not for Your Sakes

God has a personal concern in my spiritual welfare. His reputation is at stake in the success or failure of every man who names His name.

The unfaithful Israelites profaned God's name by their spiritual failure which sent them into captivity and exile. The heathen said of them, "These are the people of the Lord, and yet they had to go out of his land" (Ezekiel 36:20, R.S.V.). God proposed to put His Spirit in them and thus cleanse their lives in order to demonstrate to the heathen world that God was God.

It is not for our sakes—not for our sakes alone—that God proposes to sanctify us wholly. He wants to fill us with His Holy Spirit in order that we may be blessed and happy and useful. But that is not all. God wants to sanctify us wholly in order that our lives may be a testimony to His grace and power. He declares, "The nations will know that I am the Lord . . . when through you I vindicate my holiness before their eyes."

God is dishonored when His people are disobedient, unblessed, and defeated because of sin in their lives. He can do more than that for them and He wants an unbelieving world to know what He can do. God proposes to sanctify His people because without that help we are such poor representatives of His grace and power.

### Prayer for today

*Lord, help me to listen receptively to Your earnest prayer for the disciples—and for me: "I pray for them . . . which thou hast given me . . . I pray not that thou shouldest take them out of the world, but that thou shouldest keep them from the evil. They are not of the world, even as I am not of the world. Sanctify them through thy truth: thy word is truth"* (John 17: 9, 15-17).

308

READ: Ezekiel 36: 33-36

*In the day that I shall have cleansed you from all your iniquities I will cause you to dwell in the cities, and the wastes shall be builded* (Ezekiel 36:33).

## The Wastes Shall Be Builded

When God takes control, a man's life is transformed. And the more completely He controls, the more wonderful the change. The new heart which God promised in verse 26 is followed by a new Eden in verse 35. Isaiah sang of the way of holiness, "The wilderness and the solitary place shall be glad for them; and the desert shall rejoice, and blossom as the rose. It shall blossom abundantly, and rejoice even with joy and singing" (Isaiah 35:1-2).

But economic wastes are not the only deserts that are builded when God comes into a life—nor are they the most important. A young man whose spirit had grown bitter, and whose home had been broken by sin, returned to God. He asked the Holy Spirit to again take control of his life. He wrote, "God has given me the promise, 'And I will restore to you the years that the locust hath eaten, the cankerworm, and the caterpillar . . . And ye shall eat in plenty, and be satisfied, and praise the name of the Lord your God'" (Joel 2:25-26). That promise has been fulfilled and the waste places of his life have been builded. His spirit was transformed and his broken home mended.

God's Holy Spirit brings beauty to our faded lives, and joy to our old, weary world. Christ gives not only grace—He also adds glory. The beauty of the Lord is on the people who are wholly devoted to Him. That is why the Psalmist exhorts us, "Worship the Lord in the beauty of holiness" (Psalms 96:9).

**Prayer for today**

*Let the beauty of the Lord our God be upon us: and establish thou the work of our hands . . . yea, the . . . work of our hands establish thou it* (Psalms 90:17).

**October 25**

READ: Ezekiel 36: 37-38

*I will put my Spirit within you, and . . . as large flocks for sacrifices, as the flocks at Jerusalem during the appointed feasts; so shall the waste cities be filled with crowds of men* (Ezekiel 36: 27, 38, *Berkeley Version*).

## Full Salvation Spreads

God here promises that His kingdom shall increase as a result of His Spirit in the hearts of His people. In their religious feasts the Hebrews gathered and sacrificed great flocks of sheep and herds of cattle. When Solomon was crowned king "they sacrificed sacrifices unto the Lord . . . a thousand bullocks, a thousand rams, and a thousand lambs" (I Chronicles 29: 21). As plentiful as the flocks of sheep at a feast, so shall be the number who come into the kingdom when God's Spirit is in His people. This is the divine promise.

But the promise is not for mere numbers alone. God says, I will increase them with men *like the holy flock*. The comparison is to the special flock consecrated to God. Like begets like. When His people are consecrated—dedicated to a holy purpose—God promises that there shall be *more consecrated men*.

D. L. Moody says that before his baptism with the Holy Spirit he was powerless to reach others for Christ. But afterward God enabled him to win a million souls to his Master. Says he, "I do not know of a sermon that I have preached since but God has given me some soul . . . These are the very sermons I preached [before] . . . word for word. Then I preached and I preached, but it was as one beating the air. It is not new sermons, but the power of God. It is not a new gospel, but the old gospel with the Holy Ghost of power. Amen!"

**Prayer for today**

*O God, may Thy Holy Spirit so fill my life that others also shall long to know the wonder of Thy fullness. In Jesus' name I ask it.*

READ: Joel 2: 27-29

*And it shall come to pass afterward, that I will pour out my spirit upon all flesh* (Joel 2: 28).

## Prophecy of Pentecost

In most passages from the Old Testament that deal with a second work of grace, the teaching can be only inferred by noting facts that parallel the doctrine. However in this prophecy there is clear New Testament authority for our interpretation. On the Day of Pentecost when the Holy Spirit had been poured out on the disciples, Peter declared to the astonished and skeptical crowd: "This is that which was spoken by the prophet Joel" (Acts 2: 16).

Did the prophet himself see the meaning of his words as clearly as Peter saw it centuries later? Perhaps not. But it was God who inspired both the message in the spirit of Joel and the fuller realization of its meaning in the mind of Peter. In the Old Testament passage the translators have used a small *s*. In the New Testament that *s* has been capitalized; *spirit* has become *Spirit*. This is the Holy Spirit, whom God pours out upon all who will tarry for His coming; it is the Third Person of the Trinity, whom Jesus promised to His followers.

What time was meant when God declared, "In *those days* will I pour out my spirit"? *Those days* are the days of the Messiah and the dispensation of the Holy Spirit. The prophecy referred to the Day of Pentecost, but not to that day only. The timing of this message was for us. Peter declared the glad truth: "The promise is unto you, and to your children, and to all that are afar off, even as many as the Lord our God shall call" (Acts 2: 39).

> *Thy sanctifying Spirit pour,*
> *To quench my thirst and make me clean;*
> *Now, Father, let the gracious shower descend,*
> *And make me pure from sin.*

> —The Salvation Army Tune Book

**October 27**

READ: Joel 2:27-29

*I will pour out my spirit upon all flesh* (Joel 2:28).

## The Holy Spirit Is for All

"Blessings Unlimited"—that would be a good title for this announcement of God's plan for His people. "I am the Lord your God . . . and my people shall never be ashamed." But who are *my people?* The rabbis restricted God's blessings to certain classes even among the Jews. They said: "Prophecy does not reside on any but such as are wise, valiant and rich." But this was not God's plan; God was stretching Joel's mind and ours.

There is no gift of God's grace denied to any man who asks for it. The promise is, "I will pour out my spirit upon *all flesh.*" We tend to think that only parents—persons of maturity—can be used of God. But the promise is here given also to the young. "Your sons and daughters shall be inspired" (Moffatt). No age is excluded. God speaks to the old and to the young—though He may use a different language. He makes himself real to old men in their dreams; He speaks to young men in their visions.

Some would give men a special preference over women, but in God's gift of himself there are no sex distinctions—both sons and daughters may know and speak of the things of God. And there is no favoritism based on class or income: "Even upon the servants and the maids I will, in those days, pour out of My Spirit" (Berkeley).

We rejoice in the goodness of God that makes His grace so freely available. Of the gift of the Holy Spirit, our glad hearts sing:

> . . . *the love of God is broader*
> *Than the measure of man's mind;*
> *And the heart of the Eternal*
> *Is most wonderfully kind.*
> —F. W. FABER

READ: Joel 2: 27-29

*I will pour out my spirit upon all flesh; and . . . your young men shall see visions* (Joel 2:28).

## Young Men Shall See Visions

It does not take a special baptism with the Holy Spirit to make young men see visions. What then is this promise for the days of our youth?

All young people dream dreams of tomorrow but it takes the gift of the Holy Spirit to put God into those dreams. A young businessman naturally sees visions of wealth; but when the Holy Spirit comes to him, he begins to see how his money can be put to work for the Kingdom. A young mother sees visions of her children as successful and prosperous; the Holy Spirit enlarges the vision until she sees her children as followers of Christ—and she sets to work to make that vision become real.

To have these Spirit-given visions is to see clearly and to know surely the will of God for our lives. Adam Clarke says that those who see these visions "have true representations of divine things made upon their [minds] by the power of God." Does the Holy Spirit, then, give us specific and dependable direction in our daily decisions? Yes. In every choice of right and wrong He makes clear what we are to do. And often in decisions of less direct moral quality we may have sure guidance.

There is an inner Voice that speaks clearly to every man who is completely ready to listen. There is inner vision that is clear and convincing to all who are ready to see. When this vision of God's will is given, it is as convincing as any information that comes through the senses. It is a ministry of the Holy Spirit. Once we have known the wonder of this guidance we pray often with the Psalmist:

*Teach me thy way, O Lord, and lead me in a plain path* (Psalms 27:11).

313

**October 29**

READ: Joel 2: 27-29

*I will pour out my spirit upon all flesh; and . . . your old men shall dream dreams* (Joel 2: 28).

## Your Old Men Shall Dream Dreams

It is normal for all old men to dream dreams. But the Spirit of God makes a difference in the kind of memories that fill the minds of the aging.

There are old people who must forget great sections of their lives in order to remain sane. No man can dwell long on the sins of the past. Selfish actions, unkind words, and lifelong indifference to God are not the stuff of which satisfying dreams are made. With such background a man dare not dream; he can only run from his memories.

But God has not planned this kind of sunset years for His people. "The way of the wicked is as darkness . . . But the path of the just is as the shining light, that shineth more and more unto the perfect day" (Proverbs 4: 19, 18). When the Holy Spirit fills a human life He brings radiant vision for youth, satisfying service for mature years, and contented dreams for the aging.

A few months ago a friend and his wife stopped with us overnight. He had retired from the active ministry but before settling down he wanted to make this special journey. He was visiting his children, who were Christians; and he was stopping a few days at each church where he had served as pastor. Here were the makings of Spirit-inspired dreams. Paul never knew inactive retirement, but he penned the radiance of a moment taken out to dream when he wrote: "The time of my departure is at hand. I have fought a good fight, I have finished my course, I have kept the faith" (II Timothy 4: 6-7).

### Prayer for today

*Spirit of God, so fill my active years with a life that is pleasing to Thee that the years of dreams may be filled with Thy peace.*

October 30 *15*

READ: II Timothy 3: 14-17

*All scripture . . . is profitable . . . for instruction in righteousness* (II Timothy 3: 16).

## The Holy Spirit in the New Testament

We are grateful for all the foregleams of truth that shine from the pages of the Old Testament, but it is to the New that we must turn for clear teaching on the whole will of God.

Jesse F. Lady writes: "With the exception of the Second and Third Epistles of John, each book in the New Testament makes some reference to the Holy Spirit. Jesus claimed the possession of the Spirit as the power and inspiration of His ministry. 'The Spirit of the Lord is upon me, because he hath anointed me to preach the gospel' (Luke 4: 18). . . . In looking forward to Pentecost, Jesus predicts that the Holy Spirit will flow out from the believers as rivers of living water (John 4: 14; 7: 37-39).

"While the Holy Spirit has always been present in the world in some form, yet in a very real way Pentecost marks a new dispensation of the economy of the Spirit. To the Christian Church Pentecost was the inauguration day of the coming of the Holy Spirit. The Book of Acts is a record of the things which Jesus continued to do and to teach through the power of the Spirit working through the apostles after Pentecost. Consequently, the emphasis one is apt to find in the Acts concerning the Holy Spirit is not Christian doctrine but Christian experience. 'To the men who wrote the New Testament, and for those to whom they wrote, the Spirit was not a doctrine but an experience. Their watchword was not, believe in the Holy Ghost, but receive ye the Holy Ghost' (James Denny). They went out transformed personalities. Their lives were marked by boldness, power, unity, spiritual discernment, joy, and liberality. A new power for victorious living was the first result of Pentecost. The second result of the outpouring of the Spirit was a new power for effective service" (*Insights into Holiness*, pp. 176-82).

*(More tomorrow)*

**October 31**

READ: John 5: 36-39

*Search the scriptures; in them ye are assured ye have eternal life: and it is they that testify of me* (John 5: 39, Wesley's translation).

## The Holy Spirit in the New Testament (continued)

Regarding the truth of Christian perfection John Wesley wrote: "I tell you as plain as I can speak, where and when I found this. I found it in the oracles of God, in the Old and New Testaments, when I read them with no other view or desire but to save my own soul." Let us follow in Wesley's questing footsteps.

"When we turn to the teachings of the Pauline Epistles we are faced with abundant teaching. One Bible student states that the Holy Spirit is mentioned 120 times in St. Paul's Epistles. In Paul's teaching, 'The Spirit of Christ' and 'the Spirit of God' are used interchangeably with the Holy Spirit (Romans 8:9). "The presence of the Spirit was the presence of Christ; all that the Spirit was said to do, Christ himself did; to be filled with the Spirit was to be filled with Christ; and to live the life of the Spirit was to live a life hid with Christ in God' (Edwin Lewis).

"The work of the Spirit in regard to man's salvation may be classified by general divisions—the birth of the Spirit, imparting divine life to the soul, and the baptism of the Spirit, or the Holy Spirit as 'a sanctifying Presence,' making the believer holy and empowering him for life and service. When we receive the gift of the Spirit, we receive all of Him, for He is not divisible, but He does not receive all of us. While the child of God possesses the life of the Spirit, Paul says there is in him also the carnal mind. Thus the believer experiences also the baptism of the Spirit, which in a more restricted sense refers to the act of purifying or making holy; then the Holy Spirit receives all of us" (*Insights into Holiness*, pp. 183-86).

**November 1**

READ: Matthew 3: 11-12

*I indeed baptize you with water unto repentance: but he that cometh after me . . . shall baptize you with the Holy Ghost* (Matthew 3:11).

## The Baptism with the Holy Spirit

"John the Baptist was the last of the prophets, and the forerunner of Jesus Christ. He pointed to Jesus with the cry, 'Behold the Lamb of God, wihch taketh away the sin of the world.' John then pinpointed Jesus' age-long ministry with the words: 'He shall baptize you with the Holy Ghost, and with fire.'

"Jesus not only endorsed John's description of His ministry; He stressed it as the one indispensable element in His age-long continuing work among men. On the day of His ascension into heaven He 'commanded them that they should not depart from Jerusalem, but wait for the promise of the Father, which, saith he, ye have heard of me. For John truly baptized with water; but ye shall be baptized with the Holy Ghost not many days hence' (Acts 1: 4).

"On the Day of Pentecost the tarrying disciples were 'all filled with the Holy Ghost.' It is therefore evident that to be baptized with the Holy Spirit is to be filled with the Holy Spirit, and that the reverse proposition is likewise true. Thus this baptism is related to all those passages which exhort believers to be filled with, or to be the habitation of. the Holy Spirit.

"To be filled with the Holy Spirit is to experience the presence and work of God, the Holy Spirit, within human personality, without any barriers to His will, and in complete harmony with His purposes. On our part it means God's total access to our being, and on His part it means total possession of our personalities" (A. E. Airhart).

### Affirmation for today

*Jesus was concerned that His followers be baptized with the Holy Spirit. I shall try never to be careless about anything that Jesus considered important.*

**November 2**

READ: Matthew 3:11-12

*He shall baptize you with the Holy Ghost . . . and gather his wheat into the garner* (Matthew 3:11-12).

## He Will Gather His Wheat

"The figurative language of this scripture refers to the threshing process of that time. On the smooth, leveled top of a convenient hill the threshing floor was located. The grain was trodden out by oxen or beaten out with flails. The mixture of straw, chaff, and grain was then repeatedly tossed into the air with a 'fan' or shovel. The chaff, which the wind blew away, was later burned.

"For years I read this passage and passed over the central fact in it, the truth that Christ 'will gather his wheat into the garner.' To many, the vivid language of these verses speaks only of dividing, subtracting, and burning. They are left with the image of a smoking cinder as the symbol of their own fire-baptized hearts. But only the chaff is burned, and this only in order that the wheat—the genuine values in personality—may be garnered and set to use.

"There is potential in our personalities which only God can discern. There are possibilities of grace, dormant talents, buried treasure within believers' lives. But they are largely useless because as yet encased in the chaff of an unsanctified nature. The baptism with the Holy Spirit will provide the basis to bring to realization the personality possibilities known to the Spirit, but otherwise forever lost. This baptism with the Holy Spirit is essentially positive, liberating, and value-producing" (A. E. Airhart).

**Prayer for today**

*Spirit of God, accomplish Thy will in me. Separate and destroy the chaff. Gather and preserve all that can be of use to Thee. In Jesus' name I ask it. Amen.*

READ: Matthew 5:14-16

*Let your light so shine before men, that they may see your good works, and glorify your Father which is in heaven* (Matthew 5:16).

## Holiness and the Radiant Life

"A man stopped to chat with a little girl who was making mud pies. Her face and dress had suffered in the process. 'My,' he exclaimed, 'you're pretty dirty, aren't you?' 'Yes,' she replied, 'but I'm prettier when I'm clean!' She was right. Not only little girls, but all of life is prettier when it is clean.

"A shining countenance speaks of a radiant soul. The Psalmist knew this secret when he wrote, 'They looked unto him, and were lightened: and their faces were not ashamed' (Psalms 34:5). The Chinese translate the verse: 'All who look to the Lord have light in their faces.' Calvary is the provision for the radiant life. Beholding the brightness of the Messiah, John wrote, 'In him was life; and the life was the light of men' (John 1:4).

"This divinely bestowed radiance finds its full sunrise in spiritual life when the soul is cleansed and filled with the fullness of the Spirit. His light then not only dispels the darkness of sin about us, but penetrates the inner man until every trace of sin is gone and all is light!

"God has planned that this holy radiance shall be an ongoing quality of our lives, for He has given a continuing light. The Bible tells us, 'If we walk in the light, as he is in the light, we have fellowship one with another, and the blood of Jesus Christ his Son cleanseth us from all sin' (I John 1:7). One rendering of the verse is: 'The blood of Jesus Christ his Son *keeps on cleansing from all sin.*' The Holy Spirit within us is the Source and Sustainer of this radiant life" (C. William Ellwanger).

### Prayer for today

*O God, make me a radiant Christian. May the light Thou hast put within my heart keep a glow in my spirit. May it reflect itself to others from my life. In Jesus' name I ask it. Amen.*

**November 4**

READ: Matthew 5: 43-48

*Be ye therefore perfect, even as your Father which is in heaven is perfect* (Matthew 5: 48).

## Be Ye Therefore Perfect

Seventy percent is not passing with God. My Lord expects me to do better than that if I am to come up to His hopes and plans for me. What is the perfection that He requires? Who are to reach this high level? And when?

Our text is the summary sentence in a paragraph that begins with verse 43. Perfection therefore refers to a perfect love such as Jesus describes in these verses. God's love is not limited to men who love Him. As long as life lasts, He gives the blessings of sunshine and rain even to those who reject Him. Our Lord asks us to be like God in the liberality of our love. Can I love a man who curses me? Can I sincerely pray for God to give His blessing to one who has wronged me? Can I forgive—and keep on forgiving, and loving?

It is a difficult spiritual achievement that Jesus sets before us. But it is a blessed possibility that He opens up to us. Christian perfection is high country, but living at this level comes more from God's grace than from my achievement. If it seems an impossibly lofty height, He reaches out a hand and says, "Let Me lead you to it."

*Who* may have this kind of love? All who follow Christ. *Where* will it happen? In this life and in my own conscious experience. *How* may such grace be received? By faith in God's power and by following the urge that He puts in my heart. *When* may I expect it? The moment I hear God's call and sincerely ask to be filled with His Spirit. *Why* should I seek to be this kind of Christian person? Because my Lord points me to it, and because I want to be a child who resembles my Heavenly Father.

### Prayer for today

*Lord, could You do it for me? His answer is* YES.

READ: Matthew 22:37-39

*Thou shalt love the Lord thy God with all thy heart, and with all thy soul, and with all thy mind* (Matthew 22:37).

## Supreme Love for God

Jesus said, "If ye love me, keep my commandments" (John 14:15). To love God means to put His will first in our lives.

Some of us love God when we can also love ourselves and other things at the same time. But the perfect love of God becomes manifest when a heavenly love and an earthly affection come into conflict. In *The Pure in Heart,* W. E. Sangster tells of Henry Martyn, who gave up a brilliant career at Cambridge University to become a missionary.

After his decision to go to India "he fell deeply in love with a girl named Lydia. He told her of his love and that he was under orders from heaven for India. Would she go with him? Together, they could do great things for God. All his heart pleaded with her to go.

"She would not go. If he stayed in England, she would marry him. If he went to India, he must go alone. So the question hammered in his brain: 'India or Lydia? Lydia or India? . . .'

"He chose aright. He went to India and he went alone. He never knew that kind of affection again. He cried out in his pain: 'My dear Lydia and my duty called me in different ways. Yet God hath not forsaken me . . . I am born for God only. Christ is nearer to me than father, or mother, or sister'— and he might have added, than Lydia also."

> *Take my friends and earthly friendships,*
> *Take them, take them one and all;*
> *Give me Christ, my precious Saviour,*
> *He is sweeter than them all.*
> —N. B. HERRELL

**November 6**

READ: I Corinthians 12:31—13:13

*Be ye therefore perfect, even as your Father which is in heaven is perfect* (Matthew 5:48).

## The Wesleys on Christian Perfection

"The Wesley brothers had their differences when it came to defining Christian perfection—John declaring that Charles set it so high 'as to effectually renounce it; Charles declaring that a perfection requiring qualification was a rather strange sort of perfection! Nevertheless down deep solid unities meet. To each of the brothers the justified Christian is called to sanctification entire and complete; called to inward and outward holiness, the removal of the inbred corruption of the nature, and to the fullness of love made perfect.

" 'By perfection,' says John, 'I mean the humble, gentle, patient love of God and man ruling all the tempers, words, and actions, the whole heart and the whole life. . . . I mean loving God with all our heart and our neighbor as ourselves, I pin all its opposers down to this definition of it.' Along side of this we may set the definition of Charles:

> *A heart in ev'ry tho't renewed,*
> *And full of love divine;*
> *Perfect, and right, and pure, and good:*
> *A copy, Lord, of Thine.*

"To Charles Wesley, the sanctified life is marked by the hunger for more and more and yet more of the heaven of love in his heart. As John put it, 'Indeed, what is it more or less than humble, gentle, patient love! . . . and so I advise you to read frequently and meditate upon the 13th chapter of the first epistle to the Corinthians. There is the true picture of Christian perfection' " (T. CRICHTON MITCHELL).

> *Love divine, all loves excelling,*
> *Joy of heaven, to earth come down;*
> *Fix in us Thy humble dwelling,*
> *All Thy faithful mercies crown!*
> —CHARLES WESLEY

READ: Acts 4: 29-31

*And when they had prayed . . . they were all filled with the Holy Ghost, and they spake the word of God with boldness* (Acts 4: 31).

## Filled with the Holy Spirit

What kind of spiritual experience came to these people when on this occasion they were "filled with the Holy Ghost"? They were the same persons who a little earlier were baptized with the Holy Spirit on the Day of Pentecost. The answer to our question is given by Dr. J. B. Chapman when he says: "We believe in one baptism but many fillings."

After we have been sanctified wholly we should expect and cultivate repeated experiences in which God's Holy Spirit fills our consciousness in unusual measure. It is the nature of all conscious life to ebb and flow. Hunger comes and goes. Joy erases sorrow. Weariness of the evening gives place to strength in the morning. The lifelong love of a devoted husband and wife is most often a quiet, but deeply satisfying, song singing in the heart. But the tempo of that love also rises to all-absorbing hours of consciousness of each other. We should not expect our lifelong awareness of God's Spirit to be otherwise.

We cannot command these movings of the Holy Spirit, but we can provide the channels for His coming. It was when these Spirit-baptized Christians *prayed* that the place was shaken. In this time of special communion they were again filled to overflowing with the love of God. And this new infilling gave a new urgency to their Christian service. It was this inflow of the Spirit of God that sent sanctified disciples out to speak the word of God with boldness.

It is for just such a new infilling of the Holy Spirit that we yearn when the sanctified Christian prays:

> *Spirit of the living God,*
> *Fall fresh on me.*
> *Melt me, mold me, fill me, use me.*
> *Spirit of the living God,*
> *Fall fresh on me.*
>
> —DANIEL IVERSON

323

November 8

READ: Acts 6:1-8

*They chose Stephen, a man full of faith and of the Holy Ghost* (Acts 6:5).

## They Chose a Man Full of the Holy Ghost

What kind of service does a man render when he is filled with the Holy Spirit? Is Stephen a fair example?

It seems a clear inference from verse 3 that not all of the members even of this Early Church were Spirit-filled Christians. If they had been, why would the Apostles have said, "Look ye out among you seven men . . . *full of the Holy Ghost*" (6:3)? Although not all were sanctified—some of them were. And to these men the Apostles turned for effective service in the Church. Moreover, verse 5 makes it clear that their enthusiastic faith and deep spirituality were recognized by their fellow Christians: "The saying pleased the whole multitude: and they chose Stephen . . ."

We cannot say that sanctified Christians will always accomplish more for God than will anybody else. God makes use of every personal talent in the measure that it is offered to Him, and some have greater talent than others. We cannot truthfully say that when God sanctifies us wholly our service will be as effective as that of every other Spirit-filled Christian. There were seven men chosen, but the work of only Stephen and Philip was outstanding enough to be especially noted in the Bible.

We do know, however, that every Christian who gives himself wholly to God renders better service than otherwise. All of these Spirit-filled men made their contribution. Verse 8 tells us that after they were appointed, "the word of God increased; and the number of the disciples multiplied in Jerusalem greatly." One of them was especially effective; full of faith and power, Stephen "did great wonders and miracles among the people" (6:8).

*Would you in His service*
*Labor always at your best?*
*Let Him have His way with thee.*
— CYRUS S. NUSBAUM

READ: Acts 6: 9-15

*He, being full of the Holy Ghost, looked stedfastly
into heaven, and saw the glory of God* (Acts 7:55).

## A Man Full of the Holy Ghost

What kind of man is made when the Holy Spirit fills a
human life? Stephen was not one of the Apostles, so we know
that the Holy Spirit is given to laymen as well as to preachers.
The Bible tells us nothing about his conversion but tradition
says that Stephen was one of the Seventy. If this be so, we
may assume that he was among those filled with the Holy
Spirit on the Day of Pentecost.

We saw yesterday that such a man is fitted for God's
service and gains the confidence of God's people. But there is
more. The Holy Spirit improves even a man's countenance.
Godliness soon reflects itself in his very appearance. Even
Stephen's enemies on the Jewish council, angry as they were,
"saw his face as it had been the face of an angel" (6:15).

A sanctified man sees what others often miss, and he
sees further, because his mind is set on God. Others at
Stephen's stoning saw only an angry mob and a wretched
victim. But Stephen, "being full of the Holy Ghost, looked up
stedfastly into heaven, and saw the glory of God" (7:55).

Stephen died better than most men die. He knew that
his future was secure. He died in faith, "calling upon God,
and saying, Lord Jesus, receive my spirit" (7:59). He died as
he had lived, loving men and praying for them: "Lord, lay not
this sin to their charge" (7:60). When he was dead, "reverent
men buried Stephen and mourned deeply over him" (8:2,
Phillips). Spirit-filled men live well, die well, and they are
remembered by good people.

### Prayer for today

*Lord, grant that I may be a Spirit-filled person.
Let me so live that, when I die, good men will mourn
my passing. Amen.*

November 10

READ: Acts 19: 1-7

*They were baptized in the name of the Lord Jesus.
And when Paul had laid his hands upon them, the
Holy Ghost came on them* (Acts 19: 5-6).

## The Holy Ghost Came on Them

Who were these "certain disciples" whom Paul found at
Ephesus? And what spiritual experience came to them as a
result of Paul's ministry?

They had already professed their faith in Christ, for that
is the New Testament meaning of the word *disciples*. But,
as Matthew Henry suggests, they were as yet only in the first
grade of the Christian school. There was much they needed
to know and to experience before they could come "unto
a perfect man, unto the measure of the stature of the fulness
of Christ" (Ephesians 4: 13). With unerring spiritual insight,
Paul put his finger on the most important question for every
immature Christian: "Have ye received the Holy Ghost?"

Their answer and the reason for that answer are probably
best expressed by the Revised Version, "Nay, we did not so
much as hear whether the Holy Spirit was given." Here were
men who had not received the Holy Spirit because they had
not heard about Him. Is my reason as valid as theirs? They
had not heard about the blessing of Pentecost, but they
moved toward it as soon as they learned about it.

Paul reminded them that John the Baptist had pointed
men to Christ. These disciples at Ephesus who had obeyed
John's teaching were already on the right road but they
must go further—and they did. They accepted a clearly
understood Christian baptism of water. Their spirits were
now ready for a personal Pentecost: "And when Paul laid
his hands upon them, the Holy Ghost came on them."

> *He who has pardoned surely will cleanse thee,*
> *All of the dross of thy nature refine.*
> *Cleansed from all sin, His power will enter,*
> *Fill you and thrill you with power divine.*
> —MRS. C. H. MORRIS

READ: Romans 2: 28-29

*The real Jew is the man who is one inwardly, and real circumcision is a matter of the heart* (Romans 2: 29, Goodspeed).

## The Inwardness of Holiness

In this chapter Paul is speaking to people who have a profession of religion but whose devotion falls short of the divine requirements. Verse 17 speaks of complacency in our service to God. The Jews had God's law, they practiced the religious custom of circumcision, but there they rested. No such outward forms make a true child of God. The Apostle declares, "The real Jew is the man who is one inwardly."

"Circumcision is that of the heart." If my life is to please God, there must be a spiritual surgery. Attitudes that are unlike His love must be cut away. The disposition that chooses my own way instead of God's will must go. This is radical amputation. It hurts at the time and it is therefore natural to postpone the operation. But we shall never be better until it occurs. Once we place our lives in the hands of the great Heart Surgeon, recovery is swift; and there is a more radiant life in all the years that follow.

The Authorized Version says that this operation is "in the spirit." The Greek preposition may mean *in, on,* or *by. The New English Bible* therefore translates it, "The true circumcision is . . . directed . . . *by the Spirit.*" Phillips says such circumcision "is a God-made sign upon the heart and soul." This change is the work of the Holy Spirit.

Since it is His work in us, He fashions our lives into His own likeness. Our transformed spirits may sometimes be a mystery to men. But our lives are thus made pleasing to God.

### Prayer for today

*O Lord God, destroy and root out whatever the Adversary plants in us, that with our sins forgiven Thou mayest sow understanding and good work in our mouths and hearts; that in deed and truth we may serve Thee only* (ST. COLUMBA).

**November 12**

READ: Romans 5: 18-20

*For if many died through one man's trespass, much
more have the grace of God and the free gift in the
grace of that one man Jesus Christ abounded for
many* (Romans 5: 15, R.S.V.).

## Grace Did Much More Abound

Last Sunday morning our Sunday school teacher sought
to express an average man's reaction to the fact of our depravity because of Adam's fall. He asked, "Who is that guy? I
didn't even know Adam. How come I am involved as a
result of his sin?"

There are disturbing questions when we probe the facts
of sin, but there are satisfying answers as we explore the
grace of God. As Paul wrestled with these questions, God
gave him some of the answers for his own peace of mind—
and for ours.

As I reflect on my human situation I remember that I
am the inheritor of all that is good and glorious in the nature
of man; I can think, I can choose, I love, and I am loved.
Paul's words, "So death passed upon all men" (Romans 12: 5),
remind me that I am also somehow the inheritor of the evil
that is common to men. But I am more than an inheritor.
Honesty compels me to admit that I am also the creator of
much of the evil that I wish were not a part of my life. I have
sinned and this sin separates me from God. Paul declares in
this same verse 12, "Death passed upon all men, *for that all
have sinned.*" I have an acquired depravity as well as an
inherited carnality.

But whether inherited or acquired, sin and carnality are
not the final words in my life. Sin abounds, *but grace much
more.* In Adam's fall depravity came. Because of my own sin
more was acquired. But in Christ all can be removed, overcome, cast out.

The crucial question is not, Who is to blame for my sin?
The important question is, How can I be delivered from it?
To that question God has given a glorious answer, "Sin shall
not have dominion over you."

READ: Romans 6: 3-6

*Knowing this, that our old man is crucified with him, that the body of sin might be destroyed, that henceforth we should not serve sin* (Romans 6: 6).

## That Sin Might Be Destroyed

Shall Christians continue in bondage to inbred sin? The Bible answer rings out strong and clear, "God forbid. How shall we that are dead to sin, live any longer therein?" (v. 2). "We know that our old self was crucified with him so that the sinful body might be destroyed, and we might no longer be enslaved to sin" (v. 6, R.S.V.).

The figures of speech, "our old man" and "the body of sin," refer to the carnal mind, the sinful nature inherited as the result of Adam's fall. As surely as Christ was crucified on the Cross and died, just so surely is carnality to be crucified and destroyed. And it was our Lord's atoning death that makes our sanctification possible. "Wherefore Jesus also, that he might sanctify the people with his own blood, suffered without the gate" (Hebrews 13: 12).

This emphasis in the Bible upon the destruction of sin is the basis for the Wesleyan teaching of the eradication of carnality. Eradication is not a Bible term but the teaching has abundant support in God's Word. In answer to those who believe that God proposes only to repress carnality, Dr. Daniel Steele has noted that there are many Greek words describing repression. Ten or more of them are used in the New Testament. They are translated to bind, bruise, cast down, bring into bondage, repress, hinder, restrain, subdue, take by the throat. Yet *none of these terms is ever used of inbred sin.* The words used in relation to carnality are to cleanse, to purify, to mortify, to kill, to crucify, and to destroy.

Entire sanctification is God's provision to deal with carnality. The Bible speaks of destroying "the body of sin." Is *eradication* too strong a word for that?

**November 14**

READ: Romans 6:11-12

*Look upon yourselves as dead to the appeal and power of sin but alive and sensitive to the call of God through Jesus Christ our Lord* (Romans 6:11, Phillips).

## Shall We Continue in Carnality?

In this sixth chapter of Romans, God is certainly telling us that Christians are to be dead to sin. Many competent Bible students say that we have here specific teaching on second-blessing holiness, the eradication of the carnal mind. What is the basis for this interpretation?

The word *sin* occurs here seventeen times. In fourteen of these instances the word is preceded by the definite article, making it read *the sin*. Lange says, "The definite article before *harmartia* . . . denotes sin . . . as a power or principle which controls man and reveals itself in hereditary corruption." And Lange's interpretation has the support of other scholars.

On this basis Dr. A. M. Hills writes: "We cannot help believing that the expression 'the sin,' 'the sin,' so often repeated, means a particular kind of sin, namely 'indwelling sin,' 'inherited sin,' 'the sin principle,' 'depravity.' . . . Over and over again it is personified as an abiding state, . . . as a . . . master, as a murderer, as a body of corruption, as a ruling tendency."

It therefore seems obvious, in the language of Dr. Hills, "that, while in the earlier part of the epistle the Apostle was discussing God's method of *justification* or *pardon of sins,* here he has advanced to the discussion of the gospel cure of the sin principle or sanctification . . . He thus brought the believers of his time, and *he brings us,* face to face with the abrupt question, 'Shall we continue in sin, in depravity, in the propensity or inclination to sin?' 'Shall we remain unclean, unholy, unsanctified, unlike God?' "

The reply of the devout heart is a fervent "God forbid."

READ: Romans 6: 11-13

*Yield yourselves unto God, as those that are alive from the dead* (Romans 6: 13).

## Yield Yourselves unto God

Consecration is always more satisfying and more permanent when we pay less attention to *what* we consecrate and remember to *whom* we are dedicating our lives. It is this truth that Paul stresses when he exhorts us, "Yield yourselves *unto God.*"

The purpose for such a consecration becomes clear when we put two verses side by side. "Yield yourselves unto God, . . . that ye may prove what is that good, and acceptable, and perfect, will of God" (Romans 6: 13; 12: 2).

When God has saved me from sin, why should I hesitate to trust my whole life to Him? When in forgiveness I have learned something of God's good purpose for me, why should I hesitate to place myself completely in His hands?

To yield myself to God is to trust completely Him who is too good to do wrong and too powerful to fail. This is a yielding akin to the vows of marriage when the bride promises "to love, serve, and obey" her husband. She does not hesitate because of the love of him to whom the promise is given. In a similar way full consecration to God comes from full confidence in God.

To trust God thus is to take the real strain out of serving Him. As I yield to the will of God, I am no longer afraid of it. I am willing to ask God to show His will to me. I am ready to explore it. I am fully open to it. I read the Bible to discover it and pray to be sure of God's will in my decisions. It is this openness and trust that enables the sanctified Christian to sing:

> *Sweet will of God, still fold me closer,*
> *Till I am wholly lost in Thee.*
> —MRS. C. H. MORRIS

**November 16**

READ: Romans 8:1-4

*For the law of the Spirit of life in Christ Jesus hath
made me free from the law of [the] sin and death*
(Romans 8:2).

## Deliverance by Christ

Our scripture for today describes "the restoration of
holiness by the Holy Spirit. Sin brings death on the justified,
in whom it regains the upper hand, as well as on the un-
justified. There is, therefore, only one way of preventing sin
from causing us to perish, that is, sin itself must perish.

"The word law occurs in this second verse twice. It does
not mean any statute or legislative decree. Godet calls it
'the controlling power imposing itself on the will.' Dr. Barnes
says it means, 'the influence.' Now if we substitute one of
these phrases we shall get the meaning of the verse: 'The
*influence* of the Spirit of life in Christ Jesus made me free
from the *influence* of *the sin* and the death,' that is, *the moral
death* that accompanies *the sin*.

"This is the Apostle's wonderful testimony of deliverance
which he gladly proclaims to others. He believes that the
controlling power of the Holy Spirit, which broke the power
of *the sin* over him, can deliver others too. He knows that no
mere outward means will be sufficient to emancipate their
souls, for he has tried them. No mere intellectual methods
will set free the passions and desires that have been captured
by *the sin* principle. It is vain to seek deliverance from a
perverted will by any revelation of moral law however em-
phatic. He has tried them all, and they have miserably failed.

"Nothing can touch the necessities of the case but the
incoming Holy Spirit, as a potential indwelling Christ, whose
abiding, controlling influence in us can subvert and expel
the tendencies to sin. That communicated power must impart
life. Nothing short of a *Spirit of life,* quick and powerful,
with an immortal sense of intense energy, will avail to meet
the need" (A. M. Hills, *The Establishing Grace*).

READ: Romans 8: 9-13

*If then the Spirit of Him who raised Jesus from the dead, dwells in you, then the Resurrector of Christ Jesus from the dead will through the Spirit that dwells in you make also your mortal bodies live* (Romans 8:11, *Berkeley Version*).

## If the Spirit of God Dwell in You

What is Paul talking about in our text for today? Is he saying that the Spirit of God who raised Jesus from the dead will give us resurrected bodies? Or is he saying that if the Spirit of God lives in us, He will give us a gloriously complete spiritual life even while we live here on earth?

Standing alone, the obvious meaning of this verse seems to be a promise of immortality. But does not the context show it to be a promise of a life of holiness here and now? A footnote in *The Berkeley Version* interprets the meaning of this passage as "a glorified body later, *but now* as a Spirit-controlled body, a sacred temple."

Paul's theme throughout the paragraph is the transformed life in this world. In verse 9 he says, "But you are not in the flesh, you are in the Spirit, *if the Spirit of God really dwells in you.*" In verse 10 he speaks of God's work in our spirits: "But if Christ is in you, . . . your spirits are alive because of righteousness." In verse 11 he describes God's work in the body: "If the Spirit of him who raised Jesus from the dead dwells in you, he . . . will give life to your mortal bodies also through his Spirit which dwells in you" (R.S.V.).

It is the Holy Spirit who imparts sanctity to both the spirit and the body in this world. Having given to us eternal life here, we confidently trust Him for the preservation of both spirit and body in the world to come.

> *Praise God, from whom all blessings flow;*
> *Praise Him, all creatures here below;*
> *Praise Him above, ye heav'nly host;*
> *Praise Father, Son, and Holy Ghost.*
> —THOMAS KEN

333

November 18

READ: I Corinthians 2:1-16

*My speech and my preaching was . . . in demonstration of the Spirit and of power* (I Corinthians 2:4).

## An Exploration for Meaning

Most commentators dealing with this second chapter of I Corinthians have little to say about the nature and work of the Spirit. But eight times in sixteen verses Paul makes specific mention of these truths. One contemporary scholar writes: "The word 'spirit' in the Bible is not easily defined, meaning at times little more than 'influence,' but at other times being used in a way which indicates the full, distinct, third Person of the Holy Trinity. Verse 11 might be used as the starting point of an investigation in the matter" (*The New Bible Commentary*). Each time Paul here used the term Spirit, the translators of the Revised Standard Version have capitalized the word. In their judgment the Apostle was talking about the Holy Spirit. Let us push this investigation.

If we have here significant truth about the work of the Spirit of God, why is the teaching not set forth in more direct and definitive fashion? In answer let us remember that elsewhere in the Bible we do have such direct and definitive teaching. Let us remember also that the gift of the Spirit was widely experienced and highly valued in the New Testament Church. When talking to persons who know well our basic assumptions and practices we allude to those assumptions without detailed explanation of them. Would it not then be natural here for the Apostle to write in this way? His primary purpose was to remind the Corinthians of his ministry among them. He tells them that his work was standard Early Church ministry with full recognition of the Holy Spirit and entire dependence upon His power at work through the messenger.

Let us be grateful for this light that filters through the treetops as well as for the brilliance of a noonday sun that shines on our way. Samuel Chadwick reminds us, "The Second Blessing is not in a text; it is in the whole Bible."

**November 19**

READ: I Corinthians 2:1-16

*No one comprehends the thoughts of God except the Spirit of God. Now we have received . . . the Spirit which is from God, that we might understand the gifts bestowed on us by God* (I Corinthians 2:11-12, R.S.V.).

## The Work of the Spirit

We saw yesterday that in this chapter there are eight references to the work of the Holy Spirit. Twice Paul speaks of the Spirit in His relationships to God (vv. 10-11). The other six times he speaks of the Spirit's action in the lives of men. The Apostle testifies to the work of the Spirit in his own life (v. 4), and to God's plan for the Spirit's ministry in every Christian's life (vv. 10, 12, and 13).

Jesus promised, "Ye shall receive power, after that the Holy Ghost is come upon you." Paul testified to the fulfillment of that promise: "My preaching was . . . in demonstration of the Spirit and of power."

Before the Crucifixion, Jesus said, "I have yet many things to say unto you, but ye cannot bear them now" (John 16:12). After Pentecost, Paul could write: "Eye hath not seen, nor ear heard . . . the things that God hath prepared for them that love him. *But God hath revealed them unto us by his Spirit.*"

Does a Spirit-filled man go deeper than a casual Christian into the things of God? The Bible answers *Yes.* It is only the Holy Spirit who knows the things of God. But this same Holy Spirit is given "that we might know the things that are freely given to us of God."

And consider those two startling verses at the close of the chapter. The Spirit-filled man has the mind of Christ. Egotism? *Yes*, if such a claim is made by a man for himself apart from the gift of God. But *No*, when such rightness is the result of the very Spirit of God himself dwelling in a man's soul. He who gives himself most fully to the Spirit of God is able to judge most nearly like God. There is no spirit of egotism here. There is only glad acceptance of the grace made possible by a life filled with the Holy Spirit.

November 20

READ: I Corinthians 2:6-7; 3:1-3

*We speak wisdom among them that are perfect: yet not the wisdom of this world, . . . we speak the wisdom of God* (I Corinthians 2:6-7).

## Them That Are Perfect

Who are the perfect to whom this wisdom is given? They are not the men of this world—not even the leaders of this world. One commentator writes: "[They are] distinguished not only from *worldly* and *natural* men, but also from *babes,* who though 'in Christ' retain much that is 'carnal' " (3:1). The perfect of whom Paul speaks are a different kind of Christian from the Corinthians to whom Paul writes. Both are followers of Christ but the perfect have received the Spirit and are taught by Him. Paul cannot say this of his Corinthian converts. There is something still missing from their life in Christ. The Corinthians are unspiritual brethren; they still act like ordinary men. They are not the kind of Christians who are Spirit-filled.

The perfect are Christian men who "have received . . . the Spirit which is from God." Is it unreasonable to believe that they are those who receive the Spirit as He was received on the Day of Pentecost? Is it not probable that Paul was thinking of Spirit-filled men in the same sense that he had asked disciples at Ephesus, "Have ye received the Holy Ghost since ye believed?" (Acts 19:2) Is this assumption not given added weight when we remember that this very Corinthian letter was being written from Ephesus, where Paul had pressed the converts with the importance of receiving the gift of God's Holy Spirit?

### Question for today

*Am I "among them that are perfect"? Have I received the Holy Spirit since I became a Christian? Does God's truth come to me as a spiritually mature Christian or must I still be treated as an immature, unspiritual babe in Christ?*

READ: I Corinthians 12: 4, 7, 11

*I am telling you the truth—my going is for your good. If I do not depart, the Helper will not come to you; whereas, if I go, I will send him to you* (John 16: 7, Moffatt).

## Heart Holiness Fits My Need

"We gladly proclaim that *the baptism with the Holy Spirit is gloriously adaptable to our individual differences.* No greater mistake could be made than to suppose that we can confine the Spirit's mysterious ministries within our logic or categories of thought.

"Many of us have sometimes envied the privilege of the twelve disciples who might have joined Jesus on the sandy shore of Galilee for an evening's walk and private, earnest conversation. There, we have said, we could have shared our secret personal needs, and there learned His penetrating answers. But it was expedient *for us* that He went away in order that the Spirit might come to baptize and to indwell our hearts. When therefore the Comforter comes, His personal ministry to each individual is totally adequate.

"Paul writes: 'Men have different gifts, but it is the same Spirit who gives them . . . Each man is given his gift by the Spirit that he may use it for the common good. . . . Behind all these gifts is the operation of the same Spirit, who distributes to each individual man, as he wills' (I Corinthians 12: 4, 7, 11, Phillips). What a mistake, then, to say that, since I can never be like Brother Paul or Sister Lydia this experience is not for me! For me—me with my personal qualities, peculiarities, idiosyncracies, and personality patterns both inherited and acquired—for me, the Spirit's baptism and indwelling will be perfectly adaptable and satisfying" (A. E. Airhart).

*Saviour, to Thee my soul looks up,*
*My present Saviour Thou!*
*In all the confidence of hope*
*I claim the blessing now.*
—*Wesley's Hymns*

**November 22**

READ: II Corinthians 3:1-3

*Ye are . . . the epistle of Christ . . . written. . . with
the Spirit of the living God . . . in . . . the heart*
(II Corinthians 3:3).

## Life in the Spirit

What does this chapter teach us about the Spirit-filled
life? John Wesley found in verse 17 one of the thirty texts
on which he chiefly relied as Biblical evidence for the teaching
of entire sanctification. From this text and from this chapter
he preached a message entitled "On the Holy Spirit." There
is profound truth here but it does not lie on the surface. We
shall have to dig for it.

The first stratum of earth that needs to be removed is
the concealing language of the Authorized Version, translated
three hundred fifty years ago. The word *Spirit* occurs seven
times in these eighteen verses. In the King James Version
only four of them are capitalized; in the more recent translation of the Revised Standard Version all seven have a capital
*S*. From verse 3 onward Paul is glorying in the work of the
Holy Spirit.

The second concealing stratum is the most incidental
approach to this truth. In II Corinthians the Apostle had the
unpleasant task of defending his own ministry. His original
purpose in this chapter was to contrast the New Testament
way of salvation with the Old Testament requirements of
religion. But at verse 3 his mind was caught up with the
wonder of "the Spirit of the living God." Paul had a habit
of thus "going off at a word." Maclaren writes: "This char-
acteristic gives at first sight an appearance of confusion to
his writings. But it is not confusion, it is richness." Without
this particular detour in the Apostle's thought we would have
missed these insights into the work of the Holy Spirit.

Perhaps the force of this Bible teaching is greater just
because God's messenger came at it incidentally. Paul took
for granted that it was familiar truth to the Early Church.
He sought only to remind his Corinthian converts that a
Christian is what he is because of the Spirit of God in his
life.

READ: II Corinthians 3:4-6

*Our sufficiency is from God, who has qualified us to be ministers of a new covenant, . . . written . . . in the Spirit; . . . the Spirit gives life* (II Corinthians 3:5-6, R.S.V.).

## Life in the Spirit (continued)

We saw yesterday how Paul's thought was captured by the work of God's Spirit in the hearts of transformed men. Our scripture for today reflects the special function of the Holy Spirit in the work of the Christian minister. The Apostle here refers especially to his own ministry but he does not exclude his fellow workers Timothy, Titus, and Silas. The principles are universal. They are the testimony of every true minister of the gospel.

The trust, or confidence, of verse 4 is simply the profound conviction that God does transform human lives through the operation of His Holy Spirit. No man is sufficient for this, but the man who relies upon the help of the Holy Spirit knows that he has a sufficiency in God. The more completely and continuously he rests back upon the power of the Spirit, the greater is his realization of this sufficiency.

Is Paul here testifying to the same God-given experience that Jesus talked about before the Day of Pentecost? What else could it be? Our Lord said, "You shall receive power when the Holy Spirit has come upon you; and you shall be my witnesses" (Acts 1:8, R.S.V.). Paul here declares that God "has qualified us to be ministers of a new covenant . . . in the Spirit . . . the Spirit giveth life." The fullness of the Spirit gives a note of living authority to a man's ministry.

It is God's Spirit who convicts, forgives, and sanctifies men. We whom God has called as ministers are called to be channels through whom the Holy Spirit gets next to men. He ministers best who is most filled with the Spirit of God.

**Prayer for a preacher**

> *Have Thine own way, Lord! Have Thine own way!*
> *Hold o'er my being absolute sway!*
> *Fill with Thy Spirit till all shall see*
> *Christ only, always, living in me!**

—ADELAIDE A. POLLARD

*© By permission Hope Publishing Co.

**November 24**

READ: II Corinthians 3: 12-18

*The Israelites could not look at Moses' face because of its brightness, . . . will not the dispensation of the Spirit be attended with greater splendor?* (II Corinthians 3: 7-8, R.S.V.)

## Life in the Spirit (concluded)

What is the greater splendor of this dispensation in which the Holy Spirit has been given to us in His fullness? Is it not simply the wonder of a more direct and complete access to God? Since we have such hope (v. 12), we are more confident in our approach to God. We put no veil over our faces as Moses did.

The only real barrier between a man and God is the barrier of sin. Men without Christ still have a curtain that shuts them off from God. "But when a man turns to the Lord the veil is removed" (v. 16, R.S.V.).

Paul's theology recognizes the unity in the Trinity. He here declares, "Now the Lord is that Spirit." Wesley also saw clearly the work of the Trinity in full salvation. He wrote, "The incarnation, preaching and death of Jesus Christ were designed to . . . purchase for us this gift of the Spirit; and therefore, says the apostle, 'The Lord is that Spirit,' or *the* Spirit."

What is the freedom that comes with this experience? Is it freedom to shout, or to do whatever a man chooses to do within the bounds of his own conscience? These may follow, but this is not what Paul was talking about. Freedom in the Spirit is the freedom of unhindered access to God himself. When all sin is removed, when the Holy Spirit has full control of a man's life, then is there the completest possible fellowship with God.

In this continuing fellowship we are always drawn toward a more complete likeness to Him whom we love. "And we all, with unveiled face, beholding the glory of the Lord, are being changed into his likeness from one degree of glory to another; for this comes from the Lord who is the Spirit" (v. 18, R.S.V.).

**Praise for today**

*Now thanks be unto God, which always causeth us to triumph in Christ* (II Corinthians 2: 14).

READ: Galatians 5:16-25

*Let your lives be guided by the Spirit, and then you will not fulfil the cravings of your lower nature* (Galatians 5:16, Weymouth).

## Walk in the Spirit

Paul was here writing to converts who had all but lost their Christian faith. The Galatians were "removed from him that called you into the grace of Christ" (1:6). The Apostle gives them a formula that will save them from their failure and assure them of spiritual success. That formula is, "Walk in the Spirit."

"The lust of the flesh" is simply the desire of man's carnal nature, which is exactly opposite to the leading of the Holy Spirit. Verses 19 to 21 give a catalog of these acts which originate from the lower nature. Verses 22-23 list the attitudes and actions that grow out of living and walking as God requires.

How may I walk in the Spirit? First of all I must renounce the old nature. Paul uses strong language, "Those who belong to Christ have crucified their old nature with all that it loved and lusted for" (5:24, Phillips). When, through Christ, I am done forever with the old nature, I begin to walk in the Spirit.

If I am to walk in the Spirit I must keep myself where He is. I must try to think as He thinks, work for the things that He is interested in, and feel as He feels. As I walk in the Spirit, I do not do the works of the flesh because having crucified the old nature, I no longer want to do these things.

*Thy nature, gracious Lord, impart;*
*Come quickly from above;*
*Write Thy new name upon my heart,*
*Thy new, best name of love.*
*—Wesley's Hymns*

**November 26**

READ: Ephesians 3: 14-21

*For this cause I bow my knees unto the Father of our
Lord Jesus Christ . . . that ye might be filled with all
the fulness of God* (Ephesians 3: 14, 19).

## The Prayer for Divine Fullness

Here is as sublime a stream of intercessory prayer as ever
flowed from human lips. It is addressed to the universal
Father. I am included because the prayer is for "the whole
family in heaven and earth"—it is for all who bear the name
of Jesus Christ.

"The ultimate aim is *infillment*: 'That ye might be filled
with all the fulness of God.' Unquestionably, Paul refers
to an experience presently possible, an 'experienced divine
fulness,' as Meyer writes. The tense is aorist, denoting singleness of act, 'indicating a crisis and new attainment.' . . . This is
a petition that they might be filled, not with the gifts and
graces of God, but with the God of the gifts and graces. Phillips translates the verse, 'May you be filled through all your
being with God Himself!' It is by the infilling with the
Spirit that we become, to the extent of our human capacity,
'filled with all the fulness of God.'

"Here is a sublime prayer for a Spirit-filled experience;
an experience which *empowers* the believer against the terrific
pressure of a persecuting world; which *establishes* the believer
in the grace of love; which *enlightens* the believer with an
enlarged experiential knowledge of Christ's love-plan of salvation; which *enthrones* the triune God, unrivaled, in the
heart! This tremendous and transforming experience is *guar-
anteed* by the riches of the glory and power of God, and is
conditioned upon simple faith.

"Have you received the Holy Spirit?" (W. E. McCUMBER.)

> *Let go and let God have His wonderful way;*
> *Let go and let God have His way.*
> *Your burdens will vanish, your night turn to day;*
> *Let go and let God have His way.**
> —HARRY D. CLARKE

*© Singspiration, Inc. Used by permission.

READ: Ephesians 4:17-32

*Put away your evil nature, as displayed in your former mode of life. . . . get yourselves renewed in the temper of your minds and . . . clothe yourselves with that new and better self which has been created to resemble God in . . . righteousness and holiness* (Ephesians 4:22-25, Weymouth).

## Get Yourselves Renewed

Here is the whole doctrine of Christian holiness— (1) the need for it, (2) the nature of it, and (3) the consequences that I may expect in my life. In verses 17-19, God encourages the worst sinner by showing him from what depths Christ can lift a human spirit. In verses 25-32 we see the virtues that identify us as followers of Christ. Between these two Paul describes God's sanctifying work in the soul.

Weymouth's translation above brings us life-giving truth with convincing clarity. If I want to serve God, I must put away my evil disposition. I know that I had that kind of nature because it showed itself in my manner of life before I knew Christ. If I am unsanctified, it is still displayed in strong misleading impulses. This nature is doomed to perish. It can perish now, with my consent and by the power of the Holy Spirit. If it does not thus perish now, it is doomed to perish with me in everlasting separation from God.

God's way to make me the kind of person He wants me to be is for me to *get myself renewed.* I am to be clothed with a new and better self. This is a Greek phrase signifying to *assume the interests* of another. Eusebius says of the sons of Constantine, *"They put on their father—they seemed to enter into his spirit and views, and to imitate him in all things."* This new and better self that God gives to me is a self that resembles Him in righteousness and holiness.

### Prayer for today

*O God, this is the kind of person I want to be. Give me that new self, I pray.*

**November 28**

READ: Ephesians 6:10-18

*Put on the whole armour of God, that ye may be able to stand against the wiles of the devil* (Ephesians 6:11).

## Maximum Security

God does not propose to send His soldiers into battle without their battle equipment. Jesus said, "Tarry ye . . . until ye be endued with power from on high" (Luke 24:49). As a wise spiritual counselor, Paul closes his Ephesian letter, "You must wear the whole armour of God that you may be able to resist evil in its day of power" (6:13, Phillips).

Evil has its days of power. When Satan cannot defeat us in one way, he attacks from half a dozen directions. Then it is that we need the *whole* armor. And it is whole because it is *God's* kind of armor.

There is no spiritual defense more powerful than *truth*. When the Holy Spirit assures me that I have the facts on my side, I can stand almost any assault. And what a bulwark is *righteousness*! When under the leadership of the Spirit my attitude is right and my actions have been fair, I can boldly say to any enemy, Do your worst. It seems a strange contradiction that *peace* should be a Christian's instrument of war. But it is. Many a victory has been won for God by refusing to fight when the issues were purely personal. This is God's victory that comes to the mighty meek. And above all—most important of all—God gives me the shield of *faith*. When my faith in God is firm I do not fear what man or devil may do.

Here is the whole armor of God. Putting it on is simply giving myself completely over to God. Having done this, my life is entirely filled and surrounded with Him. I am at no point exposed to danger when His all-powerful presence stands between me and my enemy. With Luther my divinely defended spirit sings:

> *A mighty fortress is our God,*
> *A bulwark never failing.*
>
> —MARTIN LUTHER

READ: Philippians 1: 9-11

*And this I pray, that your love may abound yet more and more . . . being filled with the fruits of righteousness, which are by Jesus Christ, unto the glory and praise of God* (Philippians 1: 9, 11).

## The Prayer for Transparent Holiness

" 'And this I pray'! Surely all that follows ought to be heavily underscored, for the apostle never prayed for trivialities. That for which he poured out his soul in fervent prayer should engage our fullest attention. The object of the prayer is fivefold. Shall we today make this quintet of petitions very personal?

"The first prayer is for the *education of my love* in spiritual knowledge, 'That your love may abound yet more and more in knowledge and in all judgment.'

"The second is for the *regulation of love* by spiritual discernment. 'That ye may approve things that are excellent.' We must sharpen our faculties of moral perception until we can discern between that which is actually good and that which only appears good.

"The third request is for the *perfection of my love.* 'That ye may be sincere and without offence til the day of Christ.' The test of this sincerity is that I shall be honestly willing to let light shine through me, to evince the true character of my principles and motives . . . and that is possible only to the sanctified heart.

"The fourth petition is a prayer for the *manifestation of love.* 'Being filled with the fruits of righteousness.' As long as carnality lives in me it will seek and find occasion to act. Until we are transparent in holiness we cannot be filled with the fruit of the Spirit.

"The fifth petition, 'Till the day of Christ,' looks to the *consummation of love,* when my soul shall be joined to its Saviour in immediate and uninterrupted fellowship for all eternity" (W. E. McCumber).

## Prayer for today

*May my life be "filled with the fruits of righteousness, which are by Jesus Christ, unto the glory and praise of God."*

**November 30**

READ: Philippians 3: 12-15

*This one thing I do, forgetting those things which are behind, and reaching forth unto those things which are before, I press toward the mark for the prize of the high calling of God in Christ Jesus* (Philippians 3: 13-14).

## Christian Perfection but a
## "More Perfect" Christian

Here is the aspiration of a saint. In this passage we see the only kind of Christian perfection that is worthy of the name. Paul was a sanctified Christian when he wrote the Philippian letter. He was also a mature saint nearing the close of his active ministry. But still he was keenly aware that there were spiritual graces which he had as yet only partially developed.

Here, as elsewhere in his Epistles, Paul has in mind two aspects of perfection which we must carefully distinguish. The perfection of verse 15 is what we call evangelical perfection or entire sanctification. It may be obtained in this life. It is a glorious provision of grace that helps us in our pressing toward that other perfection of which Paul speaks in verse 12—a character and manner of conduct which are always becoming more akin to the mind of Christ.

Dean Bertha Munro has described these perfections clearly and helpfully. "The first perfection (v. 15) is of the crisis; the second (v. 12), of the process. The first is gift; the second, attainment. The first is experienced; the second is goal. The first is of heart motive; the second, of developed character. The first is received in a moment of faith; the second, completed in a lifetime of choices. The first is of disposition; the second is of habit. The first is of love; the second, of all Christian graces. The first is of Christ-loyalty; the second, of Christ-likeness. The first is grace; the second is glory."

**Prayer for today**

*O Jesus, give me a heart that is perfect in love toward Thee in order that my life may evermore perfectly resemble Thy life. This I ask in Thy name. Amen.*

READ: Colossians 3:1-4

*Ye are dead, and your life is hid with Christ in God* (Colossians 3:3).

## Hid with Christ in God

Can this passage be used fairly to support the teaching of Christian holiness? Yes. By whatever name we call it, here is described the life of evangelical perfection.

Paul exhorts us, "Seek those things which are above." This is the way of life here and now for all who pray, as Jesus teaches us to pray: "Thy will be done in earth [in me], as it is in heaven" (Matthew 6:10). The Bible teaches nothing higher than this—and asks the Christian to live no lower.

"Set your affection on things above, not on things on the earth." Another version translates it, "Set your *minds* on things that are above." God has given us the power to manage our thoughts. As we meditate on God and goodness, His power somehow creates within us a genuine desire for the things that we think about. It is thus that we set our affections where God asks us to set them. *We* set them? Not really. Only God can enable me to love what I *ought* to love. But by opening my mind to Him I make it possible for His miracle of sanctification to occur in me.

Paul says, "Ye are dead," but then he adds, "and your life is hid with Christ in God." This is the mystery of the divine-human cooperation in the life of holiness. By His power we may be dead to everything that is not like Christ. By His power we are made alive and respond *with Christ* to everything that God wills for us.

To be "hid with Christ in God"—here is Christian holiness. This is my earnest prayer every day of the sanctified life.

*Sweet will of God, still fold me closer,*
*Till I am wholly lost in Thee.*
—MRS. C. H. MORRIS

**December 2**

READ: I Thessalonians 3: 9-13

*Night and day praying exceedingly that we . . . might perfect that which is lacking in your faith* (I Thessalonians 3: 10).

## The Prayer for Completed Faith

"Paul found more to commend, less to rebuke, in this church than in any to which he wrote. Nevertheless, the defect in their faith was serious enough to drive the apostle to his knees in fervent and constant intercession, praying 'night and day.' The first defect was their ignorance of some truths of the second coming of Christ. The second was a spiritual lack manifested in imperfect love and holiness; this was their more serious need.

"Such spiritual deficiency in our Christian lives is to be supplied by the *perfection of love.* 'The Lord make you to increase and abound in love.' In a previous chapter the apostle shows us the quality of this spirit: 'We exhorted and comforted and charged every one of you, as a father doth his children' (2:11). Such a love transcends our natural affection. It results only as God works in the heart destroying all that is unlovely. Thus Paul prays, 'May the Lord give you the same increasing and overflowing love' (Phillips).

"The *immediate* result of this gift is that 'He may stablish your hearts unblameable in holiness before God. It is through love that I am confirmed and strengthened in holiness, and it is through love that the heart appears blameless before God, for 'love is the fulfilling of the law.'

"The *ultimate* result appears 'At the coming of Christ with all his saints.' To be ready for the return of Christ, to stand before God acquitted, we must be perfect in love and blameless in holiness. Have I let God put His love into my heart?" (W. E. MCCUMBER.)

**Prayer for today**

*O Lord, give us, we beseech Thee, in the name of Jesus Christ Thy Son our Lord, that love which can never cease, that will kindle our lamps, that they may burn in us and enlighten others. Lord Jesus, we pray Thee give us Thy light that we may always behold Thee, desire Thee, look upon Thee in love, and long after Thee, for Thy sake.—ST. COLUMBA.*

READ: I Thessalonians 4:1-8

*For this is the will of God, even your sanctification* (I Thessalonians 4:3).

## The Will of God

"How few people are aware that God actually did make a will! The will He made in the interest of man is, in the finest sense, as real, as bona fide, as any will ever probated in any court of man. And the specific intent of this will is clear and unmistakable. God has made absolutely clear His design for man. Its intent is so clear and its purpose so explicit that the figure of a documentary human will can be consistently used to reveal His purpose.

"God actually wills to man His own personal holiness. It is His clear purpose that through the redemptive scheme man may once more be restored to the moral image given him in the beginning. And the significance of it all is that it is a restoration, not for another age or dispensation, but for men in this present day.

"One cannot read the setting of this Thessalonian letter without seeing the implied tense. It is God's purpose that we may *now* enjoy the blessings of redemptive purpose. It is *now* that we may possess the basic benefits of His will conceived before the foundation of the world. It is God's will that we should *now* be the recipients of the provisions of His will.

"And, after all, what can surpass the value and worth of holy character? . . . It is the greatest bestowment God could possibly make to men. And this is the unmistakable intent of His will."—H. V. MILLER (*His Will for Us*).

### Prayer for today

*O God, because Thou hast loved me, Thou hast willed that I should be holy. Because I love Thee, I gladly accept Thy purpose for my life.*

"*Mold me and make me after Thy will,*
*While I am waiting, yielded and still.*"*

—ADELAIDE A. POLLARD

*© By permission Hope Publishing Co.

**December 4**

READ: I Thessalonians 5:14-24

*And the very God of peace sanctify you wholly; and I pray God your whole spirit and soul and body be preserved blameless unto the coming of our Lord Jesus Christ. Faithful is he that calleth you, who also will do it* (I Thessalonians 5:23-24).

## The Prayer for Entire Sanctification

Who can question the rightness and goodness of the kind of life that Paul asks of Christians in verses 14 to 22? Here is care for those who cannot help themselves; the returning of good for evil; an inner radiance when life is hard; consistent prayer-contact with God; thankfulness to Him in spite of difficult circumstances; ready response to the guidance of the Holy Spirit; serious consideration of godly counsels; eagerness to find the right, and care to avoid even the appearance of wrong. Who could challenge this ideal? But who can hope to live up to it?

Paul is quick to point out the possibility of the impossible. It was not the Seabees in World War II; it was Chrysostom, a leader of the Church, who first coined the words, "The impossible takes a little longer." If God can but sanctify us wholly, He can do the impossible for us. Did I say *if* God can sanctify us? From his own experience Paul is ready with the answer to my *if*: "Faithful is he that calleth you, who also will do it."

"Entire sanctification is not achieved; it is received. It is not attained; it is obtained. It is not by striving; it is by yielding. It is not by trying, but by trusting. God does it. We are not made holy by our faulty wisdom and puny efforts, but by the sanctifying energies of the Spirit of God" (W. E. McCUMBER).

The prayer of today's text is Paul's prayer that the early Christians who had these needs might also have this grace. Are my real spiritual needs any different from theirs? Would the answer to this prayer be the answer to my needs?

READ: Matthew 25:1-13

*And the very God of peace sanctify you wholly and I pray God your whole spirit and soul and body be preserved blameless unto the coming of our Lord Jesus Christ* (I Thessalonians 5:23).

## Am I Ready for the Coming of the Lord?

Jesus is coming again. God has planned it. Our Lord promised it. The Bible teaches it. The purpose of the Holy Spirit is to get us ready for it. Am I ready for the Second Coming?

First Thessalonians is crystal-clear in its call to holiness of heart and life. In this Epistle, God's Word is equally explicit in linking the call to holiness with our preparation for Christ's second coming. "The Lord . . . stablish your hearts unblameable in holiness before God, even our Father, at the coming of our Lord Jesus Christ" (3:12-13). "And the very God of peace sanctify you wholly; and I pray God your whole spirit and soul and body be preserved blameless unto the coming of our Lord Jesus Christ" (5:23).

It is not only our profession that will be tested at the coming of the Lord, but our whole manner of life. To pass scrutiny we must be holy. Only those whose hearts are pure can with joy look forward to the coming of Christ.

In this connection, what do we learn from Jesus' parable of the ten virgins? Oil is one of the Bible's symbols for the Holy Spirit. In this parable all of the ten virgins had some oil; all of them were planning to be ready for the bridegroom when he came. But five of them were shut out. Only those who had the *extra supply* of oil had enough. Does not our Lord here teach us that we need the Holy Spirit in His fullness if we are to be ready for the Second Coming?

> *When Jesus comes to reward His servants,*
> *Whether it be at noon or night,*
> *Faithful to Him, will He find us watching,*
> *With our lamps all trimmed and bright?*
> —FANNY J. CROSBY

**December 6**

READ: II Thessalonians 1: 11-12

*Wherefore also we pray always for you, that our God would ... fulfil all the good pleasure of his goodness, and the work of faith with power* (II Thessalonians 1:11).

## The Prayer for Perfected Goodness

A prayer for God's full will in my life is an earnest desire for every effective means of accomplishing that will. Paul is concerned that we may be ready for the coming of Christ, of which he speaks in verse 10. In order that we may be prepared to stand before God, he offers the earnest petition: "That our God may ... mightily perfect within you all the content of goodness, and the work of faith" (CONYBEARE).

Olshausen renders the verse, "May He fill you with all the good which is pleasing to Him." Similarly, Phillips translates, "He will effect in you all that His goodness desires to do." What is this "goodness," this "work of faith" for which Paul prays? M. F. Sadler, a great Anglican commentator, answers, "The good pleasure of God respecting any creature is that he may be as good and holy and happy as he is capable of being."

In an earlier letter Paul had prayed: "And the very God of peace sanctify you wholly, and I pray God your whole spirit and soul and body be preserved blameless unto the coming of our Lord Jesus Christ" (I Thessalonians 5:23). The petition here is the same because there is but one preparation that makes us ready to stand before God. In the first letter Paul pleads for sanctification—for the destruction of the evil; here he prays positively for the completion of the good. My heart responds to his prayer. (Adapted from W. E. McCumber.)

### Prayer for today

*Father in heaven, I would make Paul's prayer my own. Perfect in me all the goodness that is pleasing to Thee, that the name of our Lord Jesus Christ may be glorified in me.*

READ: Titus 2:1, 7-8

*Be an example [pattern] for the believers, in speech, in conduct, in love, in faith and in purity* (I Timothy 4:12, A.N.T.).

## Can My Life Stand Inspection?

Hearing the bell of the ice cream wagon, Jimmie burst into the house shouting, "Can I have an ice cream cone, Mother?" Told that it was too near lunch time, he threw himself on the floor screaming. When he had calmed down, his mother scolded him about the evil of his anger and then sent him to his room to pray about it. Interested to learn what the boy would do, she listened quietly outside the door. This is the prayer she heard: "Dear God, please help me to be a good boy. Please take away my bad temper. And while You are about it, You might take away Mother's temper too!"

Was it a child's misunderstanding of a mother's discipline, or a too clear understanding of a wrong example? Can my Christian life stand the inspection of my children? My wife or husband? My friends and associates?

The proof of my sanctification does not rest in the judgment of my acquaintances—but the effectiveness of my Christian witness does. Through sanctifying power God plans to make us worthy examples of His grace. The purpose of heart cleansing and Spirit filling is to make us Christians whom God approves, and to make us the kind of Christians whom good people can admire. Last night a sanctified friend testified: "I want to live as a Christian so that no one shall need to apologize for my attitudes and behavior." I would make that testimony my prayer for today.

*Let the beauty of Jesus be seen in me,*
*All His wonderful passion and purity.*
*O Thou Spirit divine, all my nature refine,*
*Till the beauty of Jesus be seen in me.*
—T. M. JONES

**December 8**

READ: Titus 2: 11-14

*[He] gave himself for us, that he might redeem us from all iniquity, and purify unto himself a peculiar people, zealous of good works* (Titus 2:14).

## Holy and Most Holy

"Some things are more holy than others. From the standpoint of strict logic this is, of course, impossible. Since *holy* means the thing which belongs to God it is difficult to think of God's owning one thing any more than he owns another. Nevertheless, this idea occurs in our ordinary conception of property. A millionaire owns every blade of grass on his estate. But there are certain more private belongings—his clothing, his bed, or his spectacles. These are the man's peculiar, personal property. This is exactly the meaning of the text: 'Peculiar people, zealous of good works.' That is also the meaning of the holy of holies in the ancient Temple. It was holier than the rest of the Temple because in a peculiar way it was the private, personal possession of God.

"There is a sense in which every Christian is holy. It might seem that if they are holy then there is no further holiness possible to them, but such people are exhorted to go on into the holy of holies. 'Having therefore, brethren, boldness to enter into the holiest by the blood of Jesus, by a new and living way, which he hath consecrated for us through the veil, that is to say, his flesh; and having an high priest over the house of God; let us draw near with a true heart in full assurance of faith, having our hearts sprinkled from an evil conscience, and our bodies washed with pure water [our baptism]' (Hebrews 10: 19-22).

"Here the holy people are made holier; that is, they enter into the experience of entire sanctification. As regenerated Christians they belong to God in a general sense, but as those who have passed through the second crisis, they belong to God as a private, personal possession" (CHARLES EWING BROWN, *The Meaning of Sanctification*).

**December 9**

READ: Hebrews 4:1-11

*There remaineth therefore a rest to the people of God* (Hebrews 4:9).

## The Rest of Faith

Pearl Buck had learned in the morning of the death of her husband and was flying home from Japan for the funeral. She wrote: "Sorrow cannot be assuaged. But years ago I learned the technique of acceptance. The first step is simply to yield oneself to the situation. It is a process of the spirit, but it begins with the body. There, belted in my seat, I consciously yielded my body, muscle by muscle, bone by bone. I ceased to resist; I ceased to struggle. Let come what would, I could do nothing to change what had already happened" (*A Bridge for Passing*).

Such acceptance of the inevitable is always the way for the human spirit to remain sane. But when that acceptance is based on faith in God we have life's ultimate restoration and health for the soul. There is a rest that comes to those who trust. Our scripture for today tells us the nature of this present, personal, spiritual, and practical rest.

(1) It is a rest for the people of God (v. 9). Our text reminds us that this is the heritage of every true child of the Heavenly Father. (2) It is a rest of faith (vv. 2-3). Those who had no faith were not benefited, but "we which have believed do enter into rest." (3) It is a rest from the sin of self-assertion; he who has entered "hath ceased from his own works" (v. 10). (4) It is a rest worth seeking; "Let us labour therefore to enter into that rest" (v. 11).

### Affirmation for today

*Having committed my all to God, I rest. He cares for me. No final harm can come to me while I lean back on Him. "The eternal God is . . . [my] refuge, and underneath are the everlasting arms"* (Deuteronomy 33:27).

355

## December 10

READ: Hebrews 7:24-27

*Wherefore he is able also to save them to the uttermost that come unto God by him, seeing he ever liveth to make intercession for them* (Hebrews 7:25).

### Saved to the Uttermost

Does accurate interpretation permit us to use this passage as evidence for full salvation? Dr. Charles Ewing Brown answers *Yes*.

"What are the facts? The Greek word here translated 'uttermost' occurs only twice in the New Testament. In Luke 13:11 it means 'completely.' 'Behold there was a woman who had a spirit of infirmity eighteen years, and was bowed together, and utterly unable to lift up herself.'

"In Hebrews 7, Christ is contrasted with the priests of the old law. They were priests who had infirmity; Christ was a perfected priest. They were 'not suffered to continue by reason of death,' but he had an unchangeable priesthood. Thus Christ is not only greater than the priests of the Jewish law because he lives forever, but he is also greater because he is not subject to their weakness and incompleteness. Their system was weak and unprofitable (v. 18). It made nothing perfect (v. 19). Their priests were made without an oath (v. 21). There were many of them, but only one Christ (v. 23). They had to offer sacrifices for their own sins (v. 27), and they had infirmities (v. 28). By implication they were unholy, defiled, and by nature sinners (v. 26).

"In at least three modern English Testaments this word is translated 'utterly,' that is, as indicating that Christ's salvation is complete and perfect. And with them agrees Alford. On this passage he writes: 'He is able to save (in its usual solemn New Testament sense, to rescue from sin and condemnation) *to the uttermost . . . completeness*, not *duration*, is its idea'" (*The Meaning of Sanctification*, Warner Press).

*Saved to the uttermost! Cheerfully sing*
*Loud hallelujahs to Jesus, my King.*
*Ransomed and pardoned, redeemed by His blood,*
*Cleansed from unrighteousness—glory to God!*
—W. J. KIRKPATRICK

READ: Hebrews 9:13-14

*We are his witnesses of these things; and so is also the Holy Ghost, whom God hath given to them that obey him* (Acts 5:32).

## I Have Called Thee

In his book, *Samoa Diary*, Missionary Jarrell W. Garsee testifies: "Service in Samoa would never have been a possibility if I had not yielded my heart completely to the Holy Spirit earlier in my ministry. Once I heard Dr. Vanderpool say . . . 'Unsanctified service is treason against God.' My then-carnal heart could not understand this . . . *Now* I know it is true.

"In the fall of 1957 I received a testimony in a letter, from a trusted friend, telling of a new work of God in his life. A hunger started in my own heart for an experience I had never known. I cannot yet fully understand how the years of life in a Nazarene parsonage, college, Seminary, and my own pastorate could pass by while I gave mental assent to the truth of heart holiness but had never surrendered the central citadel of my being. As the Spirit . . . probed my mind and heart, I covenanted to seek God through intensified Bible reading and prayer . . . I could not foresee that the combination of heart hunger, continual frustration because of inner weakness . . . penetrating messages from some stirring devotional books, plus the ever-present, ever-patient pull of God's Spirit would bring me to the point of complete abandonment of myself to God, but it did!

"After preaching in the closing service of a revival I was holding, God called me to seek Him at the altar. Overcoming fear of what people would think . . . I bowed to consecrate. In prayer, God gave me two promises to stand on—Hebrews 9:13-14 and Acts 5:32. By faith He was mine and I was His.

"The witness came hours later, during a sleepless night, while I tried to tell my wife what God's Spirit had done within me. As I bore witness to His work, He bore witness by His sweet, infilling, emotion-evoking presence. For the first time I was ready to serve Him, not in my own strength, but in His."

December 12

READ: Hebrews 12:1-2
*Let us lay aside every weight* (Hebrews 12:1).

## Christian Perfection in a Capsule

The two verses of our scripture suggest four essential elements of what holiness people believe and teach concerning Christian perfection. Standing alone this passage might not be used as unchallengeable evidence for the second blessing. It does, however, properly illustrate, and thus supports, the conclusion reached on other grounds.

(1) The Bible makes it clear that those who win the Christian race pay a price for their success. God's people in the past have been a heroic lot. They are the witnesses by whom we are surrounded. We believe that in some way not known to us they are aware of our progress in the race. But more important is the fact that their experience witnesses to us that we shall not finish with success unless we are willing to bend every effort to win.

That is what it means to lay aside every weight. One translator puts it, "Let us get rid of *every impediment.*" Another suggests the reason: "Let us strip off *everything that hinders.*" And a third brings out the urgency of this action: "Let us *fling aside* every encumbrance."

What are we to *fling aside?* John Wesley's mother suggested a good standard to her son. "Whatever weakens your reason, impairs the tenderness of your conscience, obscures your sense of God, or takes off the relish of spiritual things, whatever increases the authority of your body over mind, that thing for you is sin."

The Christian life requires complete consecration for success.

> *Thou, my Life, my Treasure be,*
> *My portion here below;*
> *Nothing would I seek but Thee,*
> *Thee only would I know.*
>
> —*Wesley's Hymns*

(*More tomorrow*)

READ: Hebrews 12:1-2

*Let us lay aside . . . the sin which doth so easily beset us* (Hebrews 12:1).

## The Sin Which Besets Us

We saw yesterday that God's people must lay aside every hindrance to the Christian race. And all that does not help, hinders. It is by running that we learn what the hindrances are. It is after we have been saved and have tried to serve God that we begin to feel the things that hold us back. It is only after we have tried to live without sin that we become sharply aware of (2) "the sin which doth so easily beset us."

No man who sincerely tries to serve God believes that freedom from sin comes easily. Put out at one door, sin has the frightening habit of coming back in at another. And it often comes so cleverly disguised that we have entertained the unwanted guest for a time before we recognize its true nature.

That is what it means for sin to *beset* us. Its power is subtle but relentless. Various translations of our text underline this tenacity of carnality. "Sin which clings so closely"; "every clinging sin"; "the sin that so readily entangles our feet"; "and every sin to which we cling."

*The Expositor's Greek Testament* says, "The article [the] does not point to some particular sin, but to that which characterizes all sin, the tenacity and strength of our foe calls for the greatest possible help that God can give us. But even for this, God is well able."

> *Faith to be heal'd Thou know'st I have,*
> *From sin to be made clean;*
> *Able Thou art from sin to save,*
> *From all indwelling sin.*
>
> —*Wesley's Hymns*

(*More tomorrow*)

**December 14**

READ: Hebrews 12: 1-2

*Let us run with patience the race that is set before us* (Hebrews 12: 1).

## Let Us Run with Patience

Christian perfection does not mean that we have won the race; rather it means that we have (3) accepted God's perfect provision to do our best running.

This was Paul's testimony: "My brothers, I do not consider myself to have 'arrived,' spiritually, nor do I consider myself already perfect. But I keep going on, grasping ever more firmly that purpose for which Christ Jesus grasped me" (Philippians 3: 12, Phillips). Yet three verses later Paul identified himself and his readers as *perfect*. "Let us therefore, as many as be perfect, be thus minded" (3: 15).

The Bible teaches that our hearts may be filled with perfect love for God. We can love God in a way that is entirely pleasing to Him. But a part of this attitude of perfect love is that we shall strive to serve Him better tomorrow than we did today. A static experience could never be perfect for a growing person. Paul urges us to "be thus minded"—to believe this way. If any man omits the necessity of growth from his doctrine of Christian perfection, he is neither Wesleyan nor Biblical.

The *Amplified New Testament* renders our text, "Let us run with patient endurance and steady and active persistence." Adam Clarke comments on it: "Let us start, run on, and continue running, till we get to the goal."

### Affirmation for today

*In answer to my prayer for entire sanctification God gave to me a spirit of love that I never knew before. I do now love God above all else. Today I desire to know His will and to do it fully. I expect Him to show me tomorrow some things I do not know today. I have promised that I shall walk in the light He gives. By His grace I shall keep that promise.*

*(More tomorrow)*

**December 15**

READ: Hebrews 12:1-2

*Let us run with patience the race that is set before us, looking unto Jesus the author and finisher of our faith* (Hebrews 12:1-2).

## Looking unto Jesus

The last element in this capsule of Christian perfection is (4) the way that Jesus is made the Beginning and the End of the sanctified life. To live this life of holiness is to live as Jesus lived—to live the way He asks us to live.

This is the truth that our Lord himself taught about the work of the Holy Spirit in us. "When the Spirit of truth comes, he will guide you into all truth; for he will not speak on his own authority. . . . he will take what is mine and declare it to you. All that the Father has is mine; therefore I said that he will take what is mine and declare it to you" (John 16:13-15, R.S.V.).

The word in our text that is translated *finisher* is the word for *perfect.* The verse has therefore been rendered, "Let us run with patient endurance the race that lies before us, simply fixing our gaze upon Jesus, the Leader and Perfecter of faith" (Weymouth). We have no perfection that He has not given to us. We do God's will in ways that are fully pleasing to Him only as we follow our Lord's example. In entire sanctification we seek to live lives fully surrendered to God. But it is in Jesus alone that we see complete dependence on God, implicit trust, what it is, what it costs, and what it results in.

When the spirit of Jesus captures and controls our spirits, we are thereby set apart for the service of God.

*When to me my Lord shall come,*
*Sin forever shall depart;*
*Jesus takes up all the room*
*In a believing heart.*
*—Wesley's Hymns*

**December 16**

READ: Hebrews 13: 20-21

*May God . . . perfectly fit you to do His will . . . accomplishing through you what is pleasing to Him* (Hebrews 13: 20-21, Williams).

## Perfectly Fitted to Do God's Will

The Book of Hebrews is often called *the better book*. The author speaks of a "better hope," a "better covenant," "better promises," and a "better resurrection." But even in this book of "betters," the writer today points us to the best. His prayer is, "Now the God of peace . . . make you perfect." There is nothing in spiritual gifts or growth that is better than that.

What is this perfection? It is simply that God's people may do God's will in every good work. We are sure that if our lives are to be pleasing to God our hearts must be cleansed from sin, for nothing sinful is ever "well pleasing in his sight."

How is God to accomplish in us this high level of holy character and life? We do well to remember that *it is God* who is at work in us; we do not achieve any holiness by our own unaided efforts. It is God who makes it possible— and all of His resources are available to us for this purpose. The "blood of the everlasting covenant" is available to cleanse the heart from every stain. The power "that brought again from the dead our Lord Jesus" is adequate to make our lives satisfying to God. "Through Jesus Christ" we can be entirely "well pleasing in his sight."

Holiness is high country, but by the grace of God it is not unattainable. There is in that high country the lure of a spiritual challenge. There is here the exhilaration of setting out for—and of reaching—a God-given goal.

> *I rise to walk in heav'n's own light,*
> *Above the world and sin;*
> *With heart made pure and garments white,*
> *And Christ enthroned within.*
>
> —PHOEBE PALMER

READ: Hebrews 13: 20-21

*Now the God of peace . . . make you perfect in every good work to do his will, working in you that which is well pleasing in his sight* (Hebrews 13: 20-21).

## The Prayer for Christian Perfection

"The outworking of God's pleasure is consequent upon the inworking of God's power. God works in and upon us that He might work with and through us. It is precisely this thought which underlies the prayer for Christian perfection. God is petitioned to make believers perfect by working in them, and the result is their being equipped 'in every good work to do His will.'

"When we meet God we are not what we should be, but He takes us as we are and makes us what we ought to be. The convicted sinner is aware of how far short he falls only in relation to violated law, in outward conduct. His cry is for pardon. The justified believer becomes acutely and painfully aware of a deeper and inner lack of correspondence to the character and will of a holy God, and he cries for cleansing.

"The words 'make you perfect' are translated by Adam Clarke, 'Put you completely in joint.' The bone is not bad and does not call for removal. It is out of place and calls for adjustment, that it might perform its proper function. The experience of Christian perfection involves the adjusting and rectifying of all the passions and faculties of my human personality, which are disordered by sin. When this happens the body properly serves my mind, the mind serves my spirit, and my spirit serves God. All the forces and faculties of my personality are 'tuned up' to do the will of God. This 'tune up' gives me a smoother running human motor.

"Perfection, then, is setting all of my faculties into proper relation to one another, thus equipping me to do the will of God without discord or division. There is no friction or frustration in the heart, where God's will confronts my will" (W. E. McCumber).

**December 18**

READ: Hebrews 13: 20-21

*Now the God of peace, that brought again from the dead our Lord Jesus . . . make you perfect in every good work to do his will* (Hebrews 13: 20-21).

## The Perfecting Power of God

"The appeal to reason is here the appeal to the power of God. 'Now the God of peace, that *brought again from the dead* our Lord Jesus . . .' The indescribable power by which that greatest of all miracles was wrought is here pledged for our perfection.

"When Jesus took up again His own life and strode in calm majesty from the tomb, He symbolized by that emergence an utter and final victory over every form and degree of sin. That authority over sin extends to the cleansing of indwelling sin from the heart of the believer.

"When we think of the depth and strength of the depravity and derangement of fallen nature, by which the inner life is wrenched violently out of joint with the divine will, we could easily join the ranks of those who cry, 'Impossible,' to the grace of Christian perfection. But when we stand at Joseph's tomb and see the light that streams from the empty sepulcher, we know 'what is the exceeding greatness of his power to usward who believe, according to the working of his mighty power, which he wrought in Christ when he raised him from the dead' (Ephesians 1:19-20). Then we laugh at impossibilities and cry, 'It shall be done.'

"That performance of power assures the possibility of perfection. The resurrection of Christ from the dead is mentioned only this one time in Hebrews, and it is cited here as a guaranty of God's power to make us perfect" (W. E. McCUMBER).

> *Lord of earth and heav'n above,*
> *Fill me now with perfect love;*
> *Sanctify by pow'r divine,*
> *And from dross my heart refine.*
>
> —*Hymns of the Living Faith*

READ: Hebrews 13: 20-21

*Now the God of peace . . . make you perfect . . . to do his. will, working in you that which is well pleasing in his sight* (Hebrews 13: 20-21).

## The Meaning of Christian Perfection

"Christian perfection is related to God's plan for our lives. The prayer of our text is, 'Make you perfect . . . *to do his will.*'

"Many writers and preachers who oppose the doctrine fling the term about as though it were an absolute perfection, marking the end of all weakness and all progress. It is charged that if we are made perfect we cannot sin, cannot grow, cannot be tempted, and do not need the Lord's Prayer for forgiveness. But for intelligent understanding the term must be used as the Bible uses it.

"It is useless to deny that perfection is commanded, illustrated, and promised in the Bible. But it is senseless to believe that God levies upon us the demands of absolute, angelic, or Adamic perfection. Christian perfection is a relative experience. It is not a final nor a flawless perfection. 'It does not even imply maturity, much less finality.' It is a perfection of fitness. It equips us to do the will of God, and that not necessarily without mistake, but certainly without rebellion and resentment. This is all we mean by the term—that much, no more, no less.

"Christian perfection is full acceptance of, and hearty compliance with, God's will. This certainly implies the crushing of every lurking rebel to the will of God. It demands the destruction of the carnal mind, for that is 'enmity against God.' The scripture under consideration surely implies this state of grace: 'working in you that which is *well pleasing in his sight.*' Phillips translates it, 'May He effect in you everything that pleases Him' " (W. E. McCumber).

### Praise for today

*I rejoice that the spirit of conformity which God has put within me replies with a glad Amen. The heart from which God has removed rebellion embraces His divine will "in every good work."*

365

**December 20**

READ: James 1: 2-8

*If any of you lack wisdom [finds a lack in your religion], let him ask of God . . . and it shall be given him* (James 1: 5).

## If Any of You Lack

Does our scripture reading for today speak only of a shortage of natural patience and a lack of balanced judgment or is God's Word here giving us a deeper insight into possibilities of the Christian life? Do these verses speak only of growth or do they point us to the possibilities of grace through God's generous gift of the Holy Spirit? (See Luke 11: 13.)

The answer depends in part on the unity of this passage, and in part on the meaning of the words *perfect* and *wisdom.* Some translators start a new paragraph with verse 5. But an equal number see continuity of thought and make verses 2 to 8 a single paragraph with a central theme. If this be correct, what is the theme of the passage?

The word *perfect* in verse 4 is the same word used in Matthew 5: 48 and Philippians 3: 15, where we understand it to mean Christian perfection. The word *wisdom* in verse 5 generally signifies understanding; but often in the Bible wisdom is equivalent to *true religion.* In view of these facts, is not James saying: In the midst of trials, let God make your Christian faith perfect and entire, wanting nothing? Is he not saying, If you discover, under the pressures of life, that your religion is lacking, ask God for *more*—ask Him for all He can give you?

Is this *more religion* the baptism with the Holy Spirit? We believe that it is. (1) It is under pressure that the unsanctified Christian often discovers his need. (2) It is the divine plan that every child of God should have "all the fulness of God." (3) This grace is a free gift to those who ask. (4) It is given in response to faith. (5) It brings steadiness to the wobbly Christian and (6) singleness of heart to the double-minded.

**December 21**

READ: James 1: 5-8

*A double minded man is unstable in all his ways*
*(James 1: 8).*

## Beyond Halfway Religion

"Half a loaf is better than no bread." Some religion is better than none, but halfway religion is not very satisfying. Plato described human life as a charioteer with a team of horses. One horse was white and always kept pulling upward toward goodness and God. The other was black and took every opportunity to pull downward toward evil. Always the charioteer had to be alert to keep the dark horse from setting the course and wrecking the chariot.

Plato did not know Christian theology but he had a clear insight into man's fallen nature. In our text James describes the tragedy of the divided soul: "A double minded man is unstable in all his ways." Elsewhere he tells us, "My brethren, these things ought not so to be" (3: 10). Jesus puts the impending tragedy of this division of the soul into its sharpest focus: "Every kingdom divided against itself is brought to desolation; and every city or house divided against itself shall not stand" (Matthew 12: 25).

Madame Guyon testifies to the inward unhappiness of the Christian whose heart is divided—the Christian who loves God but loves Him less than wholeheartedly: "Divine love gently drew me inward, and vanity dragged me outward. My heart was rent asunder by the contest, as I neither gave myself wholly up to the one nor the other. I besought my God . . . and cried, 'Art Thou not strong enough wholly to eradicate this unjust duplicity out of my heat?' "

Philip Doddridge found the answer to that brokenhearted prayer and wrote "O Happy Day"!

> *Now rest, my long divided heart;*
> *Fixed on this blissful Center, rest;*
> *Nor ever from my Lord depart,*
> *With Him of ev'ry good possessed.*

**December 22**

READ: II Peter 1: 2-8

*His divine power hath given unto us all things that pertain unto life and godliness* (II Peter 1: 3).

## Holiness and Everyday Living

"The majority of people do not have great, romantic experiences in life. Their course leads over a more or less undulating plain. Every day is much like every other day. The necessities of economic life drive them to their hours of labor and of rest. Their occupation brings them the large percentage of contacts with others, and hence their opportunities for doing good.

"It is our common obligation to 'attend the means of grace,' such as family and secret prayer, and the services of the church. . . . It is our obligation, without exception, to maintain a standard of conduct and conversation that will commend the profession we make and make it clear to all that we are conscious always that God sees and knows and cares and that we are responsible to Him now and at the judgment and in eternity. . . . Carelessness about keeping one's word even in small matters, and about meeting his bills or meeting his financial obligations will limit, if not actually destroy, the value of a Christian professor's influence.

"This is equivalent to saying that what we all need most is grace to live the common life in an uncommon manner. To be patient where others would become irritable, to be cheerful where others would be possessed of fear, to be kind when others would be resentful, to be pure when others would break under temptation, to reject all price offered for doing wrong, to just exemplify the spirit of the Master in the common places among common people—this, to the great majority of us, is real victory" (J. B. CHAPMAN).

*O Master, let me walk with Thee*
*In lowly paths of service free;*
*Tell me Thy secret, help me bear*
*The strain of toil, the fret of care.*
                          —WASHINGTON GLADDEN

READ: Acts 1: 7-11

*Behold, I bring you good tidings of great joy, which shall be to all people* (Luke 2: 10).

## Holiness and the Christmas Message

This is Christmas week. We hear the joyous carols, we remember the angels who sang in Judean skies, and we worship with lowly shepherds kneeling before a manger. Our minds and hearts are absorbed with the story of the first Christmas. Our spirits thrill to the realization of the angel's glad message, "Behold, I bring you good tidings of great joy."

It is well that our spirits are warmed as we remember the familiar Christmas story. But Christmas will fall short of its full meaning unless we remember all of the story. God's heavenly messenger declares that these good tidings "shall be to all people." The greater the blessings that have come to us through the gospel, the greater is our responsibility to share these good tidings with others. We who have been to Pentecost have been richly blessed.

The Babe of Bethlehem was born in order that the Man, Christ Jesus, might accomplish His work in the lives of men. It was the Babe of Bethlehem grown to manhood who said to His followers: "Ye have not chosen me, but I have chosen you, and ordained you, that ye should go and bring forth fruit" (John 15: 16). We who are followers of Christ have been saved from our sins and filled with the Holy Spirit for a purpose that is broader than the mere enjoyment of our salvation. An essential part of being a Spirit-filled Christian is to share that joy with others.

*Joy to the world, the Lord is come!*
*Let earth receive her King;*
*Let ev'ry heart prepare Him room,*
*And heav'n and nature sing.*

—ISAAC WATTS

**December 24**

READ: John 3:14-17

*God so loved the world, that he gave* (John 3:16).

## Pentecost and the Christmas Spirit

Christmas sums up in one word all the good news of the gospel. "Unto you is born this day in the city of David a Saviour, which is Christ the Lord" (Luke 2:11). "God so loved the world, that he gave his only begotten Son, that whosoever believeth in him should not perish, but have everlasting life" (John 3:16). "Wherefore Jesus also, that he might sanctify the people with his own blood, suffered without the gate" (Hebrews 13;12).

And Christmas reminds us of how we heard the story, for the spirit of Christmas is the spirit of giving. When Andrew found Jesus, he went to give the good news to Peter. Peter found Jesus and went to help Cornelius. Cornelius and other Christians of the first century gave the glad tidings to men of the second, who in turn shared the story with yet others. Across the centuries the healing streams of salvation have flowed on through the lives of Spirit-filled men and women—men and women filled with the spirit of sharing.

You and I are saved today because someone else found the Lord and then came to share his gladness with us. We enjoy the blessings of full salvation because others heard that message, were filled with the Holy Spirit, and wanted to share this joy. We are sanctified wholly in order to win others to Christ and to lead them into this blessed experience. God's plan of gospel sending is the plan of gospel sharing. Thus the good tidings of Christmas are to reach all people.

*'Twas a humble birthplace; but, oh!*
*How much God gave to us that day!*
*From the manger bed, what a path has led!*
*What a perfect, holy way!*

—W. H. NEIDLINGER

READ: Philippians 2: 5-8

*Let this mind be in you, which was also in Christ Jesus* (Philippians 2: 5).

## Christmas Is Self-giving

Heart holiness is designed to make us more like Jesus, whom God gave to us at Christmas—more like Him in sinless life and more like Him in selfless service. At Christmas it seems natural to forget ourselves and to remember others. In a sense, holiness is simply God's plan to extend Christmas through the whole year. Expecting to do some love service for God should be a part of our consecration and a normal condition of our continued sanctification. Thomas Cook has expressed it beautifully thus: "If Christ be in full possession of our hearts, it will not be long until we will be doing in our poor way some of the beautiful things He would do if He were here himself in bodily form."

The Christ of Christmas was most concerned with this kind of self-giving when He talked to the disciples about what they should expect after Pentecost: "But ye shall receive power, after that the Holy Ghost is come upon you: and ye shall be witnesses unto me both in Jerusalem, and in all Judaea, and in Samaria, and unto the uttermost part of the earth" (Acts 1: 8).

Paul exhorts us: "Make love your aim, and then set your heart on spiritual gifts" (I Corinthians 14: 1, Moffatt). Christmas reminds us again that, after our hearts have been cleansed from sin and filled with perfect love, we are to give ourselves to the service of Christ—to give ourselves as He gave himself for the service of God and the needs of men.

*Oh, holy Child, as wise men came and found Thee*
*And laid low at Thy feet their gifts of gold,*
*So we would bring our gifts of love and service*
*And pledge our faith as wise men did of old.\**
—DALE ASHER JACOBUS

*© 1943 by Lillenas Publishing Co. International copyright.

**December 26**

READ: I John 1: 5-9

*If we confess our sins, he is faithful and just to forgive us our sins* (I John 1: 9).

## Faithful to Forgive Us

"All have sinned, and come short of the glory of God" (Romans 3: 23). This brief statement of spiritual truth is the Biblical premise from which all sound thinking about the plan of salvation must start. Apart from the grace of God, men are sinful: sinful by nature because we have inherited the depravity of Adam's fall; sinful by choice because of our willful disobedience to the law of God.

We are guilty because of committed sins and polluted as a result of inherited sin. Both our guilt and our pollution separate us from God; both are factors in our sinfulness; both must be removed before we can stand in the presence of a holy God.

Our first responsibility for sin is for the sin for which we are personally responsible. We stand guilty before God, not because of Adam's sin, but because of our own. Our first conviction is conviction for transgression, and God's first work of grace in the soul is forgiveness. "If we confess our sins, he is faithful and just to forgive us our sins." The work of full salvation begins when we are saved from the guilt of personal sin against God. For the gift of this salvation we join with the Psalmist in a glad song.

**Praise for today**

> Bless the Lord, O my soul, and all that is within me, bless his holy name. Bless the Lord, O my soul, and forget not all his benefits: who forgiveth all thine iniquities; who healeth all thy diseases; who redeemeth thy life from destruction; who crowneth thee with lovingkindness and tender mercies. Bless the Lord, O my soul" (Psalms 103: 1-4, 22).

READ: I John 1: 5-9

*If we confess our sins, he is faithful and just . . . to cleanse us from all unrighteousness* (I John 1: 9).

## Faithful to Cleanse Us

We are grateful to God for the forgiveness of sins. But the Bible teaches clearly that forgiveness is only the beginning of our salvation. Great and glorious as is the work of conversion, it is but a preparatory step to our complete redemption.

Would God forgive sins and then leave the soul exposed to the grave danger of sinning yet again? Would the Redeemer die to save men only from the sins of the past and provide no protection from further guilt? John proclaims the glad answer, *No!* "He is faithful and just to forgive us our sins, *and to cleanse us from all unrighteousness.*"

If we are to be cleansed, we must feel our deep need, and we must confess the plague of indwelling sin. J. A. Wood, author of *Perfect Love*, testifies: "I was often more strongly convicted of my need of inward purity than I ever had been of my need of pardon. God showed me the importance and the necessity of holiness as clear as a sunbeam. I seldom studied the Bible without conviction of my fault in not coming up to the Scripture standard of salvation." If we confess the guilt of sin, we may have pardon. If we confess the pollution of sin, we may also have cleansing.

The work of salvation from sin is begun in regeneration it is completed in entire sanctification. This is God's provision. If we would know the joy of full salvation, we must earnestly seek both forgiveness and cleansing.

**Prayer for today**

> *Let the water and the blood,*
> *From Thy wounded side which flowed,*
> *Be of sin the double cure,*
> *Save from wrath and make me pure.*
> —AUGUSTUS M. TOPLADY

December 28

READ: I John 4: 7-12

*If we love one another, God dwelleth in us, and his love is perfected in us* (I John 4: 12).

## The Ultimate Test

Jesus taught it. Paul wrote a hymn about it in the thirteenth chapter of First Corinthians. John affirms that it is the very nature of God himself. In our scripture for today the Bible proposes it as a fair test for our experience of Christian perfection. What is this high quality of spiritual life? The answer is *love*. There is no human attitude that makes us more like God than to be filled with a spirit of love. John here seeks to show us how we may learn to love and to live according to the divine will.

There is some effort of acquaintance required for a man or a woman to walk with God. He is not as obvious as the rising sun. "No man hath seen God at any time." But still, He can be known. This knowledge is outlined in five simple and clearly related propositions.

(1) "God is love." This is not all that we know about God but this is what is most important. (2) Every loving thought and deed of mine has its origin in heaven, "for love is of God"—all love comes from Him. (3) If I do not have a spirit of love, I do not know God at all; "He that loveth not knoweth not God." (4) If I have an attitude of love, it is an evidence of my spiritual parentage and shows my family connection. "Every one that loveth is born of God, and knoweth God." (5) There is no spiritual completeness other than to have the Spirit of God himself reigning in my heart. The only Christian perfection that the Bible teaches is a perfect love. "If we love one another, God dwelleth in us, and his love is perfected in us."

### Question for today

*All that God wants from me and all that He asks of me is a spirit of sincere and honest love. Have I opened wide every door of my soul and let God's Holy Spirit fill me with that love?*

READ: Jude 20-21, 24-25

*Now unto him that is able to keep you from falling*
*. . . to the only wise God our Saviour, be glory and*
*majesty, dominion and power, both now and ever.*
*Amen* (Jude 24-25).

## Keep Yourselves in the Love of God

The sanctified life is a life of faith. If Satan cannot defeat us by the enticement of outbroken sin, he will sow seeds of doubt in the heart and try to wreck us through confusion. We must resist the devil at every point of attack— and this is one of his favorite assaults against all who seek to live the holy life. We must deliberately refuse to allow our fears to destroy us. Jude exhorts us, "Keep yourselves in the love of God." If we do our part, God will preserve us; for Jude adds, He "is able to keep you from falling."

At times when the conscious witness of the Spirit to our sanctification seems not clear, we must learn to hold steady. If Satan can get us discouraged or in confusion and then get us to doubt the work of God in the soul, he has defeated us and defeated God's work in us. If specific spiritual failures come to mind which might be evidence against our profession, we must fix them up at once—but keep our faith.

If there is only a vague sense of unrest, we must fight against it as against a mortal enemy, refusing to let it disturb our faith. We must remind God and ourselves that we have already given our lives wholly to Him and that He came to abide with us. Let us reaffirm our consecration and promise God that we will walk in all the clear light which He sends. Let us reaffirm our faith in Him who came to abide with us forever.

> *He never has failed me yet.*
> *I have proven Him true;*
> *What He says He will do.*
> *He never has failed me yet.**
> —W. J. HENRY

*© 1937 by Nazarene Publishing House.

**December 30**

READ: Revelation 22:10-12

*He that is holy, let him be holy still* (Revelation 22:12).

## Holiness in the Revelation

Rudyard Kipling in his "L'envoi" reminds us that there are finalities for us all:

*When earth's last picture is painted,*
*And the tubes are twisted and dried,*
*When the oldest colors have faded,*
*And the youngest critic has died,*

It is then that God shall have the last word in our lives. Kipling continues, "And those that were good shall be happy."

Here in the last book of the Bible we get a final glimpse of God's concern for holiness, for goodness, for Godlikeness. In 1:5-6 we join in praise "unto him that loved us, and washed us from our sins in his own blood, and hath made us . . . priests unto God." In the Old Testament the priest was an anointed man who walked close to God and served Him exclusively. But in Christ we may all draw near and serve Him continuously.

In 3:18 we hear again God's message of holy living and we remember that it is addressed, not to the sinner, but to the Church: "I counsel thee to buy of me gold tried in the fire [thus purified] . . . and white raiment [all sin removed] . . . and anoint thine eyes with eyesalve, that thou mayest see."

God's way is a holy way. His call is to every man who sincerely desires to be like Him: "The Spirit and the bride say, Come  And let him that heareth say, Come. And whosoever will, let him take the water of life freely" (22:17).

### Testimony for today

*My heart responds to that call. I have heard the invitation. I repeat it to all who read these words, Come. That water is life to my thirsty soul; it will bring strength to your drooping spirit.*

December 31

READ: Psalms 103:1-4

*We are his witnesses of these things; and so is also the Holy Ghost, whom God hath given to them that obey him* (Acts 5:32).

## Bless the Lord, O My Soul

It is always fitting that our testimony to the experience of entire sanctification be given with a deep sense of indebtedness to God. We are finders, not because we are such great seekers, but because God is such a great Giver. I testify today to the wonder of this free gift of God's grace.

Thirty-seven years ago I was a young man beginning my junior year in college. I felt my deep need to be cleansed from sin and to be filled with the Holy Spirit. I knelt at the altar in a college chapel and earnestly sought this blessing. At the altar God graciously dealt with my soul and helped me to reach a place of utter commitment to Him, but the assurance of full salvation did not come immediately. I sought on for a day or two. One morning in my dormitory room as I knelt by my window in meditation and prayer, it happened. Just as the first rays of the rising sun touched the building and lighted up my windowpane, the Holy Spirit came to my soul and illuminated all of my life.

I cannot yet testify to the end of my days, but I can testify that for these thirty-seven years He has been with me. There have been some days of uncertainty, but He has remained. He has made me a better man than I was then. He has led me into paths of Christian service of which I did not dream. The prospect has not always been bright, but the retrospect has always been luminous. In the light of this faith and with the assurance of His presence I propose to journey until traveling days are done.

*Bless the Lord, O my soul: and all that is within me, bless his holy name* (Psalms 103:1).

# Index of Scripture References